An OPUS book

A History of Western Philosophy: 7

CONTINENTAL PHILOSOPHY
SINCE 1750

OPUS General Editors

Keith Thomas
Alan Ryan
Walter Bodmer

OPUS books provide concise, original, and authoritative introductions to a wide range of subjects in the humanities and sciences. They are written by experts for the general reader as well as for students.

A History of Western Philosophy

This series of OPUS books offers a comprehensive and up-to-date survey of the history of philosophical ideas from earliest times. Its aim is not only to set those ideas in their immediate cultural context, but also to focus on their value and relevance to twentieth-century thinking.

Classical Thought
Terence Irwin

Medieval Philosophy
David Luscombe

Renaissance Philosophy
C. B. Schmitt

The Rationalists
John Cottingham

The Empiricists*
R. S. Woolhouse

English-Language Philosophy 1750–1945
John Skorupski

Continental Philosophy since 1750*
Robert C. Solomon

English Language Philosophy since 1945
Barry Stroud

*Already published

A History of Western Philosophy: 7

Continental Philosophy since 1750

The Rise and Fall of the Self

ROBERT C. SOLOMON

Oxford   New York

OXFORD UNIVERSITY PRESS

1988

Oxford University Press, Walton Street, Oxford OX2 6DP

Oxford New York Toronto
Delhi Bombay Calcutta Madras Karachi
Petaling Jaya Singapore Hong Kong Tokyo
Nairobi Dar es Salaam Cape Town
Melbourne Auckland

and associated companies in
Beirut Berlin Ibadan Nicosia

Oxford is a trade mark of Oxford University Press

British Library Cataloguing in Publication Data

Solomon, Robert C.
Continental philosophy since 1750 : the rise and fall of the self.——
(A History of western philosophy ; 7).——(OPUS).
1. Philosophy——History
I. Title II. Series III. Series
190'.9 B72

ISBN 0-19-219216-7
ISBN 0-19-289202-9 Pbk.

Library of Congress Cataloging in Publication Data

Solomon, Robert C.
Continental philosophy since 1750.
(A History of Western philosophy ; 7)
Bibliography: p.
1. Philosophy, Modern. 2. Self (Philosophy)
I. Title. II. Series: OPUS. History of Western
philosophy ; 7.
B791.S65 1988 126'.094 87-20262

ISBN 0-19-219216-7
ISBN 0-19-289202-9 (pbk.)

Printed in Great Britain by
Biddles Ltd.
Guildford and King's Lynn

For Marguerite Barnett, MD

Special thanks are due to Kathleen Higgins, Katherine Morris, Bernd Magnus, Shari Starrett, Doug Kellner, Lissa Anderson, and Jenene Allison.

Contents

Prologue.

What Rousseau Found in the Woods

Strolling in solitude through the lush forests of St Germain during the early adolescence of the modern age, Jean-Jacques Rousseau made a miraculous discovery. It was his self. This self was not, as his more scholastic predecessor Descartes had thought, that thin merely logical self, a pure formality that presented itself indubitably whenever he reflected: 'I think, therefore I am.' Nor was his the frustrated, sceptical search that led his friend Hume to declare, paradoxically, that 'whenever I look inside myself, there is no self to be found'. What Rousseau discovered in the woods of France was a self so rich and substantial, so filled with good feelings and half-articulated good thoughts, so expansive, natural, and at peace with the universe, that he recognized it immediately as something much more than *his* singular self. It was rather the Self as such, the soul of humanity. Looking deeply into himself Rousseau discovered the self that he shared with all men and women the world over, and declared that it was good—intrinsically good, despite all of the artifices and superficialities of the social whirl. In nearby Paris it might be difficult to see past the corruption and vain conventionality of modern society, but out there, free, alone, and at peace with one's nature, it was rather our innocence that was so apparent, a natural goodness that survived the sins and humiliations of social life, a true and absolute self that was not each person's alone, but which was shared with all humanity.

What Rousseau discovered—or at any rate raised to the level of first-rate philosophy—was the transcendental pretence. It appeared as innocence and common sense, but it embodied a profound arrogance that promoted self-righteousness, prohibited mutual understanding, and belied human diversity. Fully developed, the transcendental pretence has two central components: first, the remarkable inner richness and expanse of the self, ultimately encompassing everything; and secondly, the consequent right to project from the subjective structures of one's own mind, and ascertain the nature of humanity as such. It is suggestive that the transcendental pretence was discovered by a sociopath, free and alone with his self-aggrandizement, but one who inspired some of the most spectacular and successful philosophy that the world has ever known.

Introduction

Modern Continental Philosophy and the Transcendental Pretence

Himself as everything! How does Mrs Fichte put up with it?![1]

Heinrich Heine

The background of the transcendental pretence includes the whole of Western history, philosophy, and religion. It is odd and unfortunate that the story of modern philosophy is so often told as the unfolding of a small number of specialized problems in epistemology and metaphysics, so that, not surprisingly, the larger issues and implications of European philosophy are ignored or pushed aside. The story too often starts with Kant or, in an attempt to outline some larger picture, with Galileo and the New Science, with Descartes's *Meditations,* or with David Hume who woke Kant out of his 'dogmatic slumbers'. But the story of modern continental philosophy and the transcendental pretence is not about science, rationalism, or the study of human knowledge. It is rather the dramatic story of the European self-image, in which science and knowledge play an important role but only alongside the romantic imagination, unprecedented cosmic arrogance, continual reaction and rebellion, and the ultimate collapse of a bloated cosmopolitan self-confidence.

The development of European philosophy in the last half of the eighteenth century, particularly in Germany, is a thrilling cultural, intellectual, and psychological adventure story, too often told in the desiccated terms of philosophical technical invention. But the philosophers of the Enlightenment and its romantic aftermath were not all professional academics, foisting this or that system upon their captive colleagues and students, and their story is not aimed at scholars but at humanity as a whole. It is as rich and human as any epic by Tolstoy, even if expressed in the clumsy language of German theology. These philosophers really thought that they would change the world, and sometimes they did. This lack of modesty is essential in understanding their imaginative, if sometimes abstruse, efforts at comprehending the world. Too often the great thinkers of Europe have been dismissed by more down-to-earth, Anglo-American philosophers as obscurantists and charlatans, unfortunate digressions in the history of philosophy. The truth is that they were trying to attack common sense, and to change our very concept of being human. They thought of themselves as prophets, reformers, radicals, and revolutionaries, not just as philosophers and university professors.

The leading theme of this story, accordingly, is the rise and fall of an extraordinary concept of the self. The self in question is no ordinary self, no individual personality, nor even one of the many heroic or mock-heroic personalities of the early nineteenth century. The self that becomes the star performer in modern European philosophy is the transcendental self, or transcendental ego, whose nature and ambitions were unprecedentedly arrogant, presumptuously cosmic, and consequently mysterious. The transcendental self was *the* self—timeless, universal, and in each one of us around the globe and throughout history. Distinguished from our individual idiosyncrasies, this was the self we shared. In modest and ordinary terms it was called 'human nature'. In much less modest, extraordinary terminology, the transcendental self was nothing less than God, the Absolute Self, the World Soul. By about 1805 the self was no longer the mere individual human being, standing with others against a hostile world, but had become all-encompassing. The status of the world and even of God became, if not problematic, no more than aspects of human existence.

In this book I will be presenting the history of the transcendental pretence with a critical eye, aware (in retrospect) of the practical and political dangers of a viewpoint that is so universally projective and self-congratulatory. It is essential, therefore, that we also make clear how plausible, and in many ways inescapable, that viewpoint is and has been. It is also easy to appreciate the ethno- and anthropocentrism of the movement of modern

philosophy through Kant and his successors as a final development of themes that had defined philosophy from its inception.
Socrates as well as Protagoras had argued that humanity must be
the focus, if not the limit, of our inquiries, and many of the essential innovations of medieval philosophy, in Augustine, Abelard,
and Anselm for instance, might be characterized as new discoveries about the nature and importance of the self. Descartes's
epochal change in philosophy was very much a move towards
subjectivity and the self, and the method of the empiricists—
however opposed to Descartes—strengthened the emphases on
experience and introspective reflection, on the nature of the
identity of the self, and on the importance of the first-person
standpoint. Indeed, there is no question but that Descartes, 'the
father of modern philosophy', was also the founder of the modern
philosophical obsession with the self as the locus and arbiter of
knowledge, but the transcendental importance of the self only
begins with Descartes, and most of the problems and possibilities
he initiated do not reach full fruition until the nineteenth century.
But what happens to the self after 1800 in Europe is something
that could not have been imagined in classic British empiricism or
traditional Cartesianism.

 It could hardly be said that Descartes 'discovered' subjectivity
(though Heidegger comments that the Greeks, by contrast, never
had an 'experience'). Augustine, writing 1300 years earlier, had
described his 'inner' self quite thoroughly, even capping his
analysis with that precocious Cartesian insight, 'I think *ergo* I
am.' But what Descartes did, particularly in his *Meditations* of
1641, was to establish the centrality of the human mind, and set
the problems for philosophy for the next 300 years. His turn to
subjectivity involved at least three distinct radical theses: (1) his
method of doubt, the insistence that every belief be considered
guilty (false) until proven innocent (true); (2) his treatment of the
mind as a distinctive realm, with the consequent problem (in
combination with the method of doubt) known as the 'egocentric
predicament'—that is, how do we come to know, and how do we
know that we know, of a world 'outside of' our experience;
(3) his emphasis on the first-person standpoint, on experience
and knowledge from one's own point of view, with an eye to

establishing the objectivity of that experience and knowledge, and thus solving the problems raised in (1) and (2).

The first two theses constitute the problematic core of what is commonly known as 'Cartesianism', but it should be noted that the movement of European philosophy after Descartes largely dispensed with both the insistence on universal doubt, and the conception of the mind as a realm distinct from the 'external world'. It is rather the third thesis, the aim of proving the objectivity of our experience and knowledge from the first-person standpoint, that drives the movement of the philosophical *Zeitgeist*, from Rousseau's efforts to locate objective goodness within the individual to the German idealists' dramatic claims for the unity of self and world. The epistemological thrust of the argument from Cartesian doubt to the Hegelian Absolute is central, but it has too often been emphasized to the exclusion of the broader picture of subjectivity, which includes ethics, aesthetics, and religion as well as questions of knowledge.

It is with Kant that philosophical claims about the self attain new and remarkable proportions. The self becomes not just the focus of attention but the entire subject-matter of philosophy. The self is not just another entity in the world, but in an important sense it creates the world, and the reflecting self does not just know itself, but in knowing itself knows all selves, and the structure of any and every possible self. The ramifications of this view constitute the transcendental pretence. The underlying presumption is that in all essential matters everyone, everywhere, is the same. This was a thesis that was coming of age just as world-wide exploration and colonization was having its full effect, and as transportation, travel, communications, and what was then called 'the conquest of nature' were about to achieve global efficiency. The transcendental pretence is no innocent philosophical thesis, but a political weapon of enormous power. Even as it signalled a radical egalitarianism, and suggested a long-awaited global sensitivity, it also justified unrestricted tolerance for paternalism and self-righteousness—'the white philosopher's burden'. Philosophers who never left their home towns declared themselves experts on 'human nature', and weighed the morals of civilizations and 'savages' thousands of miles beyond their ken. Kant never left the provincial town of Köningsberg, insisting that in its busy port he had the opportunity to observe all of humanity.

The transcendental pretence is the unwarranted assumption that there is universality and necessity in the fundamental modes of human experience. It is not mere provincialism, that is, the ignorance or lack of appreciation of alternative cultures and states of mind. It is an aggressive and sometimes arrogant effort to prove that there are no such (valid) possible alternatives. In its application the transcendental pretence becomes the a priori assertion that the structures of one's own mind, culture, and personality are in some sense necessary and universal for all humankind, perhaps even 'for all rational creatures'. In the realms of morality, politics, and religion it is the effort to prove that there is but one legitimate set of morals (the middle-class morals of Europe), one legitimate form of government (the form of parliamentary monarchy that ruled most of Western Europe), and one true religion, to be defended not just by faith and with force of arms, but by rational arguments, by 'reason alone'.

Setting the Stage: Enlightenment and Romanticism

> The time will come when the sun will shine only on free men who know no master but their reason. . . . How consoling for the philosopher who laments the errors, the crimes, the injustices which still pollute the earth and of which he is often the victim, is this view of the human race, emancipated from its shackles, released from the empire of fate and from that of the enemies of progress, advancing with a firm and sure step along the path of truth, virtue and happiness.[1]
>
> Condorcet

The ideological cauldron from which modern European philosophy emerged is commonly called 'the Enlightenment'. This period of intense philosophical exploration and criticism began in England in the mid-seventeenth century, spread to America and France in the mid-eighteenth century, and finally reached Germany, and eastern and southern Europe just before the beginning of the nineteenth century. In its wake it fomented and rationalized several major revolutions and the Napoleonic wars, as well as initiating radical new developments in philosophy and culture. The Enlightenment was a time of lively intellectual debate and enthusiastic scientific discovery. It was also a time of far-reaching personal, political, and philosophical experimentation— Montaigne's delineation of the private self through his *Essais*, Owen's and Fourier's socialist communes, Hume and d'Holbach's radical challenges to established philosophy. Diderot, the editor of the *Encyclopaedia*, and the iconoclastic Voltaire were voluptuaries and sexual revolutionaries as well as devastating debaters, and even the Marquis de Sade can be seen as very much a part of the Enlightenment. In other words, the Enlightenment, especially in France, was first of all an attitude of rejuvenation, a spirited sense of criticism and experimentation, and an enthusiastic endorsement of change and progress. It was not a distinctive set of doctrines (the *philosophes* seemed to disagree about everything, even about the importance of disagreeing), but it is still possible to isolate some of its general characteristics, particularly its humanism, rationality, and universalism.

Humanism

Enlightenment ('secular') humanism has often been misunderstood as an attack on Christianity and religion in general, but it is important to insist that the origins of European humanism lie *within* the Church, dating from the twelfth century, and that several of the leading Enlightenment *philosophes*—notably Rousseau—were adamant theists (Rousseau recommended the death penalty for non-believers in his *Social Contract*). It is true that the Enlightenment was often at odds with Church authorities, and the religions defended by the *philosophes* were rarely orthodox, but it would be a mistake to think of Enlightenment humanism as antagonistic to religion as such.

What humanism did mean, most of all, was that the world had become a human world, determined (and threatened) by human aspirations, and delineated no longer by nature but by national boundaries. The world may have been created by God but it was now in the hands—for better or worse—of humanity. The world was a human stage, with human values, emotions, hopes, and fears, and this humanity was defined, in turn, by a universal human nature. 'In all nations and ages,' wrote David Hume, 'human nature remains still the same.' Racial, national, and cultural differences are superficial; our basic ideas, senses, and sentiments are all the same. And so the Enlightenment *philosophes* insisted on tolerance of differences, and they took it upon themselves to speak for all humanity. It was also a period of intense curiosity and an abstract sense of brotherhood. 'Nothing human is foreign to me', defined the temperament of the times. Pope's declaration that 'the proper study of mankind is man' became the working definition of the Enlightenment intellect.

Rationality

The key to human nature, for the philosophers and reformers of the Enlightenment, was its inherent rationality, the inborn faculty of *reason*. Reason enabled us to discover the intricate, abstract truths of mathematics, and to apply these to our understanding of the workings of the universe. Reason allowed us to ask and answer questions of Nature through carefully planned observations and experiments. The Enlightenment emphasis on rationality should not be confused with the rather narrowly defined philosophical orientation called 'rationalism'—which specifies a special confidence in the powers of human reason to recognize necessary non-empirical truths. The rationality of the Enlightenment includes both rationalism and empiricism. Voltaire, never patient with philosophical niceties, continually mixed the two up. Reason was basic to human nature, and with reason it was possible to guarantee universal agreement on questions about the world as well as about matters of mathematics.

This confidence in reason and rationality, however, was not confined to matters of science and mathematics. Part of Enlightenment humanism was its keen sense of humanity as part of nature, and it was one of the most fervent beliefs of the period that human social life was subject to the organization of reason according to the nature of human nature and the values of humanism—in particular 'the pursuit of happiness'. Thus the leading philosophers of the time developed a range of naturalistic theories of human nature, of man as a machine (d'Holbach), of the mind as a Newtonian microcosm (Hume), of reason as a system of built-in knowledge, guaranteed by God (Leibniz). On a larger scale philosophers developed an even wider range of models for the ideal forms of government and society. Optimism about the future of humanity was virtually the religion of the day, with an emphasis not on faith but on planning, and a sense of inevitable human progress. Even religion was subjected to the scrutiny of rational procedures: the attack was not on religion but on 'superstition', that is, on those religious doctrines (such as belief in miracles) that could not be justified by the new confidence in human reason.

Universalism

The belief in the universality of human nature, one aspect of which is universal reason, already entails the transcendental pretence. If all people are basically the same, and if that sameness lies in part in the universal reach of reason, it is not hard to conclude that everyone, everywhere, ought to believe in the same scientific truths, follow the same moral guidelines, endorse the same political structures, and worship the same god or gods. But it should not be thought that this confidence in universality considered itself to be imperialistic or coercive. Since everyone is rational then everyone would, or should, come—on his or her own—to the same conclusions. Thus the belief in universal reason becomes coupled to a confidence in individual *autonomy*—the ability of every human being to come to the right conclusions, though perhaps only after considerable education and argument. The good news was that human conflict was about to come to an end, since all disagreements could be negotiated through universal reason. The bad news was not yet evident: that not everyone would in fact agree, indeed would not even agree with the ideals of rationality, universality, and autonomy. The result would be some of the most pig-headed disagreements in history, no longer caused by pride, avarice, or religious competition, but by *ideology* bolstered with confidence in 'self-evident' truths about the nature of 'human nature'.

One philosopher develops these three themes more systematically than any other, and he was neither French, nor English, but Prussian—Immanuel Kant. But though the Enlightenment philosophy culminates in Germany its presuppositions were fully operative throughout the Enlightenment. Indeed, it is only when these canonical beliefs start to come under attack that so elaborate a defence as Kant's is required—and this attack came first of all in Germany (it can be argued that resistance to Enlightenment ideals reached similar strength in England, America, and France only very recently, perhaps only within the past few decades). The irony of this is that the wholly successful French and English Enlightenment received its most brilliant defence in Germany, where the Enlightenment never fully took hold.

The attack on the Enlightenment in Germany gave itself a distinctive name—romanticism. *Die Romantik* was first of all a reaction—to the Enlightenment and its excessive humanism, its blind confidence in human reason and rationality, and its arrogant universalism. Cosmopolitan philosophers in London or Paris might pretend that they could speak for all humanity, but equally serious thinkers stuck in the small, fragmented, still largely feudal states of Germany could not easily do so. English and French culture ruled, or aspired to rule, the world. It was all the defensive Germans could do just to get their language and culture acknowledged in their own lands. Many of the princes of Germany considered themselves enlightened, and spoke mainly in French (Frederick the Great spoke brilliantly in French, but was less than fluent in his own 'native' language). The Enlightenment, in other words, was viewed as a threat in Germany. Romanticism, however cosmic its expressions, was first of all an expression of nationalism and provincial self-assertion. But like so much of the Enlightenment, romanticism projected its provincial anxieties on to the universe itself, and in its later stages elevated the transcendental pretence to the level of an absolute. So far as the transcendental pretence was concerned, Enlightenment and romanticism turned out to be more alike than opposed.

It is possible to make too much of the social origins of intellectual currents, but the more usual problem in philosophy is the total neglect of demographic and political concerns, making the Enlightenment appear as a set of abstract claims about the source and justification of knowledge which emerges out of nowhere (or, as the proponents themselves would have put it, out of universal reason itself). Romanticism similarly appears not as a nationalistic reaction but rather as an irresponsible digression from proper philosophy by poets who did not have the patience to study Locke. But it is no historical accident that the central themes of the Enlightenment originated in cosmopolitan London and Paris, or that the romantic reaction emerged most forcefully in the smaller states of Germany, and neither movement can be comprehended in philosophical terms alone. The Enlightenment must be understood in terms of the *philosophes*' international aspirations, Voltaire's social activism and prejudices *against* philosophy, and Kant's comfortable position as a university professor in an age of violent revolutions. Romanticism was indeed a rejection of some of the most cherished Enlightenment principles, but it was also a rejection of the political imperialism of the more powerful Enlightenment nations, and a defence of traditional religion against excessive rationalism. It is not unimportant that several of the leading romantics were converted to Catholicism, endorsed mysticism, and extolled the virtues of poetry over philosophy.

Despite their opposition, both the Enlightenment and romanticism had the same social origins as expressions of middle-class— or more properly bourgeois (*bürgerlich*)—ideology. The preconditions of the Enlightenment were the growth of cities, the enlarging of the civil service, improved education, the centralization of power and government, and, as both partial cause and consequence, the rapid expansion of the bourgeoisie in France and England. In feudal Germany the middle-class was less prominent and less powerful, which helps to explain some of the differences in philosophy. But what the middle-class philosophers throughout Europe felt was an adolescent arrogance appropriate to their ascendancy, and this emerged in the transcendental pretence, whether in the unrestricted claims of universal rationality, or in the uninhibited reach of romanticism.

The attack on the Enlightenment, and its ultimate collapse was not, however, initiated by the romantics. It began with the devastating arguments of Rousseau's friend David Hume (1711–76). Although he does not fit within the European scope of this book, Hume was a typical Enlightenment philosopher. He thought that Isaac Newton was the most important intellectual and cultural figure since ancient times, and his ambition was nothing less than to construct a theory of human nature as elegant as Newton's theories of the universe. He believed in reason and the empirical appeal to the senses, and detested blind obedience to authority on such nonsensical matters as metaphysics and theology. And yet he turned the Enlightenment on its ear. He used a set of devastating arguments to show that the unqualified faith of the Enlightenment in the powers of reason and experience was limited; in fact, reason and experience could not even justify our most basic beliefs about the world such as, for instance, that such a world exists outside of our experience. He denied that we ever actually experience the necessary connections between events that we call 'causes', so that there is no way that we can rationally or empirically justify even the most common causal explanations. It was this scepticism, this deep doubt about our abilities to know the world, and for that matter ourselves, that would awaken Kant, in his own words, 'from my dogmatic slumbers' (that is, from his confidence that reason could justify, and had succeeded in justifying, such basic principles). It is Kant, reacting to Hume, who develops the intellectual machinery that will bring the Enlightenment to its peak, and then, in the hands of his romantic successors, turn against it. But if Hume did not have unqualified confidence in reason, he did share with Rousseau a profound confidence in the human sentiments. 'Reason is and ought to be the slave of the passions', he wrote in his *Treatise of Human Nature*,[2] and so expressed a thesis that would have great appeal to the romantics—though few of them had much sympathy with Hume's empiricism, scepticism, or light touch with philosophical issues.

It is the interweaving of Enlightenment and romanticism that provides the main thread of the story of modern European philosophy, even if these terms are not much used after the turn of the nineteenth century. On the Enlightenment side is the heavy emphasis on science, universal principles, and rationality. On the romantic side are deep doubts about science, and a reliance on intuition and feeling rather than reason. But what they share is as important as their disgreements. They both believe in the personal significance of the individual, and that through the individual it is possible to understand the whole. Thus it is easy to see how it is that Rousseau occupies a pivotal position in both movements. He was a bona fide member of the Enlightenment, dedicated to rational reform, and the improvement and happiness of humanity. But he was also the proponent of a provincial, simple life of sentiment, and his concept of the General Will would have a powerful appeal for later romantic authors who also sought some supra-personal self. Foremost among his followers was

Kant, usually considered the most important defender of the Enlightenment in Germany, but in fact the man who set the stage for the most dramatic romantic themes, including the elevation of the self from mere personal identity to an Absolute Self of transcendental proportions.

1

The Discovery of the Self: Rousseau

> As Newton was the first to discern order and regularity in nature, Rousseau was the first to discover beneath the varying forms human nature assumes, the deeply concealed essence of man and the hidden law in accordance with which providence is justified.[1]
>
> Kant

Our story begins not with science, or Cartesianism, or even with Kant, but with the neurotic and solitary genius of Jean-Jacques Rousseau (1712–78), at once a member of the French Enlightenment, and the founder of European romanticism, one-time friend of Diderot, Voltaire, d'Alembert, and Hume but inevitably their enemy as well. Unlike those sophisticated urban gentlemen, he was a country bumpkin who felt more at home in the woods of St Germain than in the noisy cafés of Paris. His philosophy was not so much a cry for reasonableness as a radical proposal to revise our very idea of what it is to be human.

Rousseau is often left out of standard Anglo-American accounts of modern philosophy, and the reason is not hard to find. He had no epistemology, and a post-Cartesian philosopher is expected to have an epistemology. But he had something more to offer than a theory of knowledge or another solution to the paradoxes of scepticism. He was, above all, *edifying*, bolstering his reader's confidence in themselves, and especially in that precious 'inner goodness' that Rousseau claimed to discern in himself, and by implication in all of us. He may be read today primarily for his political philosophy with its benign image of 'the state of nature', and his influential version of 'the social contract', but he was read in his own time—by Kant and Marie-Antoinette alike—as an inspiring philosopher of human nature and education, and an advocate of the inner goodness in us all.

Rousseau, of course, is not an isolated figure. He mixed with the leading *philosophes* of France, and his friend Hume was the leading light of the Scottish Enlightenment (they fell out after one of Rousseau's bouts of paranoia). However much he may have differed from these colleagues personally or philosophically, Rousseau was very much a part of the new ways of thinking. He defended the validity of original thought and criticism, believed in the rational restructuring of our major institutions, and prized the individual human being and his or her happiness above all else. Unlike Hume, however, Rousseau was not particularly concerned with the nature and limits of reason as such, and unlike his sarcastic nemesis Voltaire he had little inclination towards practical involvement in politics, and fled from the opportunity to put his theories to the test in Geneva. Some would diagnose Rousseau today as a thorough-going narcissist, concerned wholly with himself. More significant for the future of philosophy, however, was his seeing, as a result of his self-absorption, the dramatic image of the self writ large. His version of the Enlightenment was an imaginative set of suggestions about how we should conceive of ourselves anew, stripped of the artifices and artificialities of culture and (especially) the court, and removed from the deleterious effects of ambition, competition, and the ownership of private property. Other philosophers (including Descartes, Voltaire, and Hume) had presupposed and argued some universal human nature, but no one before Rousseau had presented this familiar idea with quite his flamboyance and vision. If we want to understand his powerful influence on the direction of European philosophy ever since, it is the spirit of this idea, rather than just its conceptual outlines, that we must appreciate, as did Kant and many others.

Rousseau discovered a new 'inner' self of considerable moral substance. Descartes, of course, had put enormous emphasis on the substantial, subjective self—the self as a thinking thing—but his was a concept that satisfied an appeal to logic, not to empathy and human fellowship. Rousseau emphasized feeling rather than thought as the key to the self, and the private sense of goodness rather than the logic of self-reference was its justification. Locke too had developed an empirical concept of self as introspectible memories, but while this solved some of the technical problems about the continuity of personal identity over time, it lacked the personal persuasiveness of Rousseau's moral inner self. For Rousseau the self was not just introspectible but essentially *expressive*, projecting into the world and the future. Rousseau's self, in other words, displayed not just the formal features required by the rationalists and empiricists, but the sense of universal *personality* later required by the romantics. The self was neither the first principle of metaphysics nor a consequence of empiricism; it was first of all our own inner activity—and the most important thing in the world.

Rousseau differs from Descartes and Locke most of all in his insistence that the self is distinctively moral, and he anticipates Kant in his insistence that it is the goodness of the self itself—rather than our actions—that defines us:

I drew this great maxim of morality, perhaps the only one of practical use, to avoid situations which put our duties in opposition with our interests and which show us our good in the hurts of others, sure that in such situations, however sincere our love of virtue, we weaken sooner or later without realizing it, and become unjust and wicked in our actions, without having stopped being just and good at heart.[2]

Rousseau stressed the sentiments as central to self—though this emphasis is often overplayed. He insists that reason and the sentiments work together in the moral life: 'Our natural sentiments shall guide reason to know the good, our conscience then to love it.' But he does say that 'a man who thinks is a depraved animal', and insists that even 'if all the philosophers in the world should prove me wrong', all that is important is that 'you feel that I am right'. In a famous passage he even insists that he is teaching *against* the passions, at least against those that are most destructive to civilized humanity: 'I do not want to make modern man a savage and send him back to the woods, but rather teach him, in the whirl of social life, not to be carried away by the passions and prejudices of men.'[3]

Rousseau's sense of the self was social and political as well as moral. On the one hand, he held that the self was strictly individual, even unique. In his *Confessions* he writes: 'I am unlike anyone I have ever met; I will even venture to say that I am like no one in the whole world.'[4] In the state of nature, he argues, the individual is free and independent: 'The man who stands in dependence on another is no longer a man.' He canonizes a long French tradition of 'inner freedom' even in the presence of overwhelming obstacles to physical freedom: 'As I have said a hundred times, if ever I were confined to the Bastille, there I would draw the picture of liberty.'[5] But what he means by 'freedom' is not obvious; its primary meaning is 'freedom from other people', or what Kant would later call 'autonomy'. But for Rousseau this freedom was not simply the right to self-determination; it betrayed his deep distrust of other people, and his own guilty, resentful sense of having been 'corrupted' by society. Accordingly, he develops a picture of human nature, with freedom at its centre, which stretches between the isolated individual and society writ large, where what is left out is the whole realm of personal relations and community.

It is here, of course, that Kant and much of subsequent philosophy will follow (though Descartes too had defended a philosophy that was dangerously solipsistic). In the German idealist tradition, 'inner freedom' would often eclipse political activism altogether, but this was not so for Rousseau. Because we are all free and good as individuals we are capable of entering into that grand 'social contract' which creates society. When a man enters into society he is transformed, turned from a man into a *citizen* whose self is defined by participation rather than independence, even while that participation presupposes his essential freedom. The common expression of all citizens is the *General Will*, which should be considered a living entity in its own right:

The body politic, taken individually, may be considered as an organized living body, resembling that of man. [It] is also a moral being possessed of a will, and this general will, which tends always to the preservation and welfare of the whole and of every part, is the source of the laws. . . . Each of us puts his person and all of his power in common under the supreme direction of the general will, and, in our corporate capacity, we receive each member as an indivisible part of the whole.[6]

In few other philosophers is there such an obvious battle

between individualism and communitarianism—the self as atomic and personal versus the self as irreducibly social. Rousseau emerges as the champion of free and natural living, and as one of the creators of the modern state based on popular representation rather than force or 'divine right' but no less powerful for that. The results of this conflict are sometimes shocking, as in Rousseau's infamous insistence that a citizen who refuses to co-operate with the General Will should be 'forced to be free'.[7] But it is this same sense of the General Will and the ideal of a society of non-combative individuals that gives rise to Rousseau's distrust of private property, a view that would be an important influence on the French socialists, and especially on the young Karl Marx. In England and America the demand for freedom emerged in the concept of the individual, working, acquisitive self, but in Europe the concept of self that emerged in the name of freedom was a supra-human, non-individual self, like Rousseau's General Will. Sharing property was part and parcel of sharing a self, and the invention of private property, Rousseau proclaims, was one of the great crimes against humanity:

The first man who enclosed a plot of ground and bethought himself of saying 'this is mine' and found others foolish enough to believe him, was the true founder of civil society. How many crimes, how many wars, how many murders, how many misfortunes and horrors would that man have saved the human species, who pulling up the stakes or filling up the ditches should have cried to his fellows: Beware of listening to this imposter; you are lost, if you forget that the fruits of this earth belong equally to us all, and the earth itself to nobody.[8]

The infamous underlying contrast of Rousseau's work, between happy individuals in the state of nature and the miserable creatures in civilized society, is never very far from consideration:

Savage man, when he has dined, is at peace with nature, and the friend of all his fellow creatures. . . . The case is quite different with man in the state of society, for whom first necessities have to be provided, and then superfluities; delicacies follow next, then immense wealth, then subjects, then slaves. He enjoys not a moment's relaxation; and what is yet stranger, the less natural and pressing his wants, the more headstrong are his passions, and, still worse, the more he has it in his power to gratify them; so that after a long course of prosperity, after having swallowed up treasures and ruined multitudes the hero ends up by cutting every throat till he finds himself, at last, sole master of the world. Such is in miniature the moral picture, if not of human life, at least of the secret aspirations in the heart of every civilized man.[9]

and

Nature made man happy and good, and society depraves him and makes him miserable.[10]

The point of the theory of the self is to correct this unflattering contrast by showing us that we 'really' are better than we appear to be, and this, more than anything, will be the driving force of the story of Continental philosophy. The story of modern European philosophy is the protracted prognosis of self-transformation.

Let us penetrate to the bottom of our hearts, and let us reflect on what the state of things must be in which all men are forced to caress each other and destroy each other, and in which they are born enemies out of duty and crooks out of self interest.[11]

Introspective, antisocial, and almost paranoid, Rousseau alone among the great *philosophes* of France made an enormous impact not only on the thinking of revolutionary France, but on the history of ideas. We still admire the wit and irony of Voltaire but he is rarely read for his ideas. The brilliance of Diderot is still insufficiently appreciated, and even Hume, often said (in Britain at least) to be the greatest philosopher of modern times, plays a role in philosophy that is more provocative than inspirational. Curiously, though, the great impact of Rousseau in philosophy was not felt and expressed in France but rather in neighbouring Germany. Indeed, it is almost as if French philosophy went into eclipse after the Enlightenment. Rousseau's inspirational discovery first came to fruition in the academic cloisters of provincial Prussia in the work of Kant, then through Schiller, Goethe, Hegel, and Marx it came to influence half of the civilized world.

Part I

The Rise of the Self in German Idealism

2

Kant and the German Enlightenment

Two things have always filled me with awe: the starry
heavens above and the moral law within.[1]

Kant

In an important sense, the German Enlightenment (*Aufklärung*)
developed in a vacuum. In France (and earlier in England)
Enlightenment theories were blueprints for reform or revolution,
but in Germany the political situation was such that reform was
all but unthinkable. The middle class was powerless. Germany
was fragmented into hundreds of tiny states and principalities,
and apart from Prussia, which was ruled by the iron-fisted but
'enlightened' Frederick the Great, there was no central government as in Paris or London. In 1789 Immanuel Kant (1724–1804)
wished the French revolutionaries well, but with no thought that
a similar revolution might or should be staged in Prussia. Heine
may have compared Kant to Robespierre for the bold radicalism
of his thinking, but their revolutions were not on a par. The
Enlightenment in England and France fostered a hard-headed,
visionary realism. In Germany it had to settle for an abstract
idealism, and enlightenment of the spirit only, or as Marx would
write in *The German Ideology*:

While the French bourgeoisie, by means of the most colossal revolution
that history has ever known, was achieving domination and conquering
the Continent of Europe, while the already emancipated English bourgeoisie was revolutionizing industry and subjugating India politically
and all the rest of the world commercially, the impotent German burghers
did not get any farther than 'good will'. . . . Kant's good will fully
corresponds to the impotence, depression and wretchedness of the
German burghers, whose petty interests were never capable of developing
into the common interests of a class but had their counterpart in their
cosmopolitan swollen-headedness.[2]

Immanuel Kant read and admired Rousseau; he practically worshipped Isaac Newton. From his perch on the Baltic Sea he surveyed the panorama of the world, and identified himself as the representative of humanity. As such he saw his mission in philosophy to be the defence of science, morality, and the rationality of religion. This was no easy task, for science and religion in particular had been at war for centuries. Kant was living (as we all are) in a transitional age. Science had won a long and hard-fought battle against the authority of religion, but though this was all well and good from a scientific point of view it was a disaster from the point of view of morality and religion. Kant may have worshipped Newton, but he was also a devout Lutheran, and though Newton himself had struggled to reconcile his theories of the universe with his own Christian beliefs, the conflict had not yet been satisfactorily resolved. To be sure, it was a good thing that science had won its autonomy and freedom from the dogmatic interference of religion, but if this meant that all religious and other unscientific beliefs were unjustifiable, and as such irrational, then the victory of science from a religious and humanist point of view was a disaster. Kant's mission, then, was not just to provide foundations; he had to redefine what it meant to be a rational human being. Consequently he announced his plan to 'deny *knowledge*, in order to make room for *faith*'.

Kant's philosophy is consummated in three magnificent volumes that he called 'critiques'. These were critical in the spirit of the Enlightenment, but also idealistic and speculative, with a spirit hardly known among the French *philosophes*—except in Rousseau. German idealism—often called Kantian idealism—is idealistic in the familiar sense of defending abstract ideals. In philosophy, however, it also has a technical sense: the world is constituted out of ideas. It is 'idealistic' too in its assurance that such a world is real and good, an assurance that had been shaken by Hume, who raised serious questions about the foundations of both knowledge and morals. Our knowledge, he had argued, is based only on habit, and morality is based on sentiment, not reason.

The first Critique, *The Critique of Pure Reason*, tackles the problem of knowledge and Hume's scepticism. At the heart of that formidable book, and the dramatic shift in Western thinking that begins with it, is an enormous expansion in the concept of the self, its scope, power, and richness. The primary change is a shift from the passive to the active mode, a rejection of the traditional idea of the human mind as a receptacle or receiver, to the insistence that the mind *imposes* its order on nature, an order which is fixed and immutable in all of us. 'The understanding does not derive its laws from, but prescribes them to nature.'[3] The second, *The Critique of Practical Reason*, is an attempt to analyse and justify the concept of morality, to free it from the unpredictability of sentiment and social fashion, and to defend it as a product of pure practical reason which is, as such, valid for all people at all times and under all conditions. The third Critique, *The Critique of Judgement*, has been considered the least conse-quential of the three, and is often neglected in English Kantian scholarship; but this is certainly not true on the Continent, where Kant's influence was based at least as much on this work as upon the other two. Goethe confessed that he could not read the first two Critiques, but he admired the third, as did Schiller, who reinterpreted the first two in its light, attempting a grand synthesis of Kant's version of the international Enlightenment and the uniquely German romantic *Sturm und Drang* ('Storm and Stress') reaction to it. On a superficial reading the third Critique might seem to be an unwieldy conglomeration of theses about the nature of art and beauty, the role of 'teleology' (purposive explanations) in science, and edifying remarks on the ultimate meaning of life and the universe. But what Kant has in mind in his discussion of beauty is not the protected domain of aesthetics and 'art for art's sake' but something much grander, the beauty of human life and morality, of nature, and of the universe as a whole as an expression of God's beneficence and human destiny. So understood, we can more readily appreciate how the third Critique was intended as the synthesis and culmination of the other two, and how it was the third Critique that so heavily influenced the German idealists and romantics who followed Kant.

Although the problems that drove Kant to philosophy were deeply felt, it was not in his nature to write, as had his hero

Rousseau, an elegant popular treatise or a semi-fictional novel, much less a revealing *Confessions*. His ideas had to be couched objectively and impersonally, for while Rousseau projected outward from his peculiar, personal self to the whole of humanity, Kant began with the view that human reason was universal and objective. One's personal autobiography had little relevance to the important truth about the self that Rousseau had discovered. For Rousseau, that special sense of self was something to be experienced first of all; for Kant, it was a profound metaphysical thesis to be demonstrated through the cold calculations of deductive logic. But what those deductions revealed—what Kant called his 'Copernican Revolution'—was nothing less than a revision of our view of the self in the world.

The first Copernican revolution had denied the obvious—that the sun revolved while the earth stood still. What Kant denied seemed even more obvious, that the world was 'out there' and independent of our experience of it. The whole history of metaphysics depends upon the belief in the presence of a reality independent of us, from Thales' precocious insights and Plato's brilliant defence of a World of Being beyond our own world of change and becoming, to Descartes's systematic doubts about our knowledge of the external world and the scepticism of Hume. The problem with metaphysics was that no one seemed to have the slightest hold on the true nature of reality, or as Kant put it:

metaphysics has rather to be regarded as a battle-ground quite peculiarly suited for those who desire to exercise themselves in mock combats, and in which no participant has ever yet succeeded in gaining even so much as an inch of territory, not at least in such a manner as to secure him in its permanent possession.[4]

But while Hume's conclusion was that all such metaphysical efforts should henceforth be 'committed to the flames' as nothing more than 'sophistry and illusion', Kant insists that metaphysics is inescapable:

That the human mind will ever give up metaphysical researches is as little to be expected as that we, to avoid inhaling impure air, should prefer to give up breathing altogether.[5]

In particular, there are three metaphysical questions which the human mind finds unavoidable. Kant summarizes these as 'God, Freedom, and Immortality'. But in addition there are other questions: about the nature of the self, the substantiality and the workings of the world, space and time, and the seemingly eternal verities of mathematics and geometry, as well as of religion. These questions define the structure of *The Critique of Pure Reason*, while God, freedom, and immortality are discussed in the second Critique and, to a lesser extent, in the third.

The Critique of Pure Reason has a single central thesis: knowledge of the world is possible because the self—the transcendental self or ego—determines the structure of our every experience, or as Kant puts it:

Hitherto it has been assumed that our knowledge must conform to objects. But all attempts to extend our knowledge of objects by establishing something in regard to them a priori, by means of concepts, have, on this assumption, ended in failure. We must therefore make trial whether we may not have more success in the tasks of metaphysics if we suppose that objects must conform to knowledge.[6]

The reasoning behind this revolution in philosophy can best be appreciated by referring back to Descartes and Hume. However radical Kant's suggestion that we determine our experience may be, it is more palatable and plausible than the sceptical implications of Descartes's method of doubt, and Hume's devastating conclusion that we could not really know the world at all. Descartes's first-person, subjective standpoint lies at the basis of Kant's arguments (and Hume's too), for the leading question of Kant's epistemology is how is it possible for our consciousness to know the world? So long as the world lies outside the realm of our experience, scepticism is inescapable, but to Kant it is also intolerable. What is necessary is to complete the move that Descartes began, recognizing not only the importance of the first-person point of view, but also its all-encompassing nature. The world *is* the world of our experience, not something outside of it. We are not just acted upon by a world we never know directly; we act upon the world to give it its basic forms.

The structure of the first Critique is based upon a three-part division of the 'faculties' of the human mind into sense, under-standing, and reason. Sense is our capacity to be affected by sensations, to see, hear, smell, and feel. Understanding is our ability to categorize and identify those sensations, to recognize objects and relations between them, and to employ concepts in experience. Reason is our ability to entertain and manipulate those concepts quite apart from our actual experience, as in mathematics or logic. One might say that understanding is the application of concepts to sensory experience to give us know-ledge, while reason is the application of concepts to themselves, which is why self-reflection and philosophy are primarily matters of reason, not experience. Each of these faculties has certain built-in structures which determine the nature of our experience. It is the nature of sense that all of our experiences take place in the forward flow of time and in three-dimensional space. It is the nature of understanding that what we experience are objects, not just sensations, and that these objects exist independently in the world, in various causal relationships with one another (and with us). The intriguing and somewhat paradoxical thesis here is that the human mind is responsible for the appearance of objects and their structures as independent of us, even though we can come to appreciate, through reason, that this appearance of independence is dependent upon us. But reason, because of its remarkable ability to operate independently of the facts of experience, is also capable of tying itself up in paradoxes and over-extending itself in realms where our concepts are inappropriate. Thus Kant's book is a 'critique of pure reason', an effort (in part) to curb the historical pretensions of reason, and reason alone, to gain knowledge of God, eternity, and the nature of the world beyond the realm of our experience.

But *The Critique of Pure Reason* is, first of all, an investigation into those structures that determine our experience, that is, the structures or rules of sense and understanding. Kant's stated aim may be critical but his actual method is to clarify and justify our most basic claims of knowledge about the world, those claims whose justifiability Hume had doubted: our knowledge that there is an 'external world' of objects, and that there are 'necessary connections' among them. His method is to introduce a new vision of human knowledge, a basic mode of knowledge that is something more than the passive reception and interpretation of sensations, and more substantial than the abstract manipulation of ideas, knowledge that is basic to and yet independent of experience. If this vision is correct and if it can be demonstrated that such knowledge is genuine (and not mere subjective judgement), then Kant will have succeeded in refuting Hume's scepticism, but more momentously will have succeeded in revising the traditional picture of the human mind. Kant calls such knowledge 'a priori', and it is through the display and proof of the a priori principles that rule our experience that Kant tries to show that the world has and *must* have the structures that we impose upon it, and that there is but one possible set of such structures, so that our Western scientific knowledge (with Newton's theories as its model) is and ought to be the standard of knowledge the world over.

The word 'transcendental' is central to Kant's theory, and to the story of philosophy that we are studying here. 'Transcendental' means 'necessary and universal', in contrast to the merely personal or psychological. Transcendental structures of experience are those which are basic to any experience whatever (the adjective 'transcendental' should be distinguished from 'transcendent', which means 'beyond' or 'outside of'). Kant sometimes calls his philosophy 'transcendental idealism', which refers to the thesis that certain ideas are the basic (a priori) conditions for all possible human experience. The self that is the basic source of our concepts and experience is called 'the transcendental ego', the principles that are basic to the various realms of experience are called 'transcendental principles', and the demonstrations that establish the universal validity of these principles are called 'transcendental arguments'. To say that an idea or a principle is not just personal or psychological is to say that it is not only basic to *our* experience, but that it is universal and necessary for every being or creature who can be said to have a mind at all. Thus the enormous burden that Kant takes upon himself is not just the discovery of a priori or transcendental principles, but the demonstration of their universality and necessity.

The Critique of Pure Reason is nothing less than a detailed catalogue of the a priori or transcendental principles that govern our experience, and a series of arguments to show that there could be no other such principles. The book is divided into three parts, corresponding to the three faculties of the mind, each with its own a priori structures and principles. First there is the Transcendental Aesthetic, which presents and proves the fundamental principles of all sensory experience. Since the basic structures of the faculty of sense—the 'a priori forms of intuition'—are space and time, the a priori principles presented in this first part of the Critique turn out to be none other than the familiar first principles of arithmetic and Euclidean geometry. It is sometimes said that the eternal truths of mathematics are nothing more than conventions determining the way we use certain symbols. It has also been said—notably by Plato—that mathematical propositions are true because they refer to some ethereal (transcendent) entities beyond the realm of our experience. What Kant tells us is that neither of these alternatives makes any sense. Arithmetic and geometry are not mere systems of symbolic conventions, for they apply without fail to the world, and they are not outside the world of our experience but basic to it. The propositions of mathematics do nothing less than describe the basic structures of our experience itself. But there is a further consequence of this view, and that is that the ego itself is 'outside' of time, and timeless. It projects temporality but is not itself temporal.

The Transcendental Analytic is Kant's study of the a priori or transcendental principles of understanding, the way in which we apply concepts to our sense experience to gain knowledge. Most concepts, of course, are learned through experience, as we learn to recognize different objects and the various distinctions among them. But some of our concepts—the most basic ones such as the concept of an object as such, or the concept of one event causing another—are not learned but are presupposed in every experience. Kant (following Aristotle) calls these a priori concepts 'categories'. Drawing on the psychologists of his time, Kant presents us with what he believes to be an exhaustive list of categories, which conveniently number twelve, in four sets of three. In an infamously obscure 'Transcendental Deduction of the Categories' Kant tries to show that this set of twelve constitutes the only possible conditions for experience. Along the way he refutes

Hume, who had argued that our experience never includes any observation of the necessary connection between two events, no matter how regularly one event follows the other in time. Kant agrees with this, but only to add that we necessarily apply the a priori idea of causation to every single observation, and have no choice but to do so. It is easy to miss in the labyrinthine argument of the Transcendental Analytic, but Kant is defending a most spectacular claim: that it is we ourselves who give form to the world. We know the world—and know that we know the world— not because our experience corresponds to external reality but because reality must conform to the structures of the mind. 'We can know a priori of things only what we ourselves put into them.'[7]

One of the conditions for there being any experience or knowledge whatever is the existence of a self that has these experiences and understands them. Every experience, to put it simply, must be *someone's* experience. In one sense Kant is only repeating Descartes's famous formulation of self-knowledge, but he goes beyond this when he claims that the unity of our experience can only be explained through transcendental necessity. Indeed, it has been argued that Kant's difficult deduction of the categories has a similar (though far more sophisticated) form to Descartes's demonstration of our knowledge of the external world, taking the 'possibility of the "I think" accompanying all of our experience' as its first premiss, but Kant's conception of the self and self-knowledge is far more than a mere formal inference or a mere condition for experience; it is itself one *source* of our experience, and as such the condition for the existence of the world.

In one sense this would seem to be utter nonsense, for as any philosophy undergraduate will be quick to point out, the world was here long before any of us, and presumably it—or some devastated version of it—will long survive us. But Kant does not claim that the self by itself produces our experience; it supplies only the forms, not the sensory data of experience—which are 'given'. Moreover, the self that Kant calls 'transcendental' is clearly something other than our ordinary notion of self, one that is 36 years old, blonde but balding, timid on social occasions but a tiger on the football field. This is what Kant calls the 'empirical' self, the individual self that has a certain history, body, and personality, that was born in Manchester in October 1951, and will die of causes and at a time yet unknown. But there is another transcendental self that does not share these characteristics. Sometimes Kant limits himself to the claim that this transcendental ego is a merely formal self, known only through inferences to its necessity (as in Descartes), but elsewhere he makes it clear that the transcendental self is not just inferred; perhaps it is even known directly, in each and every experience. In the second Critique Kant says that the self is not only the source of the categories, and consequently of all knowledge, but is also the source of *agency*, the will behind our actions. Furthermore, at least one of the three basic concerns of metaphysics—the idea of immortality—intimately concerns the self as well. Kant rejects Descartes's claim that the self is a substantial *thing*, independent of the body, and therefore capable of surviving the death of the body, but nevertheless defends belief in the immortality of the soul.

The transcendental ego, then, is quite different from the empirical self of everyday life, but it is also much more than the merely formal recognition that my every experience is 'mine'. It is a rich source of a priori knowledge (and, we shall see, of morality too). It is timeless and universal, and so in a profound sense not 'mine' at all. Kant writes not about transcendental ego*s* but *the* transcendental ego, 'consciousness in general'. Some of Kant's followers will make ample use of this indeterminacy.

The third part of Kant's first Critique, which concerns the faculty of reason, is called 'The Transcendental Dialectic'. It is highly critical of the pretensions of reason, and seems far more concerned with attacking the a priori claims of the great philosophers than with defending them. Indeed, Kant calls the Dialectic 'the logic of illusion', and his main concern is to show that certain principles that have been put forward as knowledge *cannot* be rationally defended.

It is in the Transcendental Dialectic that Kant attacks Descartes's notion of the self as a substantial entity, 'a thinking thing', and insists that there is no way that we could possibly know of a self that goes beyond the contingencies of human existence, and at the same time no way that the transcendental self could be an object of any possible experience. As the source of the categories the self cannot be known by the categories. It cannot even be known to be 'something'. This leads to some intriguing complications. We have noted Kant's conscientious ambiguity about the self, which leaves open such questions as 'who has one?' and 'how many might there be?' But because these are questions that fall under the categories, there can be no appropriate response in the case of the ego itself. So to the question 'who has the self?' we can only answer 'everyone', without being able to say what would seem obvious—that everyone has *one*. In view of the centrality and importance Kant gives to the self it is easy to see how this logical curiosity could be utilized by his followers (and to a certain extent by Kant himself in *The Critique of Judgement*) to defend the cosmic transcendental thesis, that the self is ultimately everything.

It is also in the Dialectic that Kant launches his famous attack on the traditional proofs of God's existence, eloquently refuting the arguments that have defined much of theology since the days of Anselm and Aquinas. But his rejection of these arguments and their ultimate conclusion—that one can *know* that God exists—does not indicate any justification for atheism or even agnosticism. God remains for Kant a transcendental *ideal*, whose existence may not be a matter of knowledge but nevertheless is an absolutely necessary condition of human existence.

The most tantalizing arguments in the Dialectic, however, are those curious pairs of contradictions called 'antinomies'. An antinomy produces two conclusions, each supported by a perfectly sound argument, which nevertheless cannot both be true. The claim that the universe has a beginning in time (the Creation), and the claim that it is timeless and has no beginning are equally valid, Kant assures us, and he presents us with proofs of both theses. So too he argues that everything both can and cannot be analysed into basic elements, that every event has natural causes but some events do not, and that there is and is not at least one being in the universe who is necessary. What is demonstrated by the antinomies, he suggests, is the illusory nature of reason. Starting with seemingly incontestable principles, philosophers throughout history have produced ingenious arguments to support a variety of conclusions that are mutually contradictory. By so displaying the antinomies Kant hoped to bring an end to these pointless squabbles. The capacity for self-contradiction is built into reason itself, and there is no point in squandering the best minds in the world in an enterprise with no possible resolution. Nevertheless, just as his refutation of the proofs of God's existence does not indicate his abandonment of religion, and his rejection of Descartes's postulation of a 'thinking thing' does not foreclose belief in the immortality of the soul, so too his attack on the pointlessness of much philosophical debate does not indicate a disillusionment with philosophy. Indeed, it is Kant more than any other figure in the modern world who represents philosophy as a serious, essential, and professional endeavour, and this attitude towards philosophy, just as much as his ideas, would have a powerful influence on many of his successors.

By the end of the first Critique Kant has given us a justification of knowledge in general and a refutation of Hume's scepticism, a bold new vision of the nature of both knowledge and reality, a rejection of much of metaphysics, and a promissory note about the transcendental ideals of God, freedom, and immortality. That note is not to be made good in the realm of knowledge, however, and for all the brilliance of Kant's first Critique it would be a mistake to think of 'Kant's philosophy' on that basis. Knowledge is important to Kant, but he summarized his own philosophy as the need to 'limit knowledge in order to make room for faith'. It is this, rather than his sympathy for and defence of Newtonian science, that would inspire generations of German philosophers. And it is not just religion that could be threatened by excessive attention to science. Art, craftsmanship, poetry, love, morals, mutual human understanding, and the exigencies of international politics—every human endeavour that does not fall under the specialized view of the scientist—tends to be ridiculed or dismissed, or distorted to fit the scientific world view. It is this part of Kant's work which sets the tone for the following century, the part linked to Goethe and Rousseau, not to Newton and the British empiricists.

To be human is not just to know; it is also to *do*. We are agents as well as observers; we are not just objects in the world, but we can change it. Thus Kant distinguishes between the world of knowledge and the world of action, between ourselves as knowers and as actors. In the first Critique he draws a problematic distinction between the world as *phenomenon*—the world as it is constituted and experienced by us—and as *noumenon*, which he cryptically calls the world as it is 'in itself', leaving open the question of what possible role this residual metaphysical notion might play in his philosophy. In the second Critique the two distinctions are brought together, and the mysterious notion of the noumenon or 'thing in itself' is given a dramatic role. It is the self as noumenon, 'the self in itself', that is the ultimate agent which accounts for the immortality of the soul. This leaves troubling questions of interpretation—about the exact relationship between the transcendental ego and the noumenal self, the interaction between the acting self, the organic body through which it acts, and the material world in which it acts. But Kant defends his 'two-world' view, and his notion of the acting self as noumenon is by no means a mere residue of prior metaphysics. It is essential to his view of morality, to the very *possibility* of moral responsibility.

Over-emphasis on science has led many modern philosophers, especially in the heady days of the New Science just before Kant's time, to insist that everything in the universe is causally determined, leaving no room for personal choice or responsibility. But such a view is disastrous outside science, where the belief that decisions and responsibility exist makes all the difference to our view of morality, and Kant accordingly takes freedom to be the presupposition (or what he calls a 'postulate of practical reason') of morality. Without freedom there could be no morality, but Kant switches this conditional around to conclude that, since there is and must be morality, we must believe in freedom (this is a version of the third antinomy: that every event has natural causes but some events do not; actions caused by choices are prime examples of such events). Science and knowledge have their limits, and one of those limits is the boundary of human action.

What is human action for Kant? It is much more than the

movement of a physical object (the human body), something more than mere behaviour, and more than mere conformity to the norms of society or the pressures of one's peers. Our actions are intentional, usually more or less deliberate, and implicitly based upon principles (or 'maxims'), whether or not we actually think about these. Most of all, they are motivated, circumscribed, and defined by ethical concerns—right and wrong, obligations and duties, virtue and selfishness. If the presupposition of morality is freedom, the nature of morality is the free and practical use of reason. Here is the critical point: when Kant denies that the realm of human action gives us knowledge he is not suggesting that we enter the domain of mere subjectivity or irrationality. Morals and religion too are matters of reason, open to argument and rational justification. He is not just concerned with the possible conditions of knowledge, but also with the necessary conditions of living a rational *life*.

Kant's view of morality, however, is uncommonly strict and uncompromisingly objective. There is no bending to fashion or cultural differences, to different times or different sentiments. Because morality is a function of reason, what defines our actions are the principles upon which they are based, and because reason is by its very nature objective and universal, those principles are not just our own personal (or 'subjective') maxims, but universal laws which define *duty*. The rule that tells us not to lie, for instance, is not just a personal preference that many of us happen to share, nor is it a rule that has been canonized by some societies to suit some particular set of circumstances. It is a moral law, a product of practical reason that applies to everyone everywhere without exception. Morality is not a matter of sentiment or social conformity but a set of universal and necessary laws of reason. Accordingly Kant refers to the laws of morality as 'unconditional' or 'categorical' imperatives. He offers several versions of 'the categorical imperative', notably that we should always act in such a way that the maxim behind our actions could be generalized as a universal law for everyone, and that we should always treat other people as ends in themselves, and never merely as means. He also formulates a Utopian notion of a 'Kingdom of Ends', an ideal, harmonious community in which everyone acts rationally all the time. The categorical imperative provides both the form of, and a general set of tests for, moral judgements of all kinds. But it also provides us with a striking analysis of 'pure' morality, not at all dependent on the contingencies of individual sentiments or cultural mores.

We see here a close parallel with the discussion of a priori knowledge in the first Critique. Just as there are principles of knowledge that are known necessarily and independently of experience, so there are principles of action that must be acknowledged as necessary independently of any particular circumstances. The rule 'do not lie', Kant argues, is not derived from experience, be it personal revulsion, contempt for liars, or observation of social calamities that have followed lies. It is a principle based on the rational argument that telling lies logically undermines the very possibility of telling the truth—for who could believe anyone if lying as such were permissible?

The distinction between the world of knowledge ('the sensible world') and the world of action ('the intelligible world') yields a thoroughgoing division that lies at the heart of Kant's ethics, between nature on the one hand, and the free, rational, moral will on the other. What is shocking is that the realm of nature includes—and freedom excludes—many of the ingredients that most moral philosophers since Aristotle have thought to be essential to ethics, for example such feelings as compassion, sympathy, pleasure, satisfaction, and happiness (which Kant collectively refers to as 'inclinations'). Morality properly speaking is motivated not by sympathy or fellow-feeling, much less by self-interest or the desire to be happy, but solely by one's sense of *duty*. One's moral worth is measured not by the quality of one's inclinations but by the fact that one acts 'for the sake of duty and duty alone'. In Kant we can see the force of Nietzsche's comment that 'morality is anti-nature', a rejection of the instincts and the passions. One unhappy consequence of this theory, as Schiller would soon point out, is that one seems to be more morally worthy the less pleasure and satisfaction one derives from the proper performance of one's duties. But Kant scholars have often replied that this is an unfair and negative reading, and that the emphasis on moral worth is not intended to exclude or minimize the importance of personal virtue and self-satisfaction.

The conceptual linkage of morality, rationality, and freedom, and the insistence that morality is not a matter of inclination or social conformity leads Kant to emphasize that the key to morality (and rational life in general) is the concept of *autonomy*. Here especially we see his deep indebtedness to Rousseau, as well as a parallel with the first Critique: Kant's notion of knowledge is born of the Enlightenment faith in reason, the confidence that the individual can, using his own resources, through observation, experiment, and careful thinking, discover what is true about the world. It is worth noting that there is no social element in this picture, no community of scientists, public opinion, or pressures from colleagues, employers, or research-granting agencies. Knowledge is purely a relationship between the autonomous individual and the world of nature, and morality is a relationship between the individual and the universal law, a product of pure practical reason. In the whole of Kant's moral theory there is hardly a word about social customs, cultural differences, or for that matter moral education. Kant's picture of the world consists of the individual and the universal, like Rousseau circumventing the conventions and interactions of society. He writes, 'Rousseau proceeds synthetically and begins with natural man: I proceed analytically and begin with civilized man'—but it is clear that they share a spectacularly self-centred image of the moral world. Rousseau discovered within himself the intrinsic worth of all humanity. Kant began with the idea that every person is autonomous and capable of discovering for himself what is right, quite apart from the conditions and opinions of his society. Rousseau's 'inner self' becomes Kant's noumenal self, and the difference is more one of method than substance. The transcendental pretence begins with this extraordinary self-confidence that one is in touch with the absolute principle of Goodness.

Kant, like Rousseau, reduces everything of importance to the 'inner self', in his case the Will, and carefully excludes almost all such factors as upbringing, socio-economic status, health, intelligence, or personality. (Kant, we should note, was well-liked and respected in Köningsberg, not at all like the paranoid outcast

Rousseau.) Thus Kant writes: 'the only thing that is good without qualification is a good will.'[8] The consequences of our actions (which are in the domain of nature and not wholly under the individual's control) are secondary. What counts is what one intends, the maxim or principle upon which one acts, the act of rational will, and not the actual results. Unfortunately this encourages moral self-righteousness, and celebrates the moral prig who obeys all of the rules and makes everyone miserable. Duty, which we usually think of as a social concept, Kant takes to refer rather to rational principles. But when the social is reduced to second-rate status, and the individual will and universal principles take priority, we lose what would seem to be the primary ground of ethics, our membership in a community and interaction with others. Instead of morality we have cosmic self-righteousness—the transcendental pretence.

Enlightenment humanism is often equated with atheism, the underlying assumption being that thinking rationally, and believing in God and a divine purpose to the universe, are incompatible. To be sure, many of the French *philosophes* were atheists, or at least denied divine significance (Voltaire commented that 'it makes no more sense to say that God is good than it does to say that He is blue'). But *Aufklärung* and atheism did not go hand-in-hand at all, and though Kant may have given up the dogmatism of traditional religion he refused to give up the dogma. For Kant the Enlightenment was another way of defending religion, and Christianity in particular could be, and had to be, justified on purely rational grounds. To confuse matters he called these rational grounds 'faith', thus marking a dramatic break from those who think of faith as belief *against* reason, but his effort to 'limit knowledge to make room for faith' in no way implied that religion is any less rational than science. It is just rational in a different way, in a different realm of reason.

Religion, like morality, is a matter of *practical* reason. Having already shown (in the first Critique) that traditional arguments for the knowledge of God's existence must fail, Kant argues in the second Critique (and in one of his last books, *Religion within the Bounds of Reason Alone*) that belief in God and the immortality of the soul can be justified (like freedom) as 'postulates of practical reason', necessary conditions of morality. In order to be moral one must believe in the ultimate justice of the world—that the good will be rewarded and the evil punished. But since this is obviously not the case in this life, where dictators live to be 80, and children are killed by drunks driving automobiles, rationality demands that we postulate a larger picture, an afterlife in which souls survive and receive their due from the divine hand of justice. Thus belief in God and immortality is justified, and religion can be shown to be rational.

This grand Christian picture is not, however, just a corollary to the discussion of morality in the second Critique. It is the over-arching image of Kant's entire philosophy, which is why he had such a positive impact on the romantics who would seem to be his opposites. And here we encounter *The Critique of Judgement*. The first Critique exposed the world of knowledge and its conceptual mechanism, and the second the nature of morality and its presuppositions; but these two portraits stand in uneasy juxtaposition next to one another, not only because it is not clear how they tie together, but also because they seem to leave unanswered the cosmic questions about the ultimate nature of the universe and the meaning of life. It is the aim of the third Critique to provide those answers.

The key to Kant's cosmology is the concept of teleology or 'purposiveness'. It is the sense of purposiveness that ties together the very different topics of the third Critique (and of a variety of essays which Kant wrote soon after)—the role of purpose in nature, art, and history. Because of the limitations on knowledge outlined in the first Critique these subjects cannot give us knowledge as such, but rather ideals, ways of comprehending that the world makes sense. Art serves Kant as a model here. It has often been noted that he had terrible taste in art, and that in the age of Haydn and Mozart he preferred the music of military bands. But art as such is not the main concern of the third Critique, where it is seen rather as the key to teleology, and therefore as a gateway to the larger vision of the world which he shared with Goethe and the romantics. He also celebrated poetic genius not because he loved poetry, but because—again like the romantics—he saw an important place for intuition in recognizing the more edifying truths about the world, in a way different from scientific know-ledge and practical reason. Art is purposive, but in itself serves no ultimate purpose (this is almost a century before the 'art for art's sake' movement in France) and thus it lifts us out of our daily, practical concerns and allows us to appreciate God's larger pur-pose. Furthermore, it is often said that the appreciation of art and the recognition of beauty, while they require some knowledge as their basis, are ultimately matters of *taste*. But Kant claims that taste, while not objective (in the sense that science and morality are objective) is nevertheless more than a matter of individual, subjective preferences. So too the ultimate truths about the universe may be communally 'felt' rather than known. In our appreciation of the beauty of the universe knowledge of science helps a great deal, though it is not sufficient; what is also necessary, according to Kant, is the religious conception of God and His design. But central to this conception of taste and aesthetic appreciation is *feeling*, by which he does not mean some dumb physiological flush. Feeling has its own intelligence; it is akin to judgement, not just a biological reaction. And genius—not in science but in the arts—has the exceptional ability to grasp and express this grand sense of beauty.

This aesthetic appreciation of the sublimity of the universe and the beauty of God's design is not the ultimate point of the third Critique. That point is moral. 'Beauty', Kant tells us, 'is the symbol of morality.' What he means is not just the moral inspira-tion provided by particular works of art (which had been argued by Diderot, among others), but the grand inspiration provided by a vision of the universe governed by God. Here is the assurance of justice defended in the second Critique, and here too is some assurance that in the secular world, in the unfolding of cosmo-politan history, God's divine plan is made increasingly evident. This powerful image, more than any other in Kant, will inspire and move the post-Kantian idealists in Germany.

3

Romancing the Self: Fichte, Schelling, Schiller, and Romanticism

From the Kantian system and its highest completion I expect a revolution in Germany.[1]

Hegel

Kant was a revolutionary, but like most revolutionaries he was unsure of the new ground he had 'liberated', and preferred to remain safely on the familiar terrain of tradition. His achievement was so great that it was almost incomprehensible to most established philosophers, and not surprisingly (like Hegel a generation later) he won his most enthusiastic adherents among the radical young students, poets, and writers, who read into him more than he ever intended. In a technical sense he destroyed the basis of metaphysics and epistemology as they had been practised for centuries, but more importantly he brought to full fruition that anthropocentric urge that had been present in Western philosophy since Socrates and Protagoras. Not only would humanity henceforth receive full attention—as it already had in Greek philosophy and in the modern Enlightenment—but even the nature of 'external' reality was now incorporated into the realm of the human mind, and made dependent upon the faculties of human knowledge. This did not mean, as in traditional metaphysics and epistemology, that the mind was merely capable of 'discovering' reality; the mind rather 'constitutes' reality, and so is in some profound sense responsible for the world's being the way it is.

Kant remained cautious. He retained the idea that there is but one possible set of categories through which one can experience and understand the world, and he held on to a residual notion of the world 'in itself' as noumenon, even if this was a notion that could not be known ('a limiting concept' he called it), and could be comprehended only in the non-scientific context of morals and religion. More substantially, while Kant gave up the dogmatism from which Hume woke him, he retained the dogmas of traditional Christianity, and kept an absolutely strict and conservative sense of morality, even while his methods ultimately undermined the foundations on which these had stood. But what bothered his radical young followers most of all was the fact that his philosophy seemed schizophrenic in that it split human life into two or three irreconcilable sections without indicating how these should be brought together. The idea of a world of knowledge and a separate world of action, which were separated again from a world of feeling and aesthetic judgement was intolerable, especially in a philosophy whose key conception was synthesis and organic unity. The third Critique had made hints in this direction; Kant's immediate followers sought to develop these, and, in their words, turn Kant's fragmentary philosophy into a 'system' (Kant, we should add, was indignant at the idea that he had left his work incomplete). This was the claim that brought together a diverse group of sometimes brilliant but always quarrelling young philosophers, to 'complete' Kant and fulfil the revolution that he had started.

One of Kant's first great disciples was the playwright Friedrich Schiller (1759–1805). Schiller is too often neglected in more formal treatments of the arguments of the philosophers, for although he did not advance the technical aspects of Kant's philosophy, he did popularize it, and apply it to the pressing conceptual problems of the day. Schiller was in a unique position in the development of German thought and culture. He was Goethe's best friend as well as one of Kant's earliest and most avid readers, and so he personally bridged the abyss between the *Sturm und Drang* tradition of German romantic poetry and the international Enlightenment. Schiller was especially concerned with the 'fragmentation' of an entire generation of Germans, who found the separation of the 'heart and the head' intolerably alienating. He emphasized the overriding importance of the third Critique with its image of organic unity, and its celebration of poetic genius as the expression of humanity—an image which

Goethe found appealing, to say the least. Schiller, like most of the post-Kantian idealists, was particularly concerned with the practical aspects of Kant's philosophy, and using the third Critique he suggested a synthesis of morality and aesthetic judgement along the lines of Kant's suggestion that 'beauty is the symbol of morality'. The result was one of those epoch-making popular books that tends to fall into the cracks between academic disciplines, *The Aesthetic Education of Mankind*. It was a book whose purpose was to encourage moral education through art, and more generally to urge the integration of the self and the unification of Germany. It would have a profound effect on Hegel and Marx. It also displayed a heady appreciation of the moral as well as the political attitudes of Rousseau.

To understand the development of Kant's philosophy in Germany it is essential to think not just in terms of the Enlightenment but also in the imagery of romanticism, which typically presents itself as an antagonist, but which is clearly embraced in the culminating work of Kant's philosophy. The Enlightenment, while international in its scope and cosmopolitan in its pretensions, was in fact very 'Western'—meaning mainly French and English—and failed to fit the 'Eastern' aspirations and traditions of the still relatively feudal Germans. England and France had secure empires, but Germany was not yet even a nation. English and French were the recognized languages of philosophy, literature, and the arts, but the German poets and playwrights were struggling to have their language recognized as a legitimate vehicle of expression. The Enlightenment thinkers speculated about the meaning of 'universal history', but the Germans were worried about their own history. All of these contrasts were to be repeated as the circle expanded to embrace other peoples in the inevitable spread of the transcendental pretence. It is ironic that the Germans, who first developed the pretence as a cosmic philosophy, were also the first to complain of its injustice and imperialism.

The German response to Enlightenment imperialism was a rebellious romanticism. The 'Storm and Stress' movement in literature was first of all an assertion of German language, expressiveness, and feelings, and not surprisingly it had strong political overtones (and was consequently quashed by Frederick the Great, the 'enlightened despot' of Prussia). The young Goethe wrote that German culture should serve as the soul of Europe, and argued that humanity would best be served not by the rational Enlightenment, but by the passionate and perhaps even 'demonic' expressions of a few inspired individuals. In many ways Goethe fathered the romantic movement, even if later he called it 'sickly'. And to make matters more confusing, both he and Schiller referred to themselves as 'classic' as opposed to romantic, even if their works rank among the most powerful expressions of early German romanticism. Just after the turn of the century Friedrich and August Schlegel stated that what they meant by 'romantic' was nothing other than 'modern' and 'progressive'. It was, in other words, a call to revolt, to an end of foreign hegemony and the already tired but intrusive reign of pure reason. It was time for the young genius of German poetry to redefine the world. The poet Novalis urged his colleagues to 'break all the rules' (whereas the more conservative Goethe recommended 'freedom within limitation'). They all accepted Kant's celebration of genius in the service of a universal cosmic vision, and it was time, according to Novalis, 'to make the world romantic', and to find in our 'lower selves' a 'higher self' that was truly transcendental and absolute. It was exuberant and inspiring talk. The hard question is whether it ever became anything else.

Romanticism was anti-Enlightenment, but it was part of the same middle-class, urban mentality that made up the core of the French and English Enlightenment—without its political opportunities. While the Enlightenment was action-oriented, romanticism remained content with passion and literary expression (and even these had their philosophical and literary roots in Blake's England and Rousseau's France). German romanticism was a revolution of ideas only, though in the century to follow these ideas would turn political and become a set of ideas, in Schopenhauer's words, whose time had come.

It is often said that the romantics placed their emphasis on enthusiasm rather than on reason, but this (like all such distinctions) must be carefully placed in the confused context of the times. Rousseau championed reason as well as sentiment, and

Hume insisted that 'reason is and ought to be the slave of the passions'. Hegel (who was, like Schiller, an ambiguous romantic) captured the central images of romanticism and, perhaps perversely, gave them the name 'reason'. Even the ultimate Enlightenment rationalist Kant insisted that 'nothing great is ever done without enthusiasm', a comment borrowed by (and usually attributed to) Hegel and Nietzsche.

Whatever else it may have been, romanticism was first of all a rebellion against an established, oppressive order, against rigidity and feudal mediocrity. The reigning metaphors, accordingly, involved organic images of 'fluidity' and growth (*Bildung*). Romanticism looked to history and change for sustenance, not to timeless categories. Nevertheless, what the romantics sought was also eternal, an inner self that was—even more than Kant's transcendental ego—universal, necessary, 'higher', and all-embracing.

The influence of Rousseau cannot be overestimated, but it is not Rousseau the champion of sentiment against reason who is so relevant here, nor the political theorist of *The Social Contract*, whose very language (not to mention his ideas) would have been treasonable in Germany. It is rather the explorer of the intrinsically good inner self who could see all of humanity in himself while taking his solitary walks through the woods, the Rousseau of the transcendental pretence. That sense of solitary freedom of thought in natural surroundings appealed to the German poets and philosophers, as did the sense of seeing the whole of the cosmos in the mirror of one's individual self—especially if one happened to be a genius. Rousseau's idea of growth, of natural education without the artificial distortions of society, also had a special appeal. So the German romantics turned their attention from the seemingly static structure of the present to an elaborate vision of history (in which the Enlightenment itself turned out to be only a 'stage'). Johann Herder, one of the early leaders of the movement, and a good Rousseauian, stressed the importance of the *Volkgeist*, the spirit of a people, in the development of history, in a dynamic version of Rousseau's 'General Will'. Like Rousseau, the romantics celebrated the role of the individual in the grand scheme of things, using the imagery of Goethe and

Sturm und Drang as well as the arguments of Kant's Critiques. The 'humanity' of the Enlightenment was replaced by something even larger, the soul of the world itself. Christianity, which had suffered from some rough handling, found a comfortable home in German romanticism. Madame de Staël lectured in France on the theme that romanticism *was* Christianity. 'Gothic' extravagance replaced enlightened clarity, and the business of philosophy was no longer to argue and clarify but to expand and alter our vision, a process that inevitably tended to confuse or deny 'common sense', and in consequence led to a certain arrogance unique to the sage. The scope and complexity of the vision also led to the realization that the world consisted of dialectical relations instead of mere antagonisms. Absolute knowledge might still be available, but only if one moved beyond the illusions of reason. For those who still clung to reason, on the other hand, Kant's antinomies pointed to new possibilities, but Kant had misinterpreted these as the limitations, rather than the promise, of reason.

The first great post-Kantian philosopher, in the narrow and increasingly academic sense, was Johann Fichte (1762–1814). Fichte took it upon himself to 'complete' Kant's philosophy and turn it into an integrated 'system', an ambition which infuriated Kant, and provoked the old man to disavow the philosophy that was developing in his name. One could not imagine two men to have been more different in temperament. As a student Fichte had been a radical firebrand, a member of the clandestine Jacobin club, and an enthusiastic follower and advocate of the French Revolution. He was later fired as a philosophy professor at the University of Jena for suspected atheism (a charge which he always denied). In 1807 he made the first major, public plea for German nationalism, in a series of 'Addresses to the German Nation', many decades before there would actually be a Germany. It is hard to imagine such a man continuing and developing the work of the pious and conservative Kant. True, Kant had also been an enthusiastic follower (from a safe distance) of the French Revolution. But whereas Kant worshipped Newton, Fichte found him 'vulgar'. Where 'freedom' for Kant meant the ability to obey the categorical imperative, the same idea would become the radical fulcrum of Fichte's entire philosophy, by which he would overturn—using Kant's own methods—much of what Kant had tried to save of traditional philosophy.

Fichte used the language of reason, but his themes and images were extremely romantic. In fact the young romantic poets turned to him at the end of the century to be their spokesman and official philosopher, only to be turned away—with characteristic Fichtean arrogance—as not worth his time or trouble. For Fichte the central idea of the Kantian system was freedom, not just as a postulate of morality but as the presupposition of human experience as such. Where Kant had separated knowledge from freedom (to 'make room for faith') Fichte insisted that freedom was the single presupposition of all experience. Where Kant had limited his cosmic and teleological speculations to the last of his Critiques, Fichte takes the image of organic growth (*Bildung*) and the concept of teleology to be central to the key concept of freedom. And where Kant sought a 'critique' of reason Fichte wanted something more positive and inspirational, a sense of 'the vocation of man', and not just of individual men but of humanity writ large.

Despite his Copernican revolution, according to which we supply concepts to objects, and objects must conform to our experience (rather than the other way around), Kant refused to consider the possibility that we might supply *different* sets of concepts to objects, and thus define different worlds for ourselves, or what contemporary philosophers call 'alternative conceptual frameworks'. Indeed, the whole purpose of the convoluted 'transcendental deduction of the categories' in the first Critique is to close off this possibility by showing that there cannot *be* any alternative set of concepts. But Fichte takes this possibility to be one of Kant's most revolutionary discoveries, and essential to the notion of freedom. Freedom is not to be found only in the realm of action, but also, and even more importantly, in the realm of thought, in the play of the imagination—as Kant himself had argued. But this must mean that we are not necessarily limited to a single way of understanding the world, and Fichte not only does away with the exclusiveness of the categories, but also cuts Kant's one remaining anchor to absolute, external reality—the notion of the noumenal world 'in itself'. Retaining such a concept, Fichte argues, was an oversight on Kant's part. It plays no role whatever in accounting for knowledge (as Kant acknowledged), and it is not needed to account for freedom of action either. Kant needed the distinction between the phenomenal and noumenal world to fortify his separation of knowledge and freedom, but as this separation is unwarranted and unwanted, so too the distinction is unnecessary.

The dramatic picture that emerges, especially in Fichte's *Science of Knowledge* of 1794, is misleadingly cast in the form of a Kantian 'deduction' in the language of presuppositions and necessity. But what Fichte has in mind far more resembles the third Critique than the first, for what he means by 'presupposition' is teleological, the *purpose* of holding certain beliefs, and this purpose is (in a broad philosophical sense) *practical*. To put it in more modern terms, like twentieth-century pragmatists (who explicitly acknowledged their debt to Fichte), he thought that what justifies our holding certain beliefs or our viewing the world in a certain way is not a matter of abstract metaphysical arguments, but rather a question of what *use* we have for such knowledge, of how it affects our lives. For Fichte what is critical here is essentially ethical, namely, what certain beliefs or a certain viewpoint indicate about one's personal character. 'The philosophy one holds', he wrote, 'depends upon the kind of man one is.'[2] There are two kinds of philosophy, he argues, and what is fundamental is the freedom to choose between them. There is the 'dogmatic' view of the world that is essential to science (as depicted in the first Critique), in which one is a mere observer, a categorizer, and then there is the 'idealistic' view of oneself as a participant in life, a responsible moral agent. There is no doubt which Fichte thinks is superior, given that the nature of the self has already been defined as a striving rather than as a knowing self, and so the 'dogmatic' position is inevitably one of self-denial and/or self-deception. What is more, he suggests that, because freedom is the basis of all experience, and the purpose of all experience (and everything in our experience) is to test and improve our moral character, the world of nature comes out looking not like a world in itself (which Fichte rejects anyway) but rather like a postulate of practical reason, a projected stage upon which we can act out our moral roles and 'prove' ourselves. It is not the world that is 'absolute' (that is, the fulcrum of our experience); it is rather the self. The world is not there to be known, but is posited in order to be acted upon. We are not here to know but to *do*. 'In the beginning was the *act*', wrote Goethe, summarizing Fichte in a line.

It should not be thought, however, that the self that Fichte so celebrates is the individual self, or that each of us creates our own world according to the dictates of our ethics. While Fichte is not entirely clear on the matter, the ego that is 'absolute' and the premiss of his entire system is more than personal; it is suprapersonal, possibly equivalent to humanity as a whole. But however grand the interpretation, it is easy to appreciate how Fichte could have been suspected of atheism, for though he occasionally peppers his prose with the name 'God', his concept of the Absolute ego is clearly less than the traditional Judaeo-Christian God (the obvious comparison is with Spinoza, the seventeenth-century Dutch pantheist who was widely read by the post-Kantians, and who was also accused of atheism in his own time). But for Fichte what is absolute and indubitable is the self, not the world, and in this he developed the transcendental pretence far beyond its comparatively humble origins in Rousseau's walks in the woods. Fichte refused to recognize the ultimate reality of the woods.

Fichte's precocious student Friedrich Schelling (1775–1854) did not offer much resistance when the same romantic poets turned to him as their official philosopher. He was closer to their age, enjoyed their temperaments even if he did not agree with all their ideas, and certainly appreciated their emphasis on creativity and the arts. Moreover, Schelling, unlike Fichte, did not give the impression of ignoring religion—like several other young romantics, he converted to Catholicism—and he did not, like Fichte, think of nature as a mere corollary of ethical life. Indeed, he accused his teacher of neglecting nature and sacrificing the heavens to the moral law. Schelling too saw his task as 'completing Kant', but it was clearly the third Critique that served as his guide. Using Fichte's style of dialectical argument Schelling rejected Newton's lifeless mechanical view of the universe, and sought to demonstrate the whole of nature as a living force, a purposeful teleological system. In his work, as in Kant's, science receives full recognition, along with ethics, religion, and the arts, but all under the single general heading of the Absolute.

'The Absolute' began as an innocent term, referring to whatever existed 'in itself' independently of anything else (including our experience or conceptions of it). But with Kant this innocent notion lost its simplicity, for there would seem to be two absolutes: the world as it is 'in itself', and the world as it must be, for us. Nevertheless, a traditional Kantian might still say that the Absolute is 'the way things are, necessarily' (referring to the phenomenal world), and perhaps add, using the arguments from the second Critique (rather than the discredited ontological argument), that God, as a necessary being, is the Absolute too. But with Fichte the Absolute shifts its ground from the world and God to the subject of experience. If there is an Archimedean point in Fichte's philosophy it is undeniably the self, the ego, and it is the self that is absolute in his work. Heinrich Heine, commenting on German idealism, mocks Fichte with the comment: 'Himself as everything! How does Mrs Fichte put up with it?!' But the mockery is not far from the target, for it is with Fichte that the transcendental pretence and the aggrandizement of the self first emerges with none of the subtlety and appeal of Rousseau or Kant. Schelling's system regains some of that subtlety, but in doing so, the word 'Absolute' had to become expanded and obscured enough to provide a cover for the most arrogant claim that one was, oneself, nothing less than all the world.

At first, the search for the Absolute was nothing more than the quest of all philosophers since Thales, the search for truth: not partial, contingent, contextual truths but truth as such. With Kant the very notion of truth becomes confused (Kant himself talks about 'knowledge'), and with Fichte truth as such plays no important role at all. So when Schelling voices the demand that philosophy must seek the Absolute, it is no longer clear what the term means, except that it must be the one inescapable, unshakeable, indubitable, all-encompassing, unifying concept of the entire system of reality. But there cannot be two absolutes, so Schelling too rejects Kant's notion of the world 'in itself', and his separation of two worlds, two selves. He also rejects Fichte's emphasis on ethics to the neglect of nature, which solves the unity problem only by sacrificing completeness. What Schelling proposes is a vision of the Absolute as One, as a single multi-faceted, self-creating, continuously developing cosmos of which nature is one aspect, the human mind another (again, much like Spinoza's vision of the universe). Schelling, unlike Fichte, has no hesitation in calling this 'God', and explicitly insists that the Absolute ego or 'World Soul' of his system is supra-individual, and encompasses not only all things human, but the universe itself. Like Spinoza, the idea of anything other than the Absolute, and the idea of anything neglected by the Absolute, is unthinkable for Schelling, and so what 'the Absolute' comes to mean for him is the unintelligibility of any attempt to distinguish 'subject' from 'object', or objective validity from universal subjective constitution. In other words, there is no way of distinguishing between those aspects of an object which we find and those which we 'posit', a claim which Schelling (like Fichte) misleadingly calls the 'Principle of Identity' (and summarizes with the unfortunate formula '$A = A$'). The claim is that no part of the universe can be comprehended without comprehending the whole as well—and we, as Absolute self, are that whole.

To the delight of his romantic friends, Schelling's vision of the universe is ultimately a vision of God as the great creator, not bringing the world into existence *ex nihilo* at some ancient time, but continuously creating it (and Himself) through time. We are not only part of that process; we are its consciousness and its instruments of expression. Poets and philosophers are not simply expressing themselves; they are expressing—and realizing—the movement of the Absolute. It was a grand image, a living universe growing and developing through history in which we ourselves played an essential, creative part (part of the picture is that nature develops too, but although the romantic idealists clearly set the conceptual stage for a theory of evolution, it is curious that none of them openly anticipated that Darwinian notion). From Kant's defence of an ego outside of time the young idealists developed the idea of the transcendental self *as* time, as itself the source and meaning of all change and development.

It was a rich and exuberant period. The excitement of the

French Revolution was still in the air, Napoleon was beginning to institute the ideological reforms of the Enlightenment and shake up the feudal German princes, German poetry was making a claim to international status, and German philosophy, thanks to Kant, was already recognized as the best in Europe. Schelling's friend Friedrich Hölderlin was fast proving himself a poetic genius on a level with Goethe, and Kantian scholarship was going in dozens of directions, all of them claiming to be the true voice of the great (and still living) philosopher, if not also the voice of the Absolute speaking in German for all of humanity. But the general shift in transcendental idealism, over-simply represented by the progression Kant–Fichte–Schelling–Hegel, was to leave behind the more conservative and commonsensical aspects of Kant's philosophy, and emphasize the more radical, visionary, self-aggrandizing elements of the Critiques. In particular German idealism came to reject the rigidity of the categories and the traditional ('transcendent') view of God as a being apart from humanity, and began to develop a remarkable appreciation of the diversity, historicity, and fluidity of forms of life and consciousness, and to accept a vision of God in some sense *as us*. Some of the dramatic excesses of romanticism passed away with the romantics themselves, but this enduring image of the cosmic self not only survived but flourished in the years to come.

4

Hegel and the Apotheosis of Self as Spirit

> The significance of that 'absolute' commandment, *know thyself*—whether we look at it in itself or under the historical circumstances of its first utterance—is not to promote mere self-knowledge in respect of the particular capacities, character, propensities, and foibles of the single self. The knowledge it commands means that of man's genuine reality—of what is essentially and ultimately true and real—of spirit as the true and essential being.[1]
>
> Hegel

Writing a quarter of a century after the publication of Kant's revolutionary first Critique, whose ideas were now as established as the slogans of the great political revolution in France, G. W. F. Hegel (1770–1831), without Kant's timidity, pursued to the limits the ideas of transcendental idealism, and the significance of the insight that it is we who give structure to our own experience. From Fichte he borrowed the now transformed notion of 'the Absolute', the rejection of the world 'in itself', and the idea that there might be alternative sets of categories—alternative 'forms of consciousness' and forms of life. From Schelling he borrowed (Schelling would later say 'stole') the idea of a dialectic of such forms, developing through time and history with ourselves (collectively) as the authors, and becoming increasingly more adequate and encompassing. According to Hegel, every form of consciousness has its truth, in a certain context and from a certain perspective. But a larger context and broader perspective will show that some forms are more satisfactory, more complete, more 'true' than others. The notion of dialectic was the ideal mean between Kant's too-dogmatic 'deduction' of a single set of categories, and the romantics' free-wheeling 'creative idealism' which made it seem as if any imagined world might be as real as any other. The dialectic is not so much a method as it is the central idea of Hegel's philosophy, and its purpose, in each of his works, is to demonstrate the ultimate necessity of an all-encompassing acceptance of the self as absolute—which Hegel calls 'Spirit' (*Geist*).

Hegel is the apotheosis of German idealism, and he has been called 'the Aristotle of our post-Renaissance world'. Viewed in itself, outside the historical context and the philosophical tradition in which it was written (a very un-Hegelian thing to do), Hegel's system appears extravagant, extreme, and almost incomprehensible, but viewed as a vision of history and as the culmination of the whole philosophical tradition, it becomes clear that Hegel's ideas were not wild 'speculations' but rather that they formed a careful synthesis of the current internationalism of history and the subjective movement in philosophy that had started with Descartes and Rousseau. Hegel saw the absurdity of scepticism, and the possibility of profound doubt is simply rejected from his system. 'Perhaps', he writes at the beginning of his first great book, 'the fear of error is itself the greatest error.' He accepted the general move of Kant's first Critique, regarding objects as being constituted by consciousness, but he also saw the manifest absurdity of making this an individual matter, as if each of us creates his or her own world; it is consciousness in general that does this, collectively and not individually, through the shared aspects of a culture, a society, and above all through a shared language. But this implies that, though we all strive for mutual agreement (even if this means, at first, imposing our own views on everyone else), our shared concepts are not in fact universal but quite particular and provincial, aspects of the truth but not the whole truth, forms of consciousness rather than—as we would like to think—human consciousness as such. But since Hegel also rejects the idea of a world 'in itself' there can be no 'truth' for human consciousness apart from its own agreement with itself, taking into account not only its many voices and perspectives but also its rich history and multitude of experiences. This explains the complexity of the Hegelian system: it is not merely an argument for the absolute truth but rather an attempt to actually *create* that truth, by moving us all through the history of human concepts and experience to an 'absolute' general agreement, or at least to the agreement that we should, ideally, all agree.

This enormous ambition also explains an inevitable tension within Hegel's dialectical method. On the one hand, he is keenly aware—as few philosophers had been before—of the variety and seeming incommensurability of human viewpoints and perspectives; on the other, he is striving, as ambitiously as any philosopher of the past, to obtain unanimity and universal agreement, even without any external standard or world to act as an anchor or guarantor of the truth. And like most thoughtful philosophers, Hegel also changed his mind, so that it often seems as if there are two Hegels, and it is not always clear which one is being praised or brought to our attention. There is more than a simple distinction of age between the young Hegel who shared the excitement of the Revolution and reforms in France, and announced the 'birth of a new age' in his *Phenomenology of Spirit* of 1807, and the older, established professor of philosophy in Berlin who wrote: 'when philosophy paints its grey on grey, then it has a shape of life grown old. . . . The owl of Minerva flies only at dusk.'[2] The younger Hegel was expressing the hope of his age, a brief period in which it looked as if Germany was at last to be united and freed of its still feudal habits, when the principles of 'liberty, equality, fraternity' seemed about to become international realities, and when philosophy was developing an exhilarating new vision of the world. The older Hegel was also expressing the spirit of his age, one of resignation, of acceptance without enthusiasm but nevertheless with a sense of satisfaction that things indeed are as they must be. The younger Hegel saw a world in transition, full of promises; the older Hegel lived through the world of Metternich's 'reaction'. Napoleon and the ideals of the Revolution were dead and buried; the enthusiasm of Kantian and romantic philosophy had turned to academic disputes and professional system-building.

These two Hegels, however, are not to be identified only by their differences in age and the ages they lived in. There were, in a more profound sense, two Hegels all along, from the revolutionary *Phenomenology* to the last dialectical lectures of the late

1820s. One Hegel was a traditional philosopher, very much the follower of Kant in search of absolute truth, a defender of (Lutheran) Christianity, a system builder, and a synthesizer. He conceived of the structure of all his works as a dialectical progression up to and establishing the Absolute, a single idea which encompassed and unified every other idea in the system. In the *Phenomenology* that idea is the idea of universal Spirit; in his later *Logic*, the Absolute idea is God, but ultimately these are the same. This apparent consistency of theme and structure hides a tension, however, between the traditional conservative search for an Absolute, and a radical, largely unacknowledged recognition that there may be no such Absolute, but only the possibly endless diversity of different forms of life and consciousness, each of them relative to and dependent upon its own historical, conceptual, and social epoch. In the *Phenomenology* this latter possibility is given remarkably free rein, and although the book is clearly designed as a kind of demonstration of the superiority of the ultimate stages, it is just as evident that there is much too much material and too many paths taken *en route* for that demonstration to mean very much. It is Hegel, accordingly, who is rightly credited with the discovery of 'alternative conceptual frameworks', at the same time that he is celebrated as the grand master of the Absolute. While not exactly contradictory these two positions sit uncomfortably with one another. Forced to choose, the older Hegel—having the advantage of hindsight— opted for the Absolute (we will see this same schizoid tendency in Hegel's followers, for example Wilhelm Dilthey and Jurgen Habermas).

More than most philosophers Hegel happily acknowledged himself as the product (and also the fruition) of an entire philosophical tradition. In his lectures on the history of philosophy he demonstrated how his ideas followed and were the culmination of the entire philosophical odyssey since the pre-Socratics, but more modestly we can see how he follows and brings to a climax the movement of ideas that begins with Rousseau. Hegel read Rousseau with his friends in college (Schelling and the poet Hölderlin were his room-mates at Tübingen), and his first essays (on the nature of 'folk religion' and early Christianity) were much in the spirit of Rousseau in their rejection of the authoritarian and corrupting influence of the organized church and theology in favour of the natural simplicity of 'subjective' folk rituals and beliefs. He was also a follower of Kant, though of Kant's writings on religion rather than the material of the Critiques. Kant had argued that religion must be 'natural'—that is, rational—and Hegel develops this idea more rigorously than Kant ever did, ultimately attacking not only Christianity but even Christ himself for appealing to authority rather than reason. But the most immediate and most profound influences on Hegel were Hölderlin and Schelling. Hölderlin seemed to have been the innovator of the group, and he inspired them all with his grand metaphor—drawn from the *Sturm und Drang* poets, from Goethe and Schiller, and, most important of all, from his imaginative reading of the ancient Greeks—of a universal life force manifesting itself in all things, and using them for its own purposes. Unlike the traditional Judaeo-Christian God, however, this spirit had no existence of its own apart from its various manifestations in the world, and yet literally everything is a manifestation of this spirit, from the tragedies of human history to the wonders of nature and the inspirations of a single young poet. Consequently everything has a purpose and a place in the overall scheme of things, whether or not, in the distractions and limitations of everyday life, we recognize this to be so.

We have already seen this image emerge in Schelling's philosophy in his portrait of the living universe, his integration of nature, religion, and human history under the singular scope of the Absolute, and his concept of the 'World Soul' or absolute ego suffusing through each of us, and pervading human history. Schelling began publishing this grand metaphor as philosophy in the 1790s, before Hegel even thought of himself as a philosopher. When he finally did decide to try philosophy as a vocation in 1801, he founded a journal (*The Critical Journal of Philosophy*) with Schelling, and began publishing his ideas. These were so close to Schelling's, however, that he was viewed merely as his disciple, and many years later Schelling complained that Hegel had become famous on *his* ideas. The justice of that charge has often been debated, since it is not easy to distinguish between cases when one author 'steals' another's idea, or when they both draw from a common source (in this case Hölderlin), or when one develops and perfects an idea that is only implicit or awkwardly expressed by the other. What is clear is that Hegel did not appear out of nowhere but was steeped in a tradition and surrounded by ideas, and that what he did (as Aristotle did in ancient times) was to unify these into a single powerful statement.

Hegel's philosophy, with all its twists, turns, and contradictions, can best be summarized in terms of two of his central concepts: 'Spirit' and 'dialectic'. The religious overtones of the word 'Spirit' are unmistakable and surely intentional, but it is clear that for Hegel—more than for Hölderlin or Schelling—this is a very *human* spirit, even if it encompasses everything else as well. Spirit is more a matter of fellow-feeling and group membership than a religious sentiment as such, much as one might have 'team spirit' or share 'the spirit of '76'. The most obvious and important historical predecessor of Hegel's spirit is Rousseau's General Will, coupled with suggestions of the Christian concepts of the 'Holy Spirit' and 'communion', but philosophically the most immediate predecessors are Kant's abstract notion of 'Humanity', and the French slogan of 'fraternity'. Although Hegel often hints at (and occasionally boldly states) religious themes, the concept of Spirit is employed most often to solve secular and ethical rather than religious problems, especially those concerning synthesis and unity. Spirit is our shared recognition of our mutual interdependence and ultimate collective identity.

This shared recognition is also the culmination of Hegel's dialectic, which is a progression based on conflict and opposition. 'Dialectic' derives from the Greek word for 'conversation', and the idea (exemplified by Socrates in the Platonic dialogues) was that through the confrontation of diverse and opposed opinions the truth will eventually emerge. Hegel saw that the history of ideas could best be understood in this way, but then went on to see that this process could be generalized, and applied to the fields of history and human events, even to the history of science and the development of nature itself. In each case conflict and confrontation of opposed ideas, concepts, and forms provokes new ideas, concepts, and forms, improved by the process until finally a set of ideas—or a single idea—emerges which satisfies the demands of all participants. According to Hegel the ultimate idea in every instance is the self-reflective recognition of an all-embracing identity. In the *Phenomenology*, this all-embracing identity is Spirit ('the self-recognition of Spirit' is in this sense a redundancy), the full realization (as well as recognition) of the unity of all humanity and the human world, which includes the world of nature as the object of human knowledge.

One of the more frightening implications of the Hegelian system is its extremely diminished role for and conception of the individual. At the end of the preface to the *Phenomenology* he comments:

at a time when the universal nature of spiritual life has become so very much emphasized and strengthened, and the mere individual aspect has become, as it should be, a matter of indifference . . . the individual must all the more forget himself . . . [and] all the less must be demanded of him, just as he can expect less from himself and may ask less for himself.[3]

Thinking of the historical context—the middle of the Napoleonic Wars—it is easy to see how Hegel could insist that only the larger picture matters, and that within that picture the individual counts for very little. Indeed, 'Spirit' was not just an abstraction Hegel created from the multitudes of actual human beings: he considered Spirit to be palpably real, and saw our concept of the individual as the abstraction—that is, plucked from its social context and given false weight, independence, and importance. Thus the overall vision of Hegel's philosophy is the development of a unified, self-reflective, international, spiritual community, and the promise of the current political situation (in 1807, at the height of Napoleon's power) seemed to make this not just a philosopher's dream but a real political possibility.

It is this enthusiastic expectation that leads Hegel to formulate his well-known philosophy of history. 'Even as we contemplate history as this slaughter bench on which the happiness of peoples, the wisdom of states, and the virtue of individuals have been sacrificed', he writes,[4] it is clear on rational reflection that these sacrifices have served some ultimate purpose—not a divine purpose (to be compensated for in the afterlife) but a human, historical purpose which he identifies as the increase and final realization of freedom in the world. To be sure, he does not mean by 'freedom' that 'negative' conception of freedom which simply means 'being left alone'. Desirable as this might be, it is cruel and meaningless if there is no context in which one's actions have any significance, if one has no opportunities, no education, and no sense of belonging and participating in some larger social entity. Hegel means by 'freedom' very much what Rousseau meant by it—identification with the whole, be it 'Spirit' or 'the General Will'. One is never free alone, but only in the context of a free and meaningful society.

Hegel is often viewed as the father of modern totalitarianism on the basis of this 'positive' view of freedom, but to be fair it should be pointed out that the modern concept of 'totality' and its conditions were hardly present in the chaotic and communicatively primitive world of Napoleon and his aftermath, and Hegel surely would have been horrified by the modern states that have borrowed some of his principles. At the time his philosophy of history was a powerful defence of the idea of historical improvement, of the transcendence of slavery and caste systems, and finally of the modern (German and Christian) achievement of consciousness of true freedom 'in the inmost realm of the spirit'. Of course one can always choose to look at history as a slaughter bench. (Dostoevsky writes in his *Notes from Underground*: 'one may say almost anything that one likes about history, except that it is rational. The very word sticks in one's throat.') But Hegel assures us that, 'to him who looks with a rational eye, history in turn presents its rational aspect'. He would not insist on the absurd thesis that history is all for the good, but would only insist that *some* good comes of it all. He would not deny the horrors of history, indeed he witnessed some of them only a few miles from his study. Nevertheless, there was a 'cunning of reason' through history, evidence of a spirit—albeit an extremely wasteful and often cruel spirit—behind the brutal actions and passions of humanity. In a world no longer willing to accept the 'will of God' as a rationalization of tragedy, in which history is all too easily dismissed as nothing more than 'one damn thing after another', even this small solace is welcome.

We said before that Spirit is the culmination of the Hegelian system, and that in a sense it is even redundant to speak of the self-recognition of Spirit. But in another sense Spirit does not always exist; like freedom, with which it is identified, it must be *realized*. Hegel explains this ambiguity by a familiar analogy with biological growth (one of the ruling metaphors of the dialectic). An acorn grows into an oak tree, and only at the end is it what it 'truly' is; nevertheless, there is a sense in which the oak has existed all along as the acorn, and the mature tree is only the realization of the potential that was in the seed. In the same way humanity has always been spiritual, in the sense that the *capacity* for spiritual growth and self-recognition have always been there, but Spirit 'truly' is what it is only at the end of history (that is, at the completion of this historical mission). To realize ourselves as Spirit is thus both to recognize, and, in so doing, to *make* ourselves into Spirit, into the grand supra-human unity that recognizes the world as ours.

It is clear that Hegel in one sense completes the development of the transcendental pretence, the exaggerated scope and importance of the self (albeit a strictly collective self), and the projection of one's own attributes onto humanity (and the cosmos) as a whole. His model of freedom is unabashedly Christian, spiritual instead of political, and later, when he does provide a political model for freedom (in *The Philosophy of Right*), he follows the barely enlightened model of the Prussian constitutional monarchy. To say that freedom is the goal of human history is to condemn or at least demean those societies that have a different conception of freedom to ours or find some other value more important than freedom (contemporary Iran comes to mind, but even the ancient Greeks, on Hegel's account, were not fully rational). What Hegel means by 'reason' is also closely linked to a very narrow and particular conception of rationality, that notion of all-embracing comprehension peculiar to the German idealists. And what Hegel has in mind by 'history', of course, is a carefully edited sample of the global commotion that has ensued since the advent of *homo sapiens*. He mentions the Orient only to dismiss it for its 'arbitrariness, savagery, and dimness of passion'. The Greeks (whom Hegel, with Hölderlin, much admired) receive disproportionate attention despite his harsh treatment of them in the philosophy of history, while most of the history of the medieval Church is ignored (Hegel was a Lutheran with a strong bias against Catholicism). The many societies now studied by anthropologists were hardly known at the turn of the nineteenth century, and there is little or no room in Hegel's system for them. One might say that even the underlying image of the dialectic, that vision of a restless, reflective, universal force seeking to express and improve itself, is distinctively 'Western', and hardly universal and essential to human existence.

Early in the *Phenomenology* Hegel tells us that 'the Truth is the Whole', but he also tells us that this should not be taken as a vacuous statement about the universal 'One-ness' of things (his criticism of Schelling's Absolute as 'the night in which all cows are black'), nor should this insistence on the whole (now called 'holism') be separated from the idea that 'the whole' includes history too. To account for truth, then, is to submerge oneself in the history of the concept and the search for truth, as well as to find the perspective from which, or within which, truth can best be comprehended. What 'truth' requires, accordingly, is such a perspective leading to complete comprehension so that nothing is left out and everything ties together. We can appreciate this requirement if we think of Hegel's immediate predecessors and their problems: Kant had an all-embracing philosophy but it was too compartmentalized, separating knowledge and action, and leaving the connection with religion and aesthetic judgement too obscure. Fichte, as Schelling had complained, neglected to account adequately for science and nature in his system. Consequently Hegel, accepting the post-Kantian demand for a system that deserved the name 'Absolute', took 'truth' to be a framework which corrected these deficiencies, and incorporated nature, ethics, religion, and aesthetics in a single grand theory.

Religion plays a key role in Hegel's philosophy, but it is by no means obvious what that role is—or what religion it is either. Hegel's followers on the 'right' (as opposed to the radical followers like the young Karl Marx) tended to take his more pious pronouncements at face value, interpreting the theological language of the Trinity and the Incarnation quite literally. In terms of structure Hegel's works do tend to culminate in religion (which, in the *Phenomenology* for example, is the penultimate stage to Absolute Knowledge). Hegel studied theology as a student (Tübingen was a seminary), and wrote his first essays on religion in general and Christianity in particular. The significance of Hegel's unabashedly theological language is by no means obvious, however, and when he explains that what the incarnation *really* means is that *every one* of us is Spirit, and Jesus is just a representation (*Vorstellung*), it is clear that this is no orthodox defence of Christianity. Hegel treats of religion not just towards the end of the dialectic but throughout, one of his treatments occurring at an early stage in the guise of 'the Unhappy Consciousness', a rather damning description of religion (Catholicism in particular) as schizoid, slavish, and miserable. Such a religion is a battle of oneself against oneself, not a spiritual endeavour but a particularly destructive form of inward self-consciousness (it is worth noting how well this description fits Kierkegaard's later conception of 'Christianity as Suffering'). On the other hand, Christianity does appear (as 'Revealed Religion') at the end of the *Phenomenology* and the *Lectures on Religion*, but one should add that so does Zoroastrianism, plant and animal worship, and Greek 'art religion', and what Hegel seems to think of as religious sensibility has more to do with his animated philosophical attitude than it does with any of the doctrines or dogmas of the Judaeo-Christian tradition. Finally, while it is true that Hegel studied theology, it is beyond dispute that he generally hated his studies, as his first essays—scathingly critical of Christian dogmatism—demonstrate. It is less likely that he underwent a total conversion in mid-life than that he simply softened his antagonism, and accepted Christianity—as he accepted everything else—within a dialectic that absorbed and went beyond it.

With the exception of the *Logic*, Hegel's works are all concerned with the necessity of a *social* conception of humanity. This seems obvious until one glances back at the history of philosophy. Of course philosophers treat people as social creatures when they are discussing politics (though even there the presumption of original individuality is quite strong, as in Hobbes's famous portrait of a state of nature in which isolated individuals, finding their lives intolerable, 'nasty, brutish, and short', finally band together to form a social covenant), but when they are discussing the nature of knowledge, consciousness, the self, or religion, they almost always treat the matter as a relationship between the individual and evidence, or reason, or his own self-awareness, or God. The idea that what we know, think, feel, and worship is circumscribed by, much less is a product of, our relations with other people is treated with disdain as popular superstition, as 'heteronomy'. The Enlightenment since Descartes honoured autonomy above all else, and romanticism valued inward feelings and intuitions just because these were untainted by social conditioning and corruption. Rousseau more than anyone else celebrated this sense of the isolated individual in touch with himself and nature, and out of touch with society. True, he developed the most persuasive theory of the social contract, but he did so against a background of a state of nature in which individuals were 'born free and happy' and were 'indifferent' to one another. The idea that there are no individuals in nature, that knowledge, self, and everything else human is a product not of nature but of culture, is an idea that comes quite new to philosophy (at least, to modern philosophy), and it comes, mainly, with Hegel.

One of the best known chapters of any of Hegel's books is devoted to showing that this is so. It is called 'Master and Slave', and occupies an early mid-section of the *Phenomenology*. It is presented without a clear context or purpose, and without any references to other philosophers, or current problems and controversies. He simply tells us the story of two wholly undescribed 'self-consciousnesses' who meet, and almost immediately enter into a fight to the death. Each tries to 'cancel' the other because his consciousness threatens the other's view of himself as free and independent. But each one is also trying to 'prove' himself, and recognizes that the actual death of the other would eliminate the only witness to that proof. So the winner lets the loser live and becomes the master, the loser the slave. The master becomes 'a consciousness existing on its own account which is mediated with itself through another consciousness'. In the process both of them learn that there is more to life than survival, and that selfhood is a complex of independence and dependency which mere individual existence cannot account for.

The story is presented wholly in the abstract. Hegel is giving us a parable which represents not a particular situation but rather the prototype of *all* human confrontations. It is set, as in Hobbes and Rousseau, in a fictitious 'state of nature', an imaginary reconstruction of what human life might be like in the absence of everything we call 'social', but unlike Hobbes, Hegel does not think that life in such a circumstance would reduce to pure selfishness: pride, vanity, and a sense of status already enter into presocial conflict. And unlike Rousseau, he does not think that the state of nature produces individuals who are happy, free, and indifferent to one another, much less 'noble savages'. What he suggests is that in the state of nature people are already pre-social and defined by the traits that Rousseau too readily blames on the corrupting influence of society. Human existence is primordially a matter of mutual recognition, and it is only through mutual recognition that we are self-aware and strive for the social meanings in our lives.

The parable develops a fascinating twist, for the master becomes dependent on the slave, not only for his food and comforts but also for his self-image. He is only master in so far as the slave truly regards him as such, but the infuriating residual independence of (other people's) consciousness is notorious, and it is even more infuriating when the other in question does not openly rebel but seems to be going through the motions of absolute obedience. One cannot obtain self-confirmation from a 'yes-man'. As the master becomes increasingly dependent on the slave, and as both of them recognize that this is the case, the power in the relationship shifts until the slave becomes the 'self-existent', and the master the dependent one. As a parable of the origins of society Hegel here lays the groundwork both for his philosophy of history (the progressive realization of freedom), and for his general theory of society and ethics, in which some less confrontational and more stable social arrangement must replace the master–slave relationship. But in this parable too Karl

Marx will find exactly the model he needs to explain the conflict between the economic master and servile classes, and its 'inevitable' resolution.

Hegel's ethical theory is too often seen as subservient to his political views—though the latter are more often understood through their unforeseen consequences in modern German history than through Hegel's own rather moderate opinions. But ethics is, in an important sense, the heart of Hegel's philosophy. His early work on religion tries—following Kant—to understand religious belief and ritual wholly within the secular framework of an ethical theory, to see religion as a vehicle (if not a 'postulate') of morality. The *Phenomenology* has as its largest part a series of explorations of various ethical systems and models (most of which is contained in the long chapter entitled 'Spirit'). The master–slave section initiates what is to become an elaborate dialectical progression of such diverse ethical theories and ways of life as hedonism (the life aimed at pleasure), romantic sensibility (especially the views of Rousseau), the pious life (for example, of a Benedictine monk), the success-motivated life of a businessman or scholar ('the Bourgeois Zoo'), a life defined wholly by one's family, and possibly in conflict with the larger 'civil society' (with Antigone as the tragic example), the sophisticated but hypocritical life of the courtier, life in a revolution (with its consequences in a reign of terror), and the theory of ethics formulated by Kant concerning morality as Practical Reason. The point of the dialectic is, as always, to provide the broadest possible view of ethics and its possibilities, while at the same time making clear what is most essential to morality and the good life.

As we can readily anticipate, Hegel does not accept the Kantian conception of morality. In his early essays, despite the Kantian flavour and his devotion to Kant's philosophy of religion, he had attacked Kant's view of morality—as did Schiller—as overly abstract, cold, and alienating. He argued that the formality of Kant's categorical imperative made it very difficult to apply it to any concrete ethical situation, at least without sneaking in personal evaluations which it was the very point of the moral law to preclude. He particularly objected to the exclusion of feeling and all 'inclination' from moral consideration, recognizing with

Schiller that a good person often acts from impulse rather than from reason, and that someone who acts on the basis of 'duty' may well, even while doing right and exhibiting Kantian 'moral worth', prove to be a wretched character. Most of all he objected to Kant's account of ethics because it lacked any social dimension; it was strictly a relationship between the individual, practical reason, and the moral law. The basis of ethics, Hegel insisted, was not this at all, but rather one's belonging to (as well as being educated by) a particular community of people. Ethics was not a matter of autonomy but (in Kant's terms) heteronomy—of being influenced by other people. Nor was it primarily a matter of rational principle, but part of a life of shared values, feelings, and customs—what Hegel calls '*Sittlichkeit*' (from '*Sitte*', meaning 'customs').

Hegel had argued for the importance of *Sittlichkeit* before he began the *Phenomenology*, and he still accepts it as the basis for all ethics in his book on politics, *The Philosophy of Right*. The emphasis on shared customs turns Kant topsy-turvy; the reason why morality is so important is not because it applies rationality downward from the heavens to particular earthly situations, but because it is a development up from those basic circumstances in which we come to value certain actions and feelings in the first place. It also places the locus of morals not in the universal and necessary laws of reason, but in the particular rules and dictates of the family. This tends to make Hegel's ethical philosophy rather conservative, for unlike those more 'liberal' thinkers who map out a grand rational scheme about the way things 'ought' to be, and try to impose it on existing society, Hegel begins with ingrained habits and expectations, and argues a kind of sanctity for them (Rousseau, interestingly, adopts both the liberal and the conservative approaches, arguing that the family is the basis of all social relationships, and then formulating an abstract but revolutionary theory of the social contract). But Hegel does not think that the dialectic stops there; Kant's overly rational view of morality ultimately deserves a place in a fully adequate ethical framework just as surely as the role of the family and the community.

One of the dialectical devices Hegel uses to show how such a movement takes place (and must take place) is to interpose the story of Antigone between his account of *Sittlichkeit* and his discussion of the ethical norms of civil society (this appears both in the *Phenomenology* and *The Philosophy of Right*). He takes Antigone (and women in general) to represent the 'divine law' of the family, of mutual affection and loyalty. When her brother is killed in an abortive attempt at a coup Antigone's duty is to bury him in accordance with religious law. But as a traitor her brother is denied burial by the king he sought to depose, and she faces a fatal conflict between her divine family duty and the 'human law' of society. She opts for her duty, and is killed by the State in return, but the point of the play for Hegel is nothing less than the nature of the dialectic as such. Life, history, and philosophy are defined by such crisis points. For the individual who is caught in the crisis there may well be no 'happy ending', but it is on the basis of such tragedies and sacrifices that the dialectic—and human history—moves forward. So understood, Kant's view of morality is an extremely sophisticated version of that forward-reaching tendency, but because it is also too narrow and limited it must be moved beyond as well.

Where does the dialectic go from here? In the *Phenomenology* it moves to the dialectic of religion, which Hegel sees not as the superimposition of Christianity on morals (which he opposes), but rather as the reintegration of *Sittlichkeit* (and the 'divine law') and more abstract conceptions of morality and society. In *The Philosophy of Right* and the *Lectures on the Philosophy of History* it moves to a new and enlarged sense of internationalism, a vision of the one self or Spirit that embraces us all, finally recognizing itself in all of us, and ending the conflicts that drive us apart. It is not only the culmination of the transcendental pretence; it is 'the end of history', according to Hegel. But this hyper-inflation of the self marks the beginning of a new era of European history, a reaction in which the premises and basic ideals of the Enlightenment will come under fire.

Part II

Beyond Enlightenment:
The Collapse of the Absolute

5

The Self Turned Sour: Schopenhauer

> In the aesthetic mode of contemplation we have found
> two inseparable constituent parts—the knowledge of the
> object, not as individual thing but as Platonic idea, . . .
> and the self-consciousness of the knowing person, not as
> individual, but as *pure will-less subject of knowledge*.[1]
>
> Schopenhauer

The transcendental pretension of identifying ultimate reality with
the self, the grandiose romantic vision of a cosmic self within the
ordinary self, and the idea that the world is in some profound
sense our own creation found a novel and perverse spokesman in
Arthur Schopenhauer (1788–1860). He was professedly a
Kantian, and he announced at the beginning of his greatest book,
The World as Will and Idea, that he assumed that his readers
were familiar with Kant's work (and also with his own). Personally as well as philosophically he was a pessimist and a notorious
crank. He was born into a wealthy family, travelled widely, and
lived well, yet insisted throughout his long and healthy life that
life was no good. He was one of the first Europeans to become
deeply engaged in Eastern philosophy, and one of his central
ideas was the Buddhist insistence on the futility of desire. He
shared with Fichte and Hegel—whom he hated—the cosmic view
of the supra-self expressing itself through us, making the individual self something of a pitiful pawn. He shared with the romantics the rejection of science, and the celebration of the aesthetic
and the creative. His metaphysical position was that the world is a
transcendental illusion; reality is first to be found within ourselves, and then not as reason but as irrational, impersonal Will.
It is the Will that throws us this way and that through desire and
emotion, but it is never under our personal control. The Will is
in no sense a personal Will (any more than Hegel's Spirit is

personal); it is ultimately the reality of all things, most obviously in the case of other living creatures whose lives are no more—and no less—meaningful than our own. On the rational foundation built by Kant, Schopenhauer demonstrates that life is intrinsically absurd. At best we might see our way through the absurdity, and achieve some sort of quasi-Nirvanic peace by denying the Will and the futile desires that are its most immediate manifestations.

If we were to take Schopenhauer at his word we might think that he could not be more opposed to the other German idealists. Despite his theoretical insistence on the absurdity of our concern for individual status he delighted in attacking his rivals in print, prefacing *The World as Will and Idea* with the comment that 'philosophy in Germany today is the product of humbug (Fichte and Schelling) and charlatanism (Hegel)'. One of the most famous stories about Schopenhauer is that when he was teaching at the University of Berlin he deliberately scheduled his classes to conflict with Hegel's lectures, just when Hegel was at the height of his fame (Schopenhauer did not register a single student). But like Fichte, Schelling, and Hegel, he took Kant as his starting point, and their differences are no more than a serious family quarrrel. Like all the idealists, Schopenhauer insisted that 'all true philosophy is idealistic', and, discussing Descartes, declared that 'the only right starting point of all philosophy is the subjective, individual consciousness'. But like Fichte, Schelling, and Hegel, Schopenhauer also ended up moving far beyond the individual self to a cosmic force within us. He did retain Kant's distinction between the phenomenal and noumenal worlds which the other idealists had rejected, though he certainly looked at the entire system from a most un-Kantian perspective, that of his pessimism. Where Hegel had insisted that if we look at the world rationally the world looks back at us with a rational aspect, Schopenhauer argued, in effect, that if we look at the world without rational expectations the world will look back at us irrationally. Where Hegel had claimed that, in spite of their cruelty and absurdities, human life and history still have meaning, Schopenhauer insisted that, no matter what meaning and brief satisfaction we might find in life, it was essentially absurd. It is a profound difference in terms of attitudes, but a mere parallax of views in terms of the structure of the philosophical theory. Both defend an idealist vision of the world in which the individual is insignificant and reality is an all-embracing holistic force, culminating in human self-recognition. But Hegel views the realization of Spirit with enthusiasm; Schopenhauer eyes the impersonal cosmic will with suspicion, and sees self-recognition as just another piece of folly.

In *The World as Will and Idea*, Schopenhauer sees himself as heir to (and fulfilment of) Plato and Kant. Both philosophers developed a view of reality divided into 'two worlds', one only apparent, the other real but beyond the realm of normal human experience. For Plato, the two worlds had been the world of becoming (appearance), and the world of being and the forms. For Kant the two worlds, both of them 'real', were the phenomenal world—the world of experience, defined by causality—and the noumenal world—the world as it is in itself, accessible to us not as knowledge but only through the activities of the will. For Plato, the contemplation of the forms gives us knowledge of the real world, and in this Schopenhauer joins with him against Kant. Knowledge of the world in itself is possible, and Schopenhauer even calls the basis of such knowledge 'Ideas' (*Ideen*), a familiar translation of Plato's term for 'Forms'. Our supposed knowledge of the phenomenal world of appearances, on the other hand, is illusory. Here Schopenhauer goes beyond both Kant and Plato, and borrows his model from Eastern philosophy; the world of appearance is an illusion (albeit a 'necessary' illusion) and reality is hidden behind the 'veil of *maya*'. Science in particular is not the road to knowledge but rather a reinforcement of just those illusions which give us a false picture of the nature of reality. Schopenhauer joins with Kant in believing that access to this knowledge is to be found, not through the contemplation of objects outside us—for instance, the admiration of beauty—but by looking within ourselves, into our inner consciousness—'the single narrow door to the truth'. What one notices there is one's own will. But 'one's own will' is not really 'one's own' at all, but only a manifestion of the one universal Will. It is only this that is real, the 'thing in itself', existing independently of our perception of it.

The phenomenal world, by contrast, exists only 'as an object for a subject'. Schopenhauer begins *The World as Will and Idea* by stating, 'the world is my idea.' In other words, *esse est percipi*: 'to be is to be perceived.' Following Kant he insists that the phenomenal world is not 'given' to us but is constituted by us, through the forms of our sensibility (space and time), and the category of the understanding (which, for Schopenhauer, is the single category of causality). He does not dismiss the phenomenal world altogether (just as Plato does not dismiss the world of becoming), but there is no question that it is less real than the Will itself (of which it is also the manifestation), and that its concepts and categories are limited. The category of causality in particular cannot be applied beyond the realm of phenomena, and attempting to do so will result in great confusion. The phenomenal world is not caused by the Will (or by anything else), but within the phenomenal world everything is explained by its cause. Schopenhauer's doctoral dissertation concerned what he called (following Leibniz) 'the Principle of Sufficient Reason'—the idea that everything has an explanation. Every event in the phenomenal world, according to this principle, has a causal explanation, which leads Schopenhauer to insist that the character of the phenomenal world is such that it is defined by relations between objects, and between concepts. The world in itself, on the other hand, stands on its own, outside of space and time, and the world of relations.

The Will, the thing in itself, is not unknown to us and beyond the reach of experience. On the contrary, it is what is closest to us and most readily known. If we look inside ourselves we realize that we are immediately in touch with (are identical with) our own actions. One might suggest, as Kant did, that what we are immediately in touch with are only our own *volitions* ('acts of will'), and that the actions following these are part of the phenomenal world. But Schopenhauer insists that there is no such distinction since volition and action are one and the same; volition is evident only in action, and action would not be action without volition. This means that one's body is something more than an appearance in the phenomenal world: it is the Will objectified, not a phenomenal object. This is the key to

Schopenhauer's philosophy. He then generalizes this observation to apply to the world as a whole, which is also a manifestation or objectification of the Will.

The Will is the centre-piece of Schopenhauer's metaphysics. It is the only thing that is truly real; everything in the universe is a manifestation of the Will, just as one's body and actions are manifestations of one's own will. The Will is *one*—there can only be one since there is no multiplicity except in the phenomenal world—whose various manifestations include the force of gravity, the growth of plants, the behaviour of animals, and the celebrated powers of human reason. But this unitary cosmic Will is not at all like the benign Spirit of Hegel's system, much less the rational will of Kant's philosophy. It is a blind, brutal force that is indifferent to human survival, and to purposes of any kind. It is capable of organizing and manifesting itself in various forms (witness the order of the world) but this is arbitrary, and any order is just as good or bad as any other. The Will is not in space or time, but has manifestations in space and time (an account borrowed from Augustine's conception of God). It is not caused, but is the pointless cause of everything.

With this concept of the double knowledge we have of ourselves, as objects in nature (phenomena) and as inwardly-known manifestations of Will (thing in itself), Schopenhauer leaves Kant and starts to sound more like Plato. With regard to phenomena we can have only 'representations' (*Vorstellungen*), but of the Will in its various manifestations we are capable of having 'ideas'. Ideas, for Schopenhauer, are more like Platonic forms than Kantian concepts, which give us representations. Representations of phenomena, and scientific representations in particular, are illusory ways of perceiving the world. Understanding the world as an orderly causal mechanism is a vicious and self-deceptive way of disguising irrationality and meaninglessness. Like Plato, Schopenhauer suggests that we have access to ideas only through a special sort of intellectual insight, and not through ordinary experience, although it is an odd sort of 'intellect' that includes art but not science. Nevertheless, again like Plato, he argues that these ideas are essentially 'perceptible' (in contrast with concepts, which are in themselves strictly abstract), though we are aware of them 'in the mind's eye', in the imagination rather than through ratio-cinative thinking. This is why these Platonic ideas are most accessible to us in art rather than science (an idea derived from the third Critique, and clearly at odds with Plato's theory of art as 'an imitation of an imitation'). The portraits and characters we know from art are not so much representations of actual people as they are ideas of a certain manifestation of Will. Shakespeare's Iago, according to Schopenhauer, had to be created in a single vision, not concocted out of a variety of real characters.

Like the other post-Kantian idealists Schopenhauer rejects individualism as illusory, and emphasizes the larger picture. But the many differences between individuals is too striking for even the most holistic idealist to ignore, and for Schopenhauer the uniqueness of the individual is captured in at least three ways. First he insists that each individual human being is a manifesta-tion of the idea of humanity, but refracted through an idea of one's own. Animals, on the other hand, are manifested only as species. Thus, even though all individuals are manifestations of one and the same idea of humanity, they are prismatically mani-fested, differently and uniquely. Secondly, what follows from this is that every individual has his or her own *character*, which Schopenhauer insists is immutable and fixed from birth. Charac-ter turns out to be the key to ethical behaviour, as opposed to the Kantian emphasis on practical reason and categorical imperat-ives. Thirdly, the significance of individuality is nowhere more important or dramatic than in the case of the isolated *genius*, a central romantic notion that Schopenhauer takes from Goethe as well as Kant, and of course applies to himself.

The Will determines everything, though it in turn is not deter-mined. In practical terms this means that everything that we do and everything that happens is determined—though not, as in more optimistic views of predestination or fate, for the sake of any ultimate purpose. There is no room for freedom of the will in Schopenhauer's system (except to say that the Will itself is free), but whatever we do as individuals is not the result of choice, but of our character, and this is determined by the Will from birth. What we call our 'acts of will' are illusions, manifestations of the Will within us, but in no sense our own or under our control. So considered, Kant's image of practical reason is something of a philosophical joke, a self-deceptive fantasy that we are obeying something other than the dictates of our desires and 'inclinations'. Not only do we not obey the dictates of reason (which Schopenhauer insists is just another equally self-interested manifestation of the Will) but we rarely even recognize our own motivation. Long before Freud, Schopenhauer suggests the existence of unconscious motives, and insists that consciousness is 'the mere surface of the mind, of which, as of the earth, we do not know the inside but only the crust'. He adds that we often rationalize and fail to recognize our own motives, and the Will itself often hides matters from memory and recognition. Indeed he sometimes writes as if we virtually never know what we are doing, as if not only the Will is blind, but we are equally blind to its impulses inside us. For such a pathetic creature the categorical imperative is of little use.

The most powerful illustration of the Will acting through us, according to Schopenhauer, is sexual desire. It is symptomatic that most philosophers have largely ignored sex, both as a phenomenon and as desire, and when they have discussed it (like Plato in the *Symposium*) they have often imposed the most absurd idealizations, and insisted on seeing it not as sex but as love, as the attraction of two individuals, and the promise, if not the guarantee, of happiness. But the truth is, Schopenhauer tells us, that sex is not at all personal or a matter of individual choice, but is inherently a source of suffering, however strong its initial attractions. It is the Will forcing its way through us and doing with us as it likes. It has little to do with our individual needs and notions but is rather the species as such operating through us as individuals, and using us for its own perpetuation. How else, he argues, could we possibly explain the urgency and importance we give to what otherwise would seem to be just another routine bodily activity? But the species does not care about individuals. We fall in love because the species determines what our progeny should be like, and accordingly determines our sexual tastes and appetites. The end of love, he assures us, is virtually always disillusion and disaster—but only after the will has had its way, and the species has been assured of its continuation.

We are aware of sexual desire as both the expression of our body and as a foreign force within us, Schopenhauer argues, and once again it is the body that gives us insight as to the true nature of reality and our place within it. In the body we are aware of the small part reason plays in our actions or volitions, and just how little control we have over ourselves. While one cannot dissociate sexual desire from the individual body, sexual desire is utterly antithetical to ourselves as individuals. But just as sex illustrates how little reason or personal purpose has to do with our lives, so too we can start to appreciate how little reason and control enter into our seemingly most deliberate, rational behaviour. One key concept in ethics, especially since Kant, has been the notion of responsibility, which is to say free choice, the ability 'to do otherwise'. But because our character, which is thoroughly determined by the Will, dictates exactly how we will respond to every situation, the deliberations of practical reason are themselves no more than an aspect of character, a part of our behaviour no less determinate—and no more responsible for our subsequent behaviour—than any other action, thought, or gesture. So too our intentions and attitudes are determined by character, and one can no more choose to be saintly or not to be moody, than one can choose to have a different body. Some people are good because they have that kind of character, and others are evil for the same reason, but there is no social programme or psychological technique that will make any significant difference to them.

What makes evil people evil, however, can be clearly stated. Evil comes into the world because of our false notion of individuality, our belief that it somehow matters what happens to each of us, that status is important in social life, that desires can be satisfied, and that it is possible for an individual to have some advantage over his or her fellow-creatures and be happy. Again we find a powerful thesis borrowed from Eastern philosophy: that belief in individuality is not only a metaphysical error but an ethical disaster. We believe that it is possible to gain competitive advantage, and the result is a war of all against all. Ironically, the most successful wicked people know this, for their success in fulfilling their desires proves to them that satisfaction is impossible since every desire is followed by another. As Goethe put it in

Faust: 'from desire I rush to satisfaction, but from satisfaction I leap to desire.' Furthermore, the wicked man suffers because he knows inwardly that the cruelty inflicted on others actually falls on himself (an argument that one also finds in different forms in Kant and Hegel). So long as we suffer from the illusion of thinking that the individual ego makes any difference we are assured of leading miserable lives. All desire is suffering, and the only way to end it is to stop desiring, give up the idea of oneself as an individual, still the Will within oneself, and turn it against itself. Schopenhauer defines his pessimism as the recognition that life is a continual fluctuation between desire and boredom, and the ultimate point of his philosophy is to make us realize this, and learn to use the Will against itself to free ourselves from this frustration.

The answer to pessimism, according to Schopenhauer, is art— and philosophy. Every aesthetic experience is a temporary escape from the dictates of the Will, because aesthetic experience, as Kant had argued, gives us a disinterested appreciation of the art object and sets us at some significant distance from our normal concerns. We become 'contemplative', and experience a metaphysical shift whereby one comes to have genuine knowledge, the knowledge of Platonic ideas which are the only 'adequate' manifestations of the Will, the thing in itself. The most adequate aesthetic experience, furthermore, is to be found in the realm of music, where we experience not just manifestations of the Will but the Will itself. Music is the art form that dispenses with representation altogether, and that is why it appeals to us so profoundly. It is 'the universal imageless language of the heart'. In aesthetic, and especially musical, experience we are elevated beyond the merely empirical, beyond the obstinately wilful individual self, and by engaging with the Will as such we free ourselves of its power.

It is in art, too, that we come to appreciate the importance of genius, which Schopenhauer defines as the ability to know things independently of causality (the principle of sufficient reason). What we experience in art are ideas rather than perceptual objects. In aesthetic contemplation we remove ourselves from our normal subjective perspective, and, in Schopenhauer's eccentric usage, become 'objective'. Equally curious, since it is not the artistic object but the idea behind the object that is critical here, the artist and the observer share the essential talent in art, not of making but of seeing. Genius is the ability to adopt this aesthetic stance, which would indicate that Schopenhauer thought that the true appreciation of art, as much as the making of it, was a very rare ability. But for most of us whatever art we can enjoy provides a temporary respite from the competitiveness and vanity of the world, a release from the power of the Will and the illusions of the individual self.

The only durable escape from the Will, however, is through philosophy. In philosophy one gives up (or ought to give up) the false optimism that everything happens for a purpose, that life is essentially good, that happiness is, after all, possible (this is why, in addition to sheer envy and competitiveness, Schopenhauer so despised Hegel). The truth is rather that of the *Upanishads*: life is suffering. The only escape is through the release of the Will, to dissolve oneself into the whole, to give up desire and the expectation that it can be fulfilled. Saints do this; it is why they become ascetic and 'deny' themselves, but becoming ascetic does not by itself release the Will. One must first see through the illusions of individuality and desire, and asceticism follows, but it is not enough to see through these illusions once or twice (we all do that, at least briefly, in a passing insight or a temporary aesthetic experience). It is not even enough to be a philosopher. Schopenhauer himself is a case in point: despite his philosophy, which he formulated as a young man, he lived a life filled with desires and their (temporary) satisfactions. But as he once commented in his own defence, it is no more necessary for a philosopher to be a saint than for a saint to be a philosopher. One cannot change one's character. At most one can look at art and accept a philosophy that minimizes one's expectations, and brings an end to our unreasonable demands for satisfaction. Philosophy can only do so much, for one cannot give instructions about how to live, and in any case, 'the translation from idea to concept is always a fall'. The end of philosophy, Schopenhauer insists, is silence.

Schopenhauer published *The World as Will and Idea* in 1819, but the immediate fame and fortune he expected did not come. He gave up university teaching soon after his foolish confrontation with Hegel, and spent the rest of his life developing his philosophy, twice rewriting his *magnum opus* and adding dozens of essays on a variety of related topics (published as *Parerga and Paralipomena*). But his anti-Enlightenment, anti-rational, anti-scientific, and pessimistic views would not find a place in the nationalistic, still-hopeful world of the early nineteenth century. After 1850, however, with the failure of popular revolutions (which Schopenhauer, needless to say, did not support), Europe seemed ready for a philosophy that called for resignation rather than hope, that recognized the evil in the world and the vanity of life, and Schopenhauer's vision of the cosmic wilful self would attract the attention of some of the most exciting philosophers in Europe.

6

After Hegel: Kierkegaard, Feuerbach, Marx

> Each age has its characteristic depravity. Ours is perhaps not pleasure or indulgence or sensuality, but rather a dissolute pantheistic contempt for individual man.[1]
>
> Kierkegaard

> The same spirit that constructs railways with the hands of workers, constructs philosophical systems in the brains of philosophers. Philosophy does not exist outside the world, any more than the brain exists outside of man because it is not situated in the stomach.
>
> The positive humanistic and naturalistic criticism begins with Feuerbach. . . . They are the only writings since Hegel . . . to contain a real theoretical revolution.[2]
>
> Marx

Hegel died of cholera in the epidemic of 1831. He was at that time the most powerful philosopher in Berlin, with an enormous following around the university (despite his notoriously dull lecture style). His philosophy allowed a variety of interpretations, however, and soon after his death his students split into two warring camps, a 'right' wing that interpreted Hegel along the lines of religious orthodoxy, and a 'left' wing that tended to emphasize the atheistic, humanistic, and revolutionary aspects. In reactionary Prussia the right wing inevitably occupied the more prestigious University chairs, while the left wing often found itself hiding from the censors, running from the police, or being driven into exile. For a while, left-wing Hegelianism was sufficiently rampant for the university to bring in a special anti-Hegel lecturer, and whom should they have chosen but Hegel's old friend and colleague, turned bitter antagonist, Friedrich Schelling.

Schelling denounced the 'negative' aspects of Hegel's system, and emphasized the religious and more conservative aspects of his own. Listening to his 1841 lectures in Berlin were a visiting Danish theology student named Søren Kierkegaard, and a young 'left' Hegelian from England named Friedrich Engels who would soon become the sponsor, friend, and collaborator of Karl Marx.

Kierkegaard (1813–55) came to Berlin knowing but already disliking Hegel's philosophy. The Danish Lutheran Church was enmeshed in a theology based upon the Hegelian system, and the young Kierkegaard was bridling against it (much as the young Hegel had bridled against the Kantian theology he was force-fed in Tübingen). Thus he welcomed Schelling's attacks, and decided that the categories of Hegel's philosophy were very different from the concepts by which ordinary men and women live their lives. The Hegelian contempt for the individual, and the abstractness of the Hegelian Idea and Spirit repelled him. It was all too objective, too collective, too abstract, too impersonal. Several years earlier he had written in his *Journals*; 'What I really lack is to be clear in my mind what I am to do, not what I am to know . . . the thing is to find a truth which is true for me, to find the idea for which I can live and die.'[3] When he went back to Copenhagen it was with a renewed antipathy toward Hegel and everything he stood for, and a resolve to come to the defence of the individual and Christian faith against the anonymity of Spirit and a dialectic that pretended to embrace the whole of the cosmos.

Engels, on the other hand, was repelled by Schelling's lectures. Like Marx, who had studied Hegel when he was an undergraduate at Berlin, he had already been deeply impressed by Hegel's work. Although Marx disagreed with much of Hegel's idealism, he liked his humanism, and he saw in the dialectic a method of criticism far more powerful than anything that he had inherited from the Enlightenment, although he had read Rousseau with enthusiasm. As a student Marx had fallen in with the crowd of young 'left' Hegelians led by Bruno Bauer, and through them met Engels a few years later—one of those seemingly insignificant events that change history. But Marx and Engels could not move away from Hegel until they had encountered another philosopher who at that time entered Berlin, Ludwig Feuerbach.

Feuerbach (1804–72) had studied with Hegel himself, and had taught philosophy for a few years until it was discovered that he was the author of a scandalous anti-Christian pamphlet. In 1841 he published a blasphemous volume entitled *The Essence of Christianity*, and immediately became a cult hero for a generation of young left Hegelians. Feuerbach attacked Hegel and idealism generally for their perverse 'inversion' of reality—taking abstract ideas and intangibles as more real than flesh-and-blood people and the seemingly solid world of objects, and he suggested that Hegel had stood the world on its head, and that it was time to set it back on its feet again. Feuerbach was a materialist as opposed to the idealists, and in addition to the appeal of his common-sense approach to philosophy he wrote in a plain style that was a great relief after the opaque prose of the idealists (as a student Marx had written to his father that studying Hegel gave him 'an endless headache'). Feuerbach was not a 'vulgar' materialist, however, insisting (with many of the French Enlightenment philosophers) that 'only matter is real'. He simply denied what the idealists all maintained, that consciousness produces the world. He did not deny the existence of consciousness, but put it back in its place in the world, as the biological consequence of our brains, combined with our social and physical circumstances. Like Schiller he celebrated the 'natural man', at home in his body and with his senses as well as with his ideas. In line with this thinking he returned to the ancient philosophical obsession with food, arguing that 'the doctrine of food is of great ethical and political significance. Food becomes blood, blood becomes heart and brain, thoughts and mind-stuff . . . Would you improve a nation? Give it, instead of declamations against sin, better food. One is what he eats' (an atrocious pun in German: 'Man ist was er isst').[4]

Feuerbach showed the new direction for Marx, Engels, and the other left Hegelians to take. Marx responded enthusiastically with a pun of his own, 'there is no other path to the truth except through the fiery stream [*feuer-bach*]', but he did not turn from Hegel to Feuerbach as much as he combined the two. From Hegel he learned how to employ the dialectic in defence of humanism, from Feuerbach, how to see the whole of philosophy, religion, and the many symbols of advanced social life as rationalizations for unsatisfactory living, and as excuses for unfair advantages and privileges, rendered as 'ideology'.

Kierkegaard's return to Denmark from Berlin brought to an end what might have been one of the least unhappy years of an extremely unhappy life. His father had been a devout but neurotic Christian, for whom religion meant a perpetual sense of guilt and inadequacy (Kierkegaard would later write, 'Christianity is suffering' and, perhaps more cheerfully, 'Christianity is not melancholy, but rather glad tidings for the melancholy'). Kierkegaard broke off his engagement to a lovely young girl, and gave up his training to be a Lutheran minister, allegedly because the promised bourgeois life would interfere with his sense of mission—to save individuality and Christianity from the Hegelian scourge. He also broke off relations with his one good friend, the writer Hans Christian Andersen, and spent the rest of his life alone, in constant conflict with the Press and the Danish Church, an object of public ridicule. And yet this unhappy recluse produced twenty volumes of witty, challenging, poetic, and personal philosophy.

Kierkegaard is often called 'the first existentialist' (when that list is not so absurdly extended as to include Socrates and Augustine as well). He had little tolerance for abstract ideas, for categories that one could only think about and not live in, and for impersonal doctrines that had no appeal or relevance to one's own inward passions. One might believe Hegel, but that had nothing to do with who one was. Indeed, Kierkegaard quipped, if a man became sufficiently steeped in Hegel he would become so anonymous that he could not even have a letter addressed to him. Similarly, one could employ the arsenal of accumulated theological tricks to prove that God must necessarily exist, but what did that have to do with belief *in* God? And wasn't it absurd, he asked, to try to prove that God exists when, if one believes, one surely believes that God is already there in front of one (listening to the proof). What counts in matters of religion and in all matters of life is personal passion, not knowledge or reason. It does not matter what others do; what matters is what one *chooses* for oneself, and then it is not *what* one chooses but *how* one chooses—passionately and personally, or just by way of 'following the crowd' (here again we have the Kantian concept of autonomy, stripped of the demands of rationality). In matters of ultimate choice—the choice of an entire way of life or a specific decision—there are no authoritative rules, objective truths, categorical imperatives, or logic of the *Zeitgeist*. There are only feelings and personal needs, 'subjective truths' for which there may be no rational defence or support.

Kierkegaard repeatedly says that his concern is ethical, a matter of what to *do*. He did not deny the charms of the sciences, but rejected them as unimportant for the business of human life. Attacking the Kantian vision at its very foundation, he rejected the 'anonymous' transcendental self of knowledge, and insisted that the only self that was of any significance whatever was the acting, 'ethical' self, the self that had feelings and intentions. Kierkegaard, like Schopenhauer (whom he much admired despite their almost total disagreement on substantive matters), retained and reinforced that Kantian schism that so offended the other German idealists, that abyss that separated questions of fact and knowledge from questions of value. In keeping with this harsh distinction, he maintained (again like Schopenhauer, and against Kant) that the realm of ethics was beyond not only knowledge, but also reason, despite the fact that ethics as such was *defined* by reason. Ironically, he accepted the Kantian view of ethics as a matter of universal rational principles, but rejected the idea that this system of rational principles could be given any rational support. Like everything else of importance in life the ethical life was a choice that one had to make, not an obligation or a duty. Obligations and duties were defined *in* the ethical life, but becoming ethical was a prior decision, an irrational 'leap of faith' in which there could be no rational assurances that one was doing the 'right' thing, no Hegelian dialectic to show the place of ethics in the overall scheme of things.

Kierkegaard, perhaps more than any philosopher since Augustine, emphasized the importance of the 'inner', individual human being. Like Rousseau he saw other people as a problem, but unlike him he not only emphasized the importance of the individual and his feelings, but rejected the idea of any larger community, which he castigated as 'the public'. His ethics was wholly asocial, a matter only of one's inner integrity, and hardly at all of one's public behaviour. Indeed, despite the rhetorical emphasis on 'doing' there is virtually no action in Kierkegaard's ethics. Even more than with Kant it is matters of intention that count; actions and their consequences are at most of secondary significance. Moreover, not only does ethics not consist of knowledge of any sort, it is not clear that what is most important in the ethical life can even be *said* (a theme picked up by Wittgenstein in this century). A person's true self—the only self worthy of the name—is an isolated individual human being, alone with his or her feelings, and with the awesome necessity of choosing, without rational guidance, what sort of being one is to be.

The particular option that concerned Kierkegaard, although he sometimes considers it under the rubric of 'ethics', is distinctively religious. Late in life he summarized his task as 'a Socratic' one: to define what it is to become a Christian. He repeatedly emphasized that being born and raised a Christian was not enough; indeed, it may be harder to become a Christian if one already is one than if one is not. He railed against 'Christendom', which he lumped together with the secular Public and Hegel's *Geist* as the very antitheses of Christianity and what it meant to be a human being. Being raised to assent to certain absurd formulations, to attend church with family and friends, and to call oneself 'Christian' by right of birth had nothing to do with being a Christian. Christianity, like ethics, was a strictly personal matter, a question of passion, of the sense that one was in personal confrontation with an all-powerful, all-knowing God, and such a confrontation was bound to provoke a profound sense of insignificance. Kierkegaard's writings are a seductive combination of edification and harsh sermonizing, a refusal to make Christianity any 'easier' than it is, or its doctrines any more plausible. The dogmas of Christianity are not plausible; they are not even intelligible, according to Kierkegaard. But this is as it should be: where would there be room, much less the need, for faith if Christian doctrines were just matters of common sense or science? Passion requires a paradox, and there is no belief more paradoxical than the belief in Christianity. Becoming a Christian is a choice of a way of life, a hard, but for some individuals like Kierkegaard, a psychologically (not logically) necessary choice. It is the point of his writing to 'seduce' the reader, to make this choice appealing, and to make sure that as a choice it is faithful to the meaning of the Scriptures.

Kierkegaard's criticism of 'the present age' (Europe in the mid-nineteenth century) began with the charges that it was an age 'devoid of passion' and with 'pantheistic contempt for the existing individual'. It was an age of grand abstractions, exemplified by the Hegelian dialectic, but with no sense of the meaning of an individual life, no sense of the absurd, no sense of the life-and-death choices that an individual—as opposed to the cosmic *Geist*—is forced to make. Indeed, Kierkegaard quips, it is an age in which a man cannot even decide to commit suicide, so 'rational' has it become. It is this climate that has allowed for the creation of 'that phantom, "the public" ', and for the loss of all sensitivity for the passion of religion—and passion in general. Of course he could not pretend to undo this damage with a broadside attack against society. Such a direct attack would simply become one more aspect of the same set of abstractions. Instead, his strategy is a form of 'indirect communication', to be teasing, personal, and creative, since every creative act is already a small destruction of the status quo.

Against Hegel, Kierkegaard develops a personal viewpoint that is in almost every way opposed to the cosmic, rationalizing philosophy of Spirit, even if it frequently (and ironically) borrows Hegel's language. In place of Hegel's celebration of universal Spirit he decries anonymity and 'the public', and insists that only 'the Individual' counts. Against Hegel's conception of God as Spirit he angrily replies that if Hegel has succeeded in saving Christianity it is only by destroying everything worth saving in Christ's teachings. Hegel emphasized the rationality of religion; Kierkegaard insists that what makes religion so powerful is precisely its irrationality: the incomprehensible nature of its doctrines, and the need for uncomprehending faith in the face of the unknown.

He even goes so far as to throw the notion of dialectic in Hegel's face, with the invention of an 'existentialist' dialectic which, unlike the Hegelian version, makes no progress and hands nothing over from people to people or from generation to generation. It is a dialectic in the sense that it proceeds through conflict and confrontation, but this always takes place *within* each individual, and though there is necessarily movement there is no resolution. There is just the individual making a choice and sticking to it, always aware that in some sense that choice is absurd and unjustifiable, and might have been quite different. One can choose to live a satisfying life ('the aesthetic life') or one can choose to live a life according to the moral law ('the ethical life'), but one cannot do both. There will always be crises and conflicts in which one will be forced to choose—'either/or'—and there is no 'higher' guide or reason to show one which is right.

This choice between the aesthetic and the ethical is exemplified by the decision to marry (indeed, it has often been said that this entire aspect of Kierkegaard's philosophy is his own rationalization of his decision not to marry Regina Olsen, and he more or less admits this). From the aesthetic point of view the only criterion for one's choosing to marry is one's own satisfaction. For the man (and Kierkegaard only really considers him), that satisfaction lies in his enjoyment as a lover, or in the degenerate case his success as a seducer. It is quite distinct from any questions of obligation, honour, or the woman's feelings, except in so far as these are directly related to one's own enjoyment (guilt might enter in here, but it is itself not at all an aesthetic feeling). Marriage, on the other hand, is an obligation; it defines duties. It is an ethical phenomenon, not a matter of self-satisfaction. Kierkegaard does not deny that marriage has its pleasures and satisfactions (indeed, his ethical spokesman Judge Wilhelm seems to go overboard with such aesthetic appeals), but he does insist that romance and marriage are two quite different and opposed options. To think that one can have both is to deny the 'either/or' necessity of choice, and ultimately to deceive ourselves about the nature of being human.

The third choice of life-styles (or 'spheres of existence')— Kierkegaard's own choice—is the religious life. Although he explicitly contrasts the aesthetic and the ethical in his early works, in his own life it was clear that the choice was more between the ethical and the religious life (he had indulged himself as an aesthete as a youth, but without great success). For the sake of his religion he gave up the considerable comforts and satisfactions of married life. The religious life is one of commitment to God. But although it was Kierkegaard's personal choice, his philosophy prevented him from ever defending it as the 'right' choice. All he could do was to choose it, live as an example, and 'seduce' the rest of us into choosing it too.

Like Rousseau, Kierkegaard turned his own resentment and anti-social nature into a spectacularly individual and appealing brand of self-righteousness and inner integrity. But unlike Rousseau he had no plans to change the world; indeed, any such 'big picture' seemed to him quite irrelevant and unappealing. When revolutions broke out throughout Europe in 1848 Kierkegaard was only a snide observer. He found such uprisings pointless and ridiculous, just another manifestation of 'the Public'.

His contemporary Karl Marx (1818–83), however, admired and shared Rousseau's social blueprints and ambitions. The precise understanding and reformulation of what Kierkegaard called 'the Public' was exactly what he wanted out of life. It was Rousseau's bold conception of the social contract, and not his romantic emphasis on the sentiments, that inspired him. He saw in Rousseau (and in Hegel) a powerful if not always explicit revolutionary doctrine, and when the revolutions of 1848 broke out all over Europe Marx was elated. His own contribution to those revolutions, co-authored with Engels, was the *Communist Manifesto*, the opening salvo of world Communism.

Criticism had been the key to the Enlightenment. In France this meant uncompromising scrutiny of all existing ideas and institutions, and a radical willingness to envisage new and better ideas and institutions into which existing society might evolve. In Germany 'critique' was far more timid, applied to the abstractions of reason and judgement rather than to institutions, and while the French Revolution left its government in tatters the Germans retained their everyday world intact. Marx clearly preferred the French version, and commented that, while the French put their world in flames the Germans 'wished the world well'. Ideas and philosophy could become the incitement to world historical change but too easily became mere rationalization and ideology, excuses for accepting the status quo. Writing about Feuerbach in 1845 Marx said, 'philosophers have only *interpreted* the world, in various ways; the point is to *change* it',[5] and in his writings of 1843 he said that the task for philosophy was the 'ruthless criticism of the existing order'. By the age of 25 Marx was becoming a Marxist.

As a youth, Marx's ambition was to become a *dichter*, a poet, and he was steeped in the romantic as well as the Enlightenment tradition. From Rousseau he inherited that familiar sense of inner integrity which a corrupt society could too easily distort and disguise, but never quash. From the German romantics and Hegel in particular he was inspired by that sweeping sense of world history moving inexorably onward powered by internal reasons of its own. From Schiller he learned to despise the 'fragmentation' of life and the dangers of increased 'specialization', as well as the ideal of a society so harmonious, integrated, and organic that the State would simply 'wither away'. From Feuerbach he learned to turn Hegel on his head, and to look for the origins and explanations of all intellectual, cultural, and social change in the 'material conditions' of society, in economics rather than in philosophy. Ideas alone would not change the world; they themselves were the product—the rationalization—of the economic needs and practices of a people. Accordingly, what Marx most had to learn was not more philosophy but economics, the new science of 'political economy' that was already flourishing in Britain and France.

In 1843 Marx married, and left Germany for Paris where he began a study of the French Revolution, started using words like 'revolution' and phrases like 'the exploitation of man', and became an international outlaw for his objections to heavy-handed censorship by the Prussian state. He had such contempt for German backwardness that he did not even address his serious criticism to Germany, saving his life's energy for a full assault on the advanced industrial world which then fully existed only in England. In Paris he met the anarchist Michael Bakunin and started working with Engels, as well as coming into contact with the French Utopians. Marx made fun of their idyllic suggestions, but the radical and conspiratorial atmosphere of Paris was suitable for the germination of his own ideas. He also began studying the British economists, Adam Smith, David Ricardo, and James Mill, and in the questions of political economy he found the ideas that would provide the substance and the driving force behind his reformulation of the Hegelian dialectic. His philosophy would not be an edifying system of abstract ideas and their (teleo)logical implications; his theories would be weapons that would change the world: 'Theory becomes a material force once it has seized the masses.'

Reading Adam Smith, Marx realized that the great economist provided not just a celebration and defence of free enterprise, but also the groundwork for a diagnosis of the contradictions and oppression that capitalism engenders. Smith was mainly concerned with the 'wealth of nations' and questions of general prosperity; Marx concerned himself with the neglected people who made industry work and who suffered most from the 'supply and demand' mechanisms of the market. The worker made prosperity possible, but he or she continued to live in wretched poverty, often working sixteen-hour days in dangerous, dirty, inhuman conditions. The plight of the worker had been examined by other economists such as Jean Baptiste Say and David Ricardo, who had argued that such wretchedness followed from—and would not be corrected by—the capitalist economic system. What Marx added to their learned studies was a sense of moral outrage. He commented that economics since Smith had become 'increasingly cynical', and in response he returned to his Rousseauian roots and began to campaign for the integrity of 'man's soul', which he distinguished sharply from the 'money-soul' of capitalism. Marx later came to consider himself a 'scientist', but his project was motivated by Schiller's ideal of the whole, harmonious person in a whole, harmonious society. 'Human individuality, human morality have become articles of commerce and the *material* that money inhabits', Marx complained; prostitution—the sale of the self—was becoming a universal phenomenon. 'Man', he concluded, 'is being alienated from himself.'[6]

That concept of 'alienation' existed in Hegel, who talked about 'self-alienation' at a variety of crisis-points in his dialectic, but for Marx alienation was not just a confrontation of 'forms of consciousness' but a very personal loss of self. Moreover, Hegel had discussed alienation as a general dilemma of the human spirit, while Marx came to see that it has specific forms, and that these forms are particular to a socio-economic *class* of society. Again, Hegel had talked about classes, indeed he had introduced the idea of 'the universal class' to refer to the bureaucrats and civil servants who supposedly acted for the benefit of society as a whole and not from self-interest, but Marx saw clearly that acting 'selflessly' from a position of power was thoroughly self-interested, and he shifted the notion of 'the universal class' from the bourgeoisie to the powerless 'proletariat', the working class. In a sense, however, the proletariat did not yet exist. The working class existed, of course; Smith, Say, Ricardo, and Fourier had all recognized the shared misfortunes of those who worked for wages, and Engels had come to Paris to write a book about them. But there was as yet no *self-consciousness* of those workers as a class, no sense of their numbers or their power, or of the system that crushed them and how it worked. Most of all there was no hope, no sense that things could be different. There was not even the recognition that poverty was a condition that one could do anything to cure. Thus Marx saw as his mission not just the development of a theory but the education of the workers in their own interests and capabilities. They, after all, make industrial society possible. Why should they not share—if not control—its wealth? Against the seeming hopelessness of the age Marx would argue that a workers' revolution was not only possible—it was 'inevitable'.

It is here that Hegel's 'Master–Slave' parable comes into play as the root metaphor of Marx's view of history. Hegel had used the parable to illustrate the essential importance of mutual recognition, but he had left the exact nature of that recognition ('as another self-consciousness') imprecise. Marx, in line with the materialism he had learned from Feuerbach, came to see the nature of mutual recognition quite precisely: it had to do with economic power. It was not the abstract fight to the death which Hegel envisioned, but a life-long struggle for ownership and the forces of production. And though the slave lost the battle for recognition in Hegel's sense, he did control the forces of production. The master—the entrepreneur—might 'own' these, but they were not his in a more profound sense, and once the slave—the proletariat—came to recognize the real fact of his power, there would be an 'inevitable' upheaval, and the slave would take control, thereby ceasing to be a slave. Here is Hegel's self-realization of spirit in real life, the overcoming of alienation not just with an improvement of ideas but by a theory-inspired alteration of the world. There would be no alienation because there would be no more socio-economic classes, no more masters, and no more wage-slaves. Greed and money would not corrupt the intrinsically creative self that is in all of us, and the 'abolition of private property [would] restore man to himself as a human being'. The Rousseauian self could be saved, and Hegel's international Spirit could become a reality, but all of this—despite its inevitability—required a politico-philosophical act. In 1848, Marx and Engels issued their invitation:

Working men of all countries, unite![7]

The Anti-Transcendental Turn: Logic, Empiricism, and the Rise of Relativism

> There is no real blood flowing through the veins of the knowing subject constructed by Locke, Hume, and Kant, only the diluted juices of reason, a mere parade of thought.[1]
>
> Dilthey

Every great period of philosophical creativity and excitement is followed, according to Franz Brentano in his *Four Phases of Philosophy*, by a predictable decline. After the flourishing of a new philosophical theory, its theoretical insights are rendered 'useful' and applied to practical problems. This is followed by a tendency to scepticism and pessimism, and finally there is a relapse into mysticism. In modern times this pattern was repeated, according to Brentano, in the explosion of ideas associated with Descartes, Locke, Leibniz, and the Enlightenment, which was followed by the scepticism of Hume, and finally by the obscurantism of Kant and the idealists who further developed his philosophy.

The late nineteenth century was not dominated by any one philosopher or school, but much of philosophy, especially in Germany, took the form of a reaction to Kant and German idealism. Franz Brentano's empiricism and Gottlob Frege's attention to logic represented two aspects of a general turn towards the natural sciences and away from abstract philosophical speculation. Straightforward scientific materialism made a come-back in a direct and obvious reaction against the excesses of idealism. Somewhat more sophisticated was a movement called 'positivism', initiated in France by Saint-Simon and Fourier as a social movement, and solidified by Auguste Comte into a general theory of history and philosophy. Central to Comte's positivism is the emphasis on scientific observation and explanation, and the rejection of theological and metaphysical speculation (though Comte himself won great acclaim late in life with a novel interpretation of the Trinity). Positivism really became a force to be reckoned with, however, at the very end of the century, when a group of physicists led by Ernst Mach, and later by Moritz Schlick formulated the creed that would become 'logical positivism', a philosophy that divides knowledge into logic and sensory experience, as in Hume, thus rejecting Kant and his successors, and almost all of the philosophy we have discussed so far.

One of the philosophers with considerable impact on the logical positivists was Gottlob Frege (1848–1925). He was a mathematician, and his concerns and his subsequent influence in philosophy were largely confined to mathematical logic and the foundations of arithmetic. Frege rebelled against the obscurity of German idealism, and looked back beyond the Cartesian and Kantian revolutions in philosophy to Aristotle and the medieval scholastics, who agreed that logic, not the theory of knowledge or any grand view of the self, was the foundation of philosophy. This perspective, which would later be adopted in Vienna by Ludwig Wittgenstein and in Cambridge by Bertrand Russell, constituted a radical rejection of the entire tradition of modern philosophy. He had little sympathy with his fellow rebels in the empiricist camp, however. They not only held on to the importance of epistemology and ontology as the bases of philosophy; they were also guilty of promulgating the error that Frege chastised as 'psychologism'—the confusion of the universal and necessary propositions of logic and mathematics with the merely empirical and contingent hypotheses of psychology. Frege insisted that the 'necessity' of which philosophers were so fond was to be found in one place only, and that was in the field of formal logic and the foundations of mathematics. Moreover, where the idealist philosophers had muddled through the fog of such Kantian notions as 'concept' and 'constitution', Frege pinned down his analyses to the structure of language. In doing so he opened the way to twentieth-century analytic philosophy, but more relevantly to our story here, he also set Edmund Husserl off in the new and different direction that he would call 'phenomeno-logy'.

There is no simple summary of the rich and often under-estimated period of European philosophy that filled the final quarter of the nineteenth century. There were no heroes like Rousseau, Kant, or Hegel, and there was no overwhelming single movement as there had been in the days of the idealists. Neverthe-less, there was great excitement, particularly in the studies of (the philosophy of) history and psychology, and much of the ground-work was being laid for the innovative movements of the early twentieth century. We will discuss only two of these here (Frege's influence on analytic philosophy being out of the scope of this study): the background of phenomenology in the work of Brentano, Meinong, and Stumpf, and the rise of historicism in the work of Wilhelm Dilthey and Henri Bergson.

Franz Brentano (1838–1917) was no enthusiast for the tran-scendental revolution in philosophy. Like many philosophers and scientists in the late nineteenth century he despised the speculation and obscurity that Kant and the German idealists had brought to philosophy, and sought a return to the solid testimony of the senses. He was an empiricist much in the mould of John Locke, and the psychology, ontology, and ethics he developed in the final years of the last century were explicitly based on 'the empirical standpoint'. He saw himself combating the deleterious effects of Kantianism, and encouraging renewed, careful attention to the details of conscious experience, not only in standard epistemology but also in regard to such neglected mental processes as 'emotive phenomena', especially love and hate.

Brentano was a realist in the sense that he insisted that every act of consciousness must have an object other than itself. In other words, what we know (perceive, believe, and so on) are not in any sense ideas (as in idealism) but things, objects, states of affairs. This essential property of consciousness—that it is always 'directed toward an object'—is now known as 'intentionality'. Of course some of these objects do not exist, as in a false belief or a hallucination, but this familiar phenomenon, which Brentano called (following the scholastics) 'intentional inexistence', never-theless presupposes the general realist thesis that consciousness is not self-enclosed and concerned only with itself or its ideas but is always 'about' an object of some sort, even if it turns out that the object does not exist.

This concept of intentionality came to define consciousness for Brentano. It was the heart of his rejection of idealism. A mental or psychological process is necessarily directed toward an object, but one cannot infer from this that such an object exists. That is, from the fact that one desires or thinks about roast beef one cannot infer—as one could from the fact that one was eating it—that the roast beef in question exists. But this raised a number of questions for the realist about the kind of existence such 'inexistent' objects had. They were not real objects, but if he said that they were ideas then he would find himself back in the idealist camp. When he published his *Psychology from an Empirical Standpoint* in 1874, Brentano entertained the possibility that they had some special kind of existence, but in his later works he returned to his hard-headed realism, and insisted that nothing exists except concrete, particular objects in the world. This leaves the problem of how we are to conceive of the objects of consciousness in general. When the thing that we desire or think of does not exist, the object of consciousness is not a real existing object. But if that thing were to exist it would seem that the object of consciousness is nevertheless the same, and this means that the object of consciousness is *always* something other than a real or 'genuine' object. Brentano toyed with a theory of 'fictions' and 'abbreviations' to account for our use of general terms, but the question of the existence of 'inexistent' objects of consciousness remained a problem for the realists.

Alexius Meinong (1853–1920) was a student of Brentano in Vienna, and in response to the realist dilemma formulated his 'Theory of Objects'. It was clear to him that objects of consciousness that do not exist could not simply be dismissed from ontology but required some special status, and so he distinguished between 'existence' (or 'being') and 'subsistence' ('non-being'). Possible objects that did not exist (for example, a golden mountain or a flying horse) had subsistence, even though they did not have existence. They were also incomplete, however: William James noted that an imaginary horse need not be of any particular colour or height, as every real horse must. Meinong excluded from this analysis impossible objects (round triangles, for example); they have 'character' but neither existence nor subsistence. Indeed, all objects have character, and this is in every case independent of whether they exist or subsist. Thus Meinong avoids idealism, since neither existence nor subsistence is a property of consciousness. His theory bears some resemblance to Plato's view, but he is not a Platonist; he does not claim, as Plato seems to, that non-existent objects nevertheless have being. But neither is he exactly a realist as Brentano was; indeed, Meinong sometimes suggests that he should be called an 'objectivist' instead.

Although they are best known for their theories of consciousness and objects respectively, both Brentano and Meinong carried their researches far beyond the narrow boundaries of traditional ontology. They developed sophisticated moral philosophies, beginning with the rejection of Kant's separation of values and knowledge, and his subsequent separation of morality and the inclinations, including emotions as well as desires and such motives as self-interest. For Brentano and Meinong, emotions in particular have objects, just as thoughts and judgements do, and values are just as much objects of consciousness as facts. Consequently, they base their ethics not on the isolated Kantian sense of practical reason but rather on basic 'value feelings'. Brentano analyses these as varieties of love and hate; Meinong develops a more complex set of moral categories which include such 'objectives' as meritorious action. Emotions, like judgements, may be correct or incorrect; they are not dumb sensations which are without value and merely 'inside', of no relevance to the world. But one might note that, with this return to feeling and the rejection of Kant, they bring us back once again to Rousseau, and it should not surprise us that they would have some effect on the return of romantic sensibilities, on Freud and Heidegger, and on Husserl's best ethics pupil, Max Scheler.

Karl Stumpf (1848–1936) was not a philosopher on a par with Brentano and Meinong, but he is an excellent illustration of productive late nineteenth-century empiricism. Stumpf admired Kant, and did not reject idealism so vehemently as Brentano and Frege. Yet he preferred Locke to Kant and rejected Kant's central notions of a priori knowledge and transcendental argument. He did allow for the existence of some a priori knowledge, but only straightforward deductions and statements of mathematics (which he insisted, with Frege and against Kant, could not be construed as 'synthetic a priori' but only as what Kant would have called 'analytic'). He did not hold the extreme empiricist view (for example, that of John Stuart Mill) which insisted that all knowledge, even mathematics, was directly based upon empirical observations. From Brentano he developed a notion of 'self-evidence', and insisted that some propositions, for example, '2 + 2 = 4', could be known to be true without any further argument. Adopting a position midway between Brentano's realism and Kantian idealism, Stumpf held that truth was a property of the contents of consciousness, but he also followed Frege in insisting that truth was a function of thought, not the thinker. Nevertheless, Stumpf remained a thoroughgoing empiricist, and there are suggestions that even such self-evident propositions as those of mathematics might ultimately be based upon experience. His main work, accordingly, concerned the fundamental units of experience, a study of the nature of sensations. Against both traditional empiricism and idealism, he argued that sensations had to be understood holistically, as a *Gestalt* (in the terms of one of his students, Wolfgang Kohler).

Wilhelm Dilthey (1833–1911) also considered himself a strict empiricist but he had no compunctions about tracing his allegiance to Kant and Hegel, and aspiring to formulate an all-embracing theory of human life. He was greatly influenced by Kant, Schelling, and especially Hegel, and his philosophy—which he called a 'philosophy of life'—is devoted to the appreciation of the richness and variety of human life. In particular he was concerned with the changes in our various world-views (or *Weltanschauungen*) through history, and Dilthey is the primary figure in the movement called 'historicism'. He began by rejecting the unexamined premiss that lay at the basis of almost all empirical psychology and social science at the time, namely that the study of human life was on a par with the study of nature, and that in both cases the challenge was to gather observable data and formulate general theories of explanation. According to Dilthey there is a great difference between the explanation of natural phenomena and the *understanding* of human acts and institutions. We can understand human behaviour only because we can see it 'from the inside', because we too are human, and recognize the *meaning* of what people say and do. This is the special realm of the human sciences—or *Geisteswissenschaften*—which consists not of explanations and general laws but rather of meanings and their interpretation. Like Hegel he emphasized the importance of historical development in our understanding, and rejected any notion of an unknowable 'thing in itself' beyond human experience. The business of philosophy, as the key to the human sciences, was just this historical and holistic reflection on life. Like Hegel again, he insists that there is no absolute starting point for such reflection, but he differs from him in rejecting the assurance that we shall ultimately reach some absolute end-point. We never escape from our own historical circumstances, and though we can see beyond our own horizons, it is by no means certain that we shall find any necessary and universal meaning that ties all of humanity together.

In the natural sciences we classify and categorize phenomena; they do not classify and categorize themselves. In the human sciences, however, we find ourselves already provided with a wealth of organizing principles and categories, for human life does not come to us as 'data' but rather as life already lived, and lived through interpretations and meaning. The philosopher does not impose meanings or categories on human life but rather 'reads' the meanings and categories already evident in every word, act, and gesture. Social institutions represent enormous complexes of interpretations of human aims and actions, and art, literature, and morality exhibit interpretations on a still more expressive level. All that a philosopher can do is to articulate these many pre- or semi-conscious meanings on a fully explicit level. Our lives are already thoroughly organized and interpreted, and already embody the philosophical tendency to an all-encompassing *Weltanschauung*. But there is no single such world-view, as is evidenced by the dramatic differences in philosophies. Dilthey explicitly distinguishes Kant and Hegel here as proponents of very different and incommensurable philosophical views, Kant as a 'freedom idealist', Hegel as an 'objective idealist', and contrasts both of them with the materialist realism that he calls 'positivism'. But Dilthey suggests no possible synthesis or common viewpoint here, and one might well wonder whether his appreciation of the variety of *Weltanschauungen* and philosophies is sufficient to defuse the charge of relativism that has been levelled against him. Knowing the options is not the same as obtaining absolute knowledge.

The problem is complicated by Dilthey's historicism, the thesis that all human events and institutions must be understood (at least in part) in historical terms, as having developed in a certain way in certain contexts which may well have changed dramatically over time. The philosopher himself is in no privileged position, and cannot pretend to assume a transcendental standpoint outside of history from which history and the variations of human meanings can be viewed. He too is bound by a historical context from which the past will inevitably be interpreted through the concepts and concerns of the present. His understanding will be limited by his own 'horizon', and though one can expand one's horizon it is impossible to go beyond it (Heidegger will make extensive use of this 'horizon' metaphor). Concepts as well as contexts vary with history and horizons. Even the concept of 'humanity' is different in different times, and we have no right to assume that the all-embracing concept that we use to study humanity is shared by the various individuals or cultures which we include therein. The people of other ages can be understood only by entering into their point of view, but we are always bound by the horizons of our own age, and can never obtain a transcendentally adequate view of the whole.

Nevertheless, it should not be thought that Dilthey himself ever accepted the relativist tendencies of historicism. It was his belief that the study of hermeneutics—the systematic interpretation of human experience—would allow us to understand the social and cultural meaning systems that underlie every human expression. This understanding involved a technical difficulty, however. One can understand an underlying system only if one first understands the particular expressions that are its manifestations. But one can understand any particular manifestation only if one already understands the system as a whole. To take the most obvious example, one can understand the meaning of a sentence only if one already knows the language of which that sentence is a part. So too one understands a play in a football game only if one already understands the rules of the game. This is the infamous 'hermeneutical circle', and while it is obviously involved in interpretation of any kind it can also lead to the charge of relativism, the idea that any human institution or enterprise can be understood only in its own terms, and may be ultimately incomprehensible from some different point of view.

This new emphasis on the importance of history, which had played a minimal role in philosophy before the nineteenth century, brings us back to France and to perhaps the first great French philosopher since Rousseau, Henri Bergson. Bergson (1859–1941) was vehemently opposed to materialism and most contemporary forms of realism and empiricism. Like the later German idealists he had some sympathy with mysticism, and with the romantics he distrusted rational thought and preferred to rely on *intuition*. He rejected the realist insistence that consciousness is always consciousness of objects, and insisted that we are immediately aware only of our own experience, and can know the objects that cause that experience only by inference. What we know best and immediately, therefore, is the flow and duration of our own consciousness, of the passing of the past and the continuing arrival of the future. But this is knowledge that does not yield easily to concepts; one knows it rather by living it, through intuition (remember that Kant called time a 'form of intuition', not a concept). Furthermore, our knowledge of other people and their experience resists conceptualization, and must be known through intuition too. Concepts are useful for the scientific study and description of the material, spatial world, but not for the understanding of human experience. Here we have a somewhat extreme, quasi-mystical parallel to Dilthey's hermeneutics.

The most obvious parallel with Dilthey, however, is Bergson's insistence on the 'flow of life' itself which can only be understood through time and history. Much more than Dilthey (or any of the German philosophers preceding him) Bergson was a serious student and disciple of Darwin's theory of evolution, but he rejected Darwin's overly mechanical theory of 'natural selection' and defended instead his concept of 'creative evolution'. Darwin sought to explain the enormous variety of species on earth and throughout history with a model of random adaptation which, according to Bergson, could not possibly explain why simple organisms—many species of which are still alive and thriving after hundreds of millions of years—should have been supplemented by animals at higher and higher levels of organization, culminating in the arrival of humanity. Accordingly Bergson substituted a teleological theory for Darwin's mechanistic model, and postulated a 'vital force' that pervaded the entire evolutionary process. Except for its inherent optimism, his theory reminds us very much of Schopenhauer's conception of the cosmic Will manifesting itself in all living things as a 'will to live'. Unlike Schopenhauer and like Hegel, however, Bergson believes in progress, not only in the realm of human history but in the history of the world as a whole.

We know this vital force (as we know Schopenhauer's Will) through our own consciousness. We should not suppose that it was always in every organism as we know it in ourselves, of course. The first physio-chemical complexes in which the vital force situated itself surely were not conscious, and they in no sense 'intended' to evolve into higher organisms, nor can we conclude that the vital force has always had some ultimate endpoint in mind. Bergson rejects determinism, even of this teleological sort, such as the suggestion that evolution is a process in which the emergence of humanity is prefigured. He insists that the vital force explains 'progress' but not the particular path of progress, and yet he does not shy away from suggesting that the emergence of humanity is the reason for life on earth. Dilthey's and even Hegel's appreciation of the importance of human history pales next to such a grand teleology.

Just as his account of evolution avoids mechanistic explanation, so too Bergson's account of human life avoids determinism and maintains a firm belief in the centrality of human freedom. History demands the influence of the past on the present, but it is a mistake, he suggests, to think that this influence must be one of causal determination. All living organisms, Bergson argues, retain their past as a kind of memory, in habits and learned, instinctual responses. In addition human beings have proper memories, and memory, Bergson insists, is the essence of consciousness. Being conscious is not defined by the perception of objects, nor by the self-reflective 'I think', nor even by the awareness of one's own body, but by the 'spiritual' functions of memory which make the past explicit and readily available to us. But the past does not 'determine' that we act in a certain way; indeed, determinism as such is a false picture created through the underestimation of the importance of time in our definition of ourselves. It is the flow of time that is the essence of consciousness, but this flow is difficult to capture in concepts, and so we try to capture it in spatial terms, and thus misunderstand not only time but freedom.

Bergson distinguishes two kinds of time—time in natural science, and our experience of time (a distinction later adopted by both Heidegger and Sartre). In the natural sciences the concept of time is mathematical, which means measured by clocks. But clocks (mechanical clocks, water clocks, rope clocks, or sundials) are all spatial; they measure units in space, not the flow of time. In our own experience, however, we are immediately aware of the flow of time as a concrete indivisible process, as 'real duration'. Space, Bergson suggests, is time arrested; concepts are dead intuitions. Scientific determinism cannot account for the flow of consciousness where there are no causes and effects, and no rigid causal patterns, but rather creativity. Determinism misconstrues choice as a spatial choice 'point', represented by a drawing where one line turns into two (or more), but choice is not progress along a path: it is a temporal act. Like the flow of consciousness itself, freedom can be directly experienced by us. A free act is an act that emanates from one's whole personality and is spontaneous. We can grant that such acts are the exception rather than the rule, without insisting that human action in general is determined by causes outside of consciousness, just as we can accept the natural sciences without allowing them to pretend that they are capable of comprehending the essential creativity of human life.

When the enthusiasm for idealism had waned in Europe

(curiously enough just as it was becoming influential in England and America) philosophy became fragmented, a situation which historians too readily identify as a problem for intellectual life rather than as a period of healthy pluralism. But pluralism entered into the substance of these various philosophies as well, as Europe became increasingly aware of other parts of the world and of its own 'decadence', and as the promise of the Enlightenment became less and less evident in both social and intellectual life. Dilthey's historicism already heralded a new era in which the incommensurability of world-views would become more of a premiss than a hesitant conclusion. Bergson's unique combination of Cartesian dualism, evolutionary theory, and mysticism suggested a softening of the philosophical spirit which would be vigorously opposed in Britain but which remained influential in France. There would be less of Descartes's 'clear and distinct ideas', and more emphasis on the inner flow of the self. In Germany there would be a transcendental reaction to Dilthey's historicism, but first there had to be a completion of the anti-absolutist impulse. This was accomplished by Friedrich Nietzsche (1844–1900), whom even Dilthey took as 'a warning of where the brooding individual mind leads when it tries to grasp the essence of life within itself'. But this warning applies not just to a single brooding philosopher: it encompasses the pretensions of an epoch, and the extremes of Nietzsche's philosophy represent nothing less than the disintegration of the whole movement in European philosophy since Rousseau.

8

The Attack on the Self: Nietzsche and Nihilism

> Gradually it has become clear to me what every great
> philosophy so far has been: namely, the personal con-
> fession of its author and a kind of involuntary and
> unconscious memoir; also that the moral (and immoral)
> intentions in every philosophy constituted the real germ
> from which the whole plant had grown.[1]
>
> Nietzsche

Like many great philosophers Nietzsche saw himself as a new
beginning. In spite of this claim, he was entrenched in the tradition which he claimed to reject, and while he eliminated some of
its central features he retained others even more crucial. It was
not entirely perverse of Heidegger to identify him as 'the last of
the metaphysicians', even though Nietzsche took the destruction
of metaphysics as one of his main projects. He did attack the
absolutist conception of 'the one true world' in the name of what
he called 'perspectivism', but as he did so he sometimes
presupposed the Cartesian distinctions that gave rise to both
scepticism and absolutism. Similarly, he attacked the very idea of
morality, but he himself was—as he sometimes noted—the most
severe of moralists. Nietzsche often announced the need for new
philosophers and new values, but his philosophy—though strik-
ingly original—is very much a part of the story we have been
telling.

Nietzsche's attack on the modern conception of the self should
be viewed in the context of his admiration for the ancient Greeks.
He was trained as a classical philologist, and from his childhood
he admired the Homeric heroes above all. He despised what he
called 'the herd' and its conformist thinking. In an early work he
wrote that 'the goal of humanity cannot lie in the end but only in

its highest specimens'. In his prophetic prose-poem *Thus Spake Zarathustra* he even postulates a 'superman'—an *Übermensch*— who should serve as our ideal and who might some day replace us in history: 'Man is a rope tied between beast and *Übermensch*.'[2] In contrast to most of the philosophers we have discussed Nietzsche was an unabashed elitist. He worshipped warrior virtues, and despised the mediocrity and banal morality of the bourgeois German life in which he felt himself trapped.

However, Nietzsche by no means wished to go 'back' to ancient Greece—any more than Rousseau wanted to take us 'back' to the state of nature. He was an entirely forward-looking philosopher, and his attention to the past was largely aimed at destroying it, or rather clearing it away, for in his view it had already disintegrated: 'What is falling, that one should also push.'[3] The values and virtues that Nietzsche admired may have been very old, but he was well aware of the fact that nearly two thousand years of Christianity had so altered and improved the human spirit that it could never return to the non-introspective mentality of Achilles and Agamemnon. His warrior virtues applied more to the spirit than to the battlefield, and his heroes tended to be writers and artists rather than military or political leaders (in *Beyond Good and Evil* more than 100 of the 125 examples of 'higher men' are writers). Napoleon and Caesar are mentioned occasionally, and then more as metaphors than as human beings; Goethe appears quite frequently (as Wagner did in the early works). When Nietzsche speaks of 'the will to power' ('*macht*', not '*reich*'), we should be ready to interpret this as the power of great souls, not the might of dictators.

This admiration of creativity clearly aligns Nietzsche with the romantics. Indeed, his most powerful philosophical influence was Schopenhauer, and though he rejected his mentor's pessimism he accepted much of its foundations. Admiring Schopenhauer he naturally despised Hegel, in particular his vacuous optimism, and (like Kierkegaard) his elevation of the 'herd' to the level of Spirit. Indeed, Nietzsche's attacks on Christendom often resemble those of his Danish predecessor (whom he never had the chance to read); he found modern Christianity anonymous, passionless, self-righteous, and hypocritical, but he did not at all agree with Kierkegaard's insistence that the vital task was to recapture the true meaning of being a Christian. Nietzsche's attitude toward Jesus was quite ambivalent. He despised Christ's teachings ('the meek shall inherit the earth'), but admired—one is tempted to say envied—the personal power of the man. Similarly, he had an ambivalent attitude toward Socrates whom he often called a buffoon but whose creative power and influence he idolized. But he saw Socrates, not Christ, as the real beginning of the 'other-worldly' mentality that he so loathed in Western philosophy and religion. It was Socrates who appealed to reason as an antidote to the passions and an escape from the harsh and humiliating realities of everyday life. Before Socrates, Nietzsche believed (following the work of Heinrich Heine), the Greeks were an earthy, heroic people, not at all the proto-academic theoreticians admired by the Enlightenment.

In many ways Nietzsche's philosophy was a harsh reaction to the Enlightenment and in particular to the transcendental pretence. He had much to say against Kant and Rousseau, against their rich and pretentious sense of self, their glib identification with humanity, and their optimism that declared that humanity is essentially good. He even goes so far as to suggest that the self is an illusion, as is the notion of free will. But unlike Schopenhauer he does not give up the notion of individual identity, and though he questions both the concept of the Will and the idea that we are free, his philosophy is a steadfast defence of eccentricity, the privileges of genius, and the overwhelming importance of creative and original action. He objects to Kant's idea of a priori truth—as if truths were more than simply necessary 'for us', as instruments of survival not foundations of knowledge—and to his idea of the categorical imperative, as if action could be divorced from the inclinations and instincts, and commanded universally for all people at all times, whatever their situation and abilities. And more than for any particular doctrine he attacks Kant himself as a dogmatic system-builder who failed to question his own basic prejudices: his piety, his middle-class morality, and his Enlightenment pretensions of speaking for humanity as such. Despite his 'Copernican' revolution, as a man Kant was not radical enough for Nietzsche, who left his own University post in order to spend the rest of his life free from the fetters of any academic establishment.

Nietzsche's philosophy begins with a book on the Greeks, *The Birth of Tragedy*, which in many ways provides the key to all his future writings. In it he writes, 'only as an aesthetic phenomenon is the world justified eternally',[4] but the quest for justification will soon drop out of his philosophy, and the concept of 'eternity' will play a problematic role at best. But the exclusive emphasis on the aesthetic, on 'living one's life as a work of art', remains central to all of his attacks and admonitions, as its basic standard and unspoken ideal. The problem with morality and religion is that they defend the ugly and the misshapen, whereas Nietzsche's leading insight in *The Birth of Tragedy* is: 'how much these people [the Greeks] must have suffered in order to be so beautiful!' The Enlightenment may have looked back at the Greeks and imagined a happy society of enlightened philosophical souls, but Nietzsche—who read the literature before the philosophy—saw a people filled with anguish, who instead of escaping to other-worldly religions turned their hardships into a magnificent and glorious civilization.

In this context it is appropriate to introduce the term 'nihilism'. Nihilism—'believing in nothing'—is emphatically *not* the outcome of Nietzsche's philosophy. He used 'nihilism' as a diagnostic term to attack modern society, and traditional morality and religion, claiming that they, not his philosophy, were nihilistic. The modern sense of the self had become so emptied of content, and at the same time so arrogant, that it was as if there were no longer any real values at all. Of course those most responsible for this nihilism sounded as if they had the firmest beliefs and ideals—'liberty, equality, fraternity', 'duty', and 'being a good human being', the teachings of Christ, and the promise of eternal salvation—but in every case such fine ideals are only masks for disillusion with, if not contempt for, life. They deny our instincts and the dramatic differences between us, reject human nature as it is, and substitute an imaginary pure self and a harmonious community of equals, a 'kingdom of ends', and the promise of an eternal, blissful life after the end of this brief, brutal one. Nihilism is not necessarily the explicit denial of values (and atheism, Nietzsche insists, is certainly not nihilism); much more often it is a despair and resentment that covers itself with grand illusions. Getting rid of the illusions does not leave us with nihilism, however; instead it removes much of the motivation that makes nihilism so seemingly unavoidable.

Nietzsche's most dramatic portrayal of the nihilism that currently threatens the world is summed up in the thesis usually summarized as 'the Death of God' (the phrase itself had been used, with a different meaning, by Hegel and Martin Luther). The death of God obviously did not refer to some cataclysmic cosmological event, nor did Nietzsche intend to 'disprove' the existence of God in the fashion of some of the Enlightenment atheists (he calls himself 'an atheist by instinct'). It was rather the quasi-sociological insight that even people who considered themselves pious believers did not behave as if they believed in God at all, an insight reminiscent of Kierkegaard and sharing his indignation that so many people could treat the sense of being in the divine Presence with so little regard or feeling as to class church-going with any other kind of public activity, rather than engaging in personal and passionate confrontation with God. But Nietzsche's attack goes deeper, in part because, unlike Kierkegaard, he has no interest in salvaging Christianity in a renewed form. He suggests that what motivates Christianity is not at all the selfless, spiritual piety that Christians routinely refer to, but rather resentment and the spirit of revenge against those who are wealthier, healthier, happier, stronger, more intelligent, or even just 'different'. It is not an attitude of humility before God but of vengeance against their fellow citizens. The death of God refers to a very tangible change in the modern frame of mind. Whatever power the belief in God and divine rewards and punishments may have had in the past, they have it no longer, but neither has any set of values taken the place of the old fear of divine retribution, except for those instincts that have always been with us, no matter how vehemently denied. One of these, which Nietzsche calls 'the will to power', was in fact the motivation of all of those seemingly selfless, spiritual acts, but it will also be the basis of the new values he seeks to introduce in his philosophy.

The will to power plays a multitude of roles in Nietzsche's unsystematic thought. Most of the time it is a reasonable hypothesis about the primary motive of human behaviour—playing a role parallel to John Stuart Mill's utilitarian hypothesis that all human behaviour is motivated by the pursuit of pleasure (broadly interpreted) and the avoidance of pain. Occasionally Nietzsche allows himself a degree of Schopenhauerian speculation, and suggests that the will to power—like Schopenhauer's Will—is the underlying force behind all living things, or even behind *all* things. Often it represents a kind of pragmatism, the suggestion that the only meaning to be given to such metaphysical concepts as 'truth' is that they allow a certain species or people to survive. We can expect that, with this view, Nietzsche would have a life-long struggle with Charles Darwin, whose ideas (like those of virtually anyone he admired) he both borrowed and lambasted. The will to power explains the survival of ideas too, especially those that Kant considered a priori, or universal and necessary. In fact these are the ideas that we most need 'for the sake of the preservation of such creatures like ourselves; though they might, of course, be false judgements for all that'.[5]

This peculiar view, which sometimes parades under the title 'epistemological nihilism', is in fact a form of relativism, or what Nietzsche calls his 'perspectivism'—the view that there are only truths *for* a certain sort of creature or a certain society, there is no truth as such. Perspectivism is a technique as well as a claim, and in his 'middle' works (of the late 1870s and early 1880s) Nietzsche treated philosophy as an experimental discipline in which one would 'look now out of this window, now out of that', never settling down with any one view (which he considered a form of cowardice and corruption). Against such systematic philosophers as Kant, Hegel, and Schopenhauer he complains that 'the will to a system is a lack of integrity'. But the image of 'perspectives' leaves open the embarrassing question, 'perspectives on what?', and, indeed, much of Nietzsche's epistemology foundered on his retention of traditional Cartesian and metaphysical metaphors. He writes, for example, that 'the apparent world is the only one, the "real world" is merely added by a lie'.[6] Such a pronouncement leaves intact the traditional polarity of appearance and reality, then simply denies one pole. Similarly when he declares that 'truth is error' he is covertly appealing to some standard according to which our various perspectives can be judged. Slowly he saw his way beyond this confusion, but his real interests were never in the arena of knowledge but always in the realm of morals. Like Kierkegaard he was interested mainly in how to live; what we could know was, at most, of secondary importance. 'There is no pre-established harmony between the pursuit of truth and the welfare of mankind.'[7]

Every philosopher, Nietzsche announces at the beginning of *Beyond Good and Evil*, really reveals only his own 'prejudices', though typically in the name of some transcendental truth. They all seek to solve the riddles of human existence—and more—with a single stroke, but in fact they corrupt themselves and 'appear more stupid' than they really are. Modern philosophers pretend to be interested in knowledge, but the fact is that the quest for values—and the need to overcome nihilism—motivates all of them, even though they unwittingly contribute to nihilism rather than provide an answer to it. Kant's moral system is exemplary in this regard. In one sense Kant himself admitted limiting the pretensions of knowledge to make room for an unconditional defence of freedom and responsibility, and an absolute foundation for a universal morality—based, of course, on the pious bourgeois morals that Kant had himself been taught as a child. Terrified by the suggestion that morality might be no more than local custom or an expression of undependable sentiments, he formulated his a priori conception of the categorical imperative, presupposing cross-cultural similarity as well as an ultimate moral equality among all human beings. But if there is one thing that is clear to Nietzsche (and must have been to Kant) it is that human beings are basically different in circumstances, talents, and abilities. To impose a single universal set of standards is inevitably to limit those who have the greatest abilities, to 'level' society to the lowest common denominator, even if in the honorific name of 'autonomy'. Kant spoke of genius in his third Critique, but did not seem to consider the unusual attitudes and circumstances that went into the expressions of genius, and although he was keenly aware of the importance of 'intuition' in art, he had little tolerance for instinct or any other value that could not be rationally justified.

Kant is not alone, of course, in valuing rationality above all else, especially those non-rational (and sometimes irrational) biological promptings of the instincts. Rousseau and Hume praised our 'natural' sentiments, but it must be said, from a Nietzschean perspective, that their conception of nature was far more benign and bourgeois than any observation of creatures both in and out of society would warrant. Even Schopenhauer, who came closest to recognizing the undeniable reality of the instincts as Will, thought of them as purely destructive and undesirable. Thus Nietzsche is quite original in elevating the instincts to an exalted philosophical status. Indeed he even suggests that reason is no more than 'a system of relations between various passions and desires'.[8] He calls himself a 'naturalist' and is, perhaps, more of a biologist in temperament than any philosopher since Aristotle. It is the instincts that move us, and make us creative, perceptive, and wise, but they also make us stupid, and 'drag us down with their own weight'. The business of philosophy, morality, and reason is not to deny the instincts but to discriminate among them, encourage those that are 'life-enhancing', and resist or rechannel those that are 'life-stultifying'. But this is very different from the traditional prejudice against the instincts and the passions, 'the moralists' mania which demands not the control but the extirpation of the passions', the view which says, 'only the emasculated man is the good man'.[9] Anticipating Freud's central notion of sublimation, Nietzsche argues: 'instead of employing these great sources of strength, those impetuous torrents of the soul that are so often dangerous and overwhelming and economizing them, this most short-sighted and pernicious mode of thought wants to make them dry up.'[10]

If morals and the pursuit of the good life are to be based on the instincts instead of on the principles of practical reason, then much of the traditional emphasis in philosophy on the need to justify morality is misplaced. This had been seen as one of the leading tasks of the Enlightenment, and Kant's second Critique had only developed far more rigorously and systematically the project that had occupied philosophers for many years. It is true that some of these—the Scots Hume, Smith, and Hutcheson for instance—had tried to justify morality by appeal to the sentiments, but such a justification was weak at best, as Hume saw. Kant's attempted justification was magnificent in its ambition, taking the principles of morality as a priori principles of reason, and then showing (as he had for the basic principles of knowledge) that these were universal and necessary. But Nietzsche's objection to these various attempts is not aimed at their success or failure but at their very motivation. Why should one feel the need to justify morality he asks, unless one feels that morals are crumbling, are perhaps even without foundation? And furthermore, why should we have accepted those principles which we call 'moral' at all for so long, much less elevated them to the status they enjoy in our lives? This is a matter that calls not for a justification (which presupposes the status of morality, and only seeks a foundation for it) but rather for an explanation of our choice of values. Why should we have taken on the burden of morality at all and pretended that these principles are the only possible ones under which we could be secure and happy?

How does one explain morality? One way would be to show how a set of principles or customs allows a society to 'fit into' its environment, warlike virtues for a society like ancient Athens, surrounded by hostile neighbours, or environmental sensitivity for a society like some early American Indian tribes whose survival depended on a close and conservative working relationship with nature. Another way would be to demonstrate how certain forms of relationship made possible a secure and harmonious way of life within a society, for instance the different moral codes associated with marriage and sexuality in feudal society and modern bourgeois capitalism. A quite different way would be to examine the history of morals in a particular society or group of societies, and show how current attitudes developed through time. Nietzsche calls this a 'genealogy of morals', and in combination with the first two ways it provides him with a unique perspective on the nature of the moral principles that Kant took for granted and approached only 'analytically'.

The first thing to notice is that what we call morality in the ancient world originated among the slave population of the Hebrews, and developed during the long periods of martyrdom of the early Christians. It was, in other words, a 'slave morality', a morality formulated by, and suited to, those who suffered at the bottom of society, who had good reason to fear those who were more powerful and equally to celebrate virtues that minimized suffering and maximized group solidarity, for only in numbers could the weak have any strength at all. Slave morality succeeded by a combination of humility and hopeful arrogance. It encouraged a view of life as intrinsically unhappy and unfulfilling, and pointed to the vanity of even the greatest accomplishments in life. It showed the emptiness of the greatest luxury and the futility of all ambition. Above all it emphasized the evils of power, wealth, and leisure time—all things enjoyed by the master class and unattainable by slaves. But slave morality also made bold promises and pronouncements: that the slaves were 'the chosen people', and that, whatever the current political prognosis of history, 'the meek shall inherit the earth'. Thus it rationalized the plight of the slaves and at the same time provided an abstract reassurance, even a sense of superiority, and in this dramatic reversal we see again that curious phenomenon of master and slave that Hegel captured so elegantly in his parable in the *Phenomenology*.

The history of Western morality is the story of the reversal or 'transvaluation' of two moralities, that of a downtrodden group of slaves, and that of the powerful masters whom they served. Slave morality, as we have noted, rationalizes humbled circumstances and disappointment with life. It is also aimed at *getting even*, or at least maintaining one's self-esteem in the face of constant humiliation. The superiority felt by slaves who see themselves as the chosen people, and look forward to a day when they will take over from their present masters, provides not just a rationalization but also a weapon (whose political manifestation is what Marx called 'class consciousness'). The morality of the masters, on the other hand, does not initially look like a 'morality' at all. It places little emphasis on what one should not do, and seems to leave out many or most of the virtues that are essential to (slave) morality. Humility is viewed as a weakness rather than a strength; 'turning the other cheek' is a sign of cowardice, and wealth, far from being the root of evil, is rather a necessary presupposition of the good life. The question is, how did an impoverished and for many years unarmed group of slaves manage to impose their values on the proud and powerful masters of the ancient world, indeed even to eclipse master morality altogether so that today 'morality' means nothing other than what the slaves meant by it?

This 'incredible act of revenge', Nietzsche says, was made possible by a metaphysics learned from Plato (or Socrates), and augmented by a powerful set of theological sanctions. 'Christianity is Platonism for the masses', he wrote, and, indeed, Plato's metaphysics combined with the Hebrew God resulted in a most appealing and powerful idea. The ancient Hebrews already had the conception of an all-powerful God who looked over them, but his protection was far from dependable in the Old Testament, and His jealousy and anger occasionally resulted in more damage to the chosen people than to their enemies. Socrates' appeal to the otherworldly emphasized, as ancient Judaism did not, the transience and unreality of this world compared to another 'world of being', which was eternal. Together they could be forged into the weapon that could be used not only in defence of the weak but also offensively, if the Hebraic God were to extend his concern beyond the small group of chosen people to every human soul. Belief in God was no longer optional but mandatory, with the most awful penalties for refusal to believe, and with belief in God came Christian (slave) morality, with its emphasis on humility, equality under God, and charity, precisely what was needed by the unfortunate slave populations for them to demand the right to equality and an end to bondage. This process took place over many hundreds of years, and achieved success only in the past hundred years or so, just when, ironically, belief in the metaphysics that had made it possible was on the wane, and victorious (slave) morality was about to betray its inner nihilism.

(Slave) morality was (and is) essentially a *reaction* against the humiliation and oppression of slavery, and the superiority of the ruling class. It has, in an important sense, no values of its own.

The masters enjoyed the luxuries that wealth could obtain, and so the slaves in reaction insisted that luxury and wealth were evil. The masters had the advantage of superior military power and physical strength, so the slaves reacted and protected themselves by insisting that power and strength were evils, and that meekness, by contrast, was a virtue. The masters were proud and boastful, and the slaves reacted by declaring pride a sin. The masters gave free vent to their emotions, and so the passions in general were said to be evil. Such sentiments as faith, hope, and love were, not surprisingly, elevated to special status. In other words, what the masters valued as good, the slaves declared to be evil, and what turned out to be good, consequently, was the absence of evil. Thus the good man could be a man with few charms or talents, and probably with few overwhelming passions: 'the emasculated man is the good man', and the virtues tend to involve abstinence rather than enjoyment and achievement. Morality consists, not of values, but of principles that tell us what not to do, and it is this strange conception of human life that is canonized by Kant with his categorical imperatives. But that this is a façade for an absence of values is, Nietzsche says, becoming dangerously apparent in the treacherous world of late nineteenth-century politics.

It is Nietzsche's intention to pull down this façade for nihilism, whether it takes the form of traditional Christianity or the formidable structure of Kant's second Critique. But it must not be thought that, in attacking morality, Nietzsche is rejecting the possibility of values. He sometimes speaks of 'moralities' (as in 'master and slave morality'), indicating that his objection is to one variety of moral thinking, and not to morals as such. Furthermore he often defends such traditional virtues as courtesy and courage, clearly indicating that in rejecting traditional morality he does not intend to reject all of the values that it embodies. Similarly, in giving up the quest for a justification of morality he is not thereby admitting that values are, in general, unjustifiable. Rather he sees the very quest as mistaken and unnecessary; we could no more give up values than we could give up breathing, and the values that we *really* value are as much a part of our make-up as the 'reason' with which so many philosophers have denied these. Nietzsche keeps insisting that 'philosophers must be legislators' and 'invent new values', but the truth is that he defends some of the very oldest values, and insists that these are already an essential part of our being.

We introduced 'master and slave' as two historical classes (in Hegel they refer to two tenuous power roles), but Nietzsche sees master and slave rather as two types of person, defined not by class or culture but rather by natural constitution. Some people are strong, independent, energetic, creative, and ambitious, and others (the majority) are weak, dependent, easily tired, conformist, and resigned. These temperaments are not achievements but innate characteristics, and one could no more aspire to be the other than a lamb could aspire to be an eagle. Accordingly, Nietzsche's ethics must, like the history of morality itself, be divided into two. But where history favours slave morality and neglects that of the master, Nietzsche encourages a masterly morality (not a return to the brutality of ancient times) in which individual excellence and creativity are prized above obedience and conformity. But this is not a matter of choice, and in a sense he is not giving us an ethics or telling us what to do at all. One does what one must; Nietzsche has little patience with the notion of free will. He rejects the Schopenhauerian myth of the Will, and concludes that 'if there is no will, then there is no free will (or unfree will either)'.[11] We each have our fate, and one of the more joyful if vacuous recommendations of Nietzsche's philosophy is that we should each 'love our fate'—*amor fati*. Moreover, there is no point in forming moral principles because each of us has to go our own way in any case. 'This is my way; where is yours?' teaches Zarathustra. As for those of us who are still 'slaves', hopelessly unoriginal and conformist, it will always be the case that 'any rule is better than none'.

This dichotomy—or perhaps we should call it 'this moral prejudice'—between strong and weak, 'higher' and 'lower' men (women are virtually always 'lower'), between what is healthy and what is sickly, lies at the heart of Nietzsche's philosophy. It may even be—to use his own genealogical metaphor—the germ from which the whole philosophy has grown. Even without delving into the medical facts of Nietzsche's own lifelong losing

battle for health, sleep, and painless writing time, we can appreciate the ferocious emphasis on sheer *energy* that dominates his
philosophy, a welcome change from the ideals of stasis, security,
and nirvana that dominate so much of the philosophical tradition. What moves Nietzsche's readers is the enthusiasm and love
of life that is the ultimate point, as well as the driving force, of his
work. His celebration of strength should not be taken (as it so
often is) as a recommendation of brutality and aggressiveness;
more to the point is the private exhilaration of the creative artist
or writer. Nor should his condemnation of weakness be taken to
mean that ordinary people are worthless and mere pawns for the
ambitions of the strong (he says at one point that the strong have
a *duty* to protect the weak). It is unfortunate that he so
emphasized the supposed genetic differences between the weak
and the strong, and failed to employ his own perspectivism concerning the wide variety of human types, but like his predecessors
he was moved by the overriding ambition to reduce all of humanity to some single principle—or at least a single dichotomy. The
result has been that one of the greatest challenges to traditional
'transcendental' ethics has often gone unnoticed because of the
belligerent tone of its presentation.

In this regard we should briefly mention Nietzsche's most celebrated ideal, the *Übermensch*. The fact is that this much touted
and much lampooned superhuman character is discussed very
rarely in his work. He is introduced in *Thus Spake Zarathustra*,
and even there described hardly at all. Throughout his writings
Nietzsche discusses those whom he calls 'higher men', but he
makes it quite clear that none of these qualifies to be an
Übermensch: every one of them is still 'human all-too-human'.
The *Übermensch* is clearly something more than human, but
Nietzsche's description is so thin that one must conclude that the
very concept is more of an expression of disgust with human
beings as they are than an actual ideal of what they might be.
Moreover, Nietzsche seems to feel that we are locked into our
present pathetic nature; there is no way that we can be upgraded,
and he often makes fun of those (like Rousseau) whom he calls
'the improvers of mankind', who think that people are basically
good, and need only a restructuring of society to make them act

well. Furthermore, it is clear that he does not envision the *Übermensch* as the next step up evolution's ladder. Rejecting what he considers to be the Darwinian model (which he evidently did not adequately understand), he insists that there is no guarantee whatever that subsequent species will constitute an improvement. In *Zarathustra* he gives us a frightening portrait of what man will probably become, in his caricature of 'the last man', a particularly feeble bourgeois who is thoroughly content with his lot in life, and says, with a smile and a blink, 'we have invented happiness'. Here is the ideal of the Enlightenment in a revolting guise.

The one more or less concrete suggestion that Nietzsche does give us by way of identifying the *Übermensch*—though this too is to be found only in a scattering of paragraphs in his various books—is that what sets him apart is a matter of *attitude* rather than ability or accomplishment. This attitude is what we have called '*amor fati*' or the love of one's fate, in other words, the sheer love of life. The test of this attitude is an act of the imagination (which Nietzsche suggests in his notes might be a fact of physics) called 'the eternal recurrence', the hypothesis that whatever has happened and whatever will happen has been, and will be, repeated an infinite number of times (the physical basis for the hypothesis is the 'fact' that there are a finite number of 'energy states' and an infinite amount of time). The importance of the hypothesis becomes evident when one asks oneself: 'how would I react to this terrifying idea?' The *Übermensch*, Nietzsche suggests, would react with joy, having so loved his life in its every detail that he would gladly live it again. None of us, however, is capable of such an attitude, although eternal recurrence might still serve as a test for our relative satisfaction with our lives—whether we see what we have done and are doing as at all worthwhile. The myth of eternal recurrence is also a direct antidote to the teleological thinking of Christianity, much of German idealism, and even of Marx. 'In the long run', according to all of these philosophies, 'this all will add up to something.' But with eternal recurrence nothing adds up to anything; it just happens, again and again. 'This life, with every pain and every joy and every thought and every sigh . . . thou must live it once more and also innumerable times.'[12]

What does such a philosophy do to our already mangled concept of self? Having been provoked to transcendental arrogance by Rousseau and Kant, expanded to cosmic proportions by Hegel and the other idealists, tossed to the vicissitudes of the Will by Schopenhauer, and reduced to a pawn of global economics by Marx, the poor self might rightly wonder whether there is anything left of it in Nietzsche. We (most of us) are told that in the eyes of history we do not count (although it is the seductive charm of Nietzsche's writing that he often lets the reader think that he might be one of 'the few'). We are told that we have no will, much less free will, and that 'the "subject" is only a fiction'. All that seems to be left is self-interest, underlying all of what we thought were our noblest actions and beliefs. Nietzsche even denies us the right to be egoists, for 'the ego of which one speaks when one censures egoism does not exist at all'.[13] It looks as if the self, which had been raised to transcendental then cosmic status, has now disintegrated into nothingness.

Part III

The Self In and For Itself:
Phenomenology and Beyond

9

The Transcendental Reaction: Husserl's Science of the Ego

> Phenomenology is as it were the secret longing of the whole philosophy of modern times. The fundamental thought of Descartes is already pressing toward it. Hume almost enters its domain, but his eyes are dazzled. The first to perceive it truly is Kant, whose greatest intuitions first become quite clear to us after we have brought the distinctive features of the phenomenological field into the focus of full consciousness.[1]
>
> Husserl

Twentieth-century continental philosophy begins with Edmund Husserl (1859–1938), who in 1900–1 published a series of *Logical Investigations*, setting the stage—along with his colleague Gottlob Frege—for the technical inventiveness and intense interest in logic and mathematics of the coming decades. He was an influential leader in the concern with 'method' that marks so much of contemporary philosophy, and his 'phenomenology' was the chosen method, or at least the starting point, for many of the main figures of recent European philosophy including Heidegger, Sartre, Merleau-Ponty, Gadamer, and Derrida. On the other hand, Husserl might with some justification be viewed as one of the last strongholds of the nineteenth century, a reactionary who was dismayed by the historicist and relativist direction of Nietzsche and Dilthey, and longed to turn philosophy back to the Absolute.

That Absolute, for Husserl, had to be found in consciousness. He is thus the heir of Kant, Fichte, and Hegel, but also looks back to Descartes as his ultimate philosophical predecessor. Although Husserl had little interest in the history of philosophy, he openly longed for the days when scepticism was not taken so seriously, when philosophy could call itself a 'science' without qualification, and could declare itself a search for certainty and absolute truth without embarrassment. Husserl perceived the loss of absolutes as a genuine 'crisis', not only in the philosophical sciences but in civilization as well. Scepticism was like a disease, an admission of failure, and Nietzsche's relativism and Dilthey's historicism were tantamount to scepticism. The simple rejection of philosophy and its foundations among scientists and empiricists was no better, for their taking the 'natural standpoint' for granted, without any attempt to show its validity, was also a virtual admission of failure. Phenomenology had as its aim nothing less than the return of philosophy to scientific status, and of European thought to the road of rationality.

Husserl's starting-point, following the model of Descartes, was the 'self-evidence' of one's own consciousness. Phenomenology, despite Husserl's sometimes radical pronouncements about starting philosophy anew and without presuppositions, was very much a part of the mainstream tradition of modern philosophy, a turn to subjectivity with the intention of arriving at objective truth. The grand presumption, never sufficiently questioned by Husserl, is that the truth is to be found in consciousness, in the ego, and nowhere else. Sometimes this claim is just the reasonable demand that experience counts for something, as in *Ideas* where he writes, '. . . if we ascribe no value to the reply, "I see that it is so", we fall into absurdity',[2] but it does not follow that this is absolute evidence rather than, at best, one possible piece of evidence. It also leaves the status of what is seen quite undetermined. In *Cartesian Meditations*, on the other hand, Husserl proclaims that: 'The monadically concrete ego includes also the whole of actual and potential conscious life. . . . Consequently the phenomenology of this self-constitution coincides with phenomenology as a whole (including objects).'[3] In one's own experience one can discover the world, and realize the nature of everyone else's experience as well.

Phenomenology is the close examination of the essential structures of consciousness, with an eye to deriving (describing) necessary and universal truths of experience. With Husserl's phenomenology philosophy was finally to become a science, but not an empirical science. The object of phenomenological description was to get to the essences or ideas (*eidos*) that presented themselves in experience, to go beyond the various 'facts' of experience and the relativity of theories and practices to those features of experience which are 'absolutely given in immediate intuition'. As opposed to Descartes and Kant (as well as Fichte and Hegel), Husserl's phenomenology is an appeal not to deduction or dialectic but directly to 'evidence', not the evidence of the senses but of the consciousness as such, 'apodeictic' evidence that can be directly intuited, with a specially trained method of philosophical investigation. To recover philosophy as a science meant to discover a body of indubitable necessary truths with this new method.

Phenomenology is typically presented as a method rather than as a philosophical stance, but this is misleading. Philosophy, the one discipline that is forever picking itself up by its own bootstraps, is never merely methodological; it always involves some substantial, metaphysical position, a set of doctrines about the world, the self, and where the truth is to be found. It is often said, against Husserl, that he spent so much effort tinkering with his method that he never had time to actually work out philosophical problems, but every one of his reformulations of the phenomenological method—and there were many—was at the same time a revision in philosophy, a different view of the nature of the world's existence and our knowledge of it, a different theory about the self and its extent.

We might note that, compared to Kant, Hegel, or Nietzsche, Husserl's interests in philosophy were extremely narrow. He came into it from mathematics, and he remained exclusively interested in epistemological questions concerning necessary truth (at the end of his life he made an enormous concession when he suggested—but did not pursue—the importance of the 'life-world' (*Lebenswelt*) as the foundation of scientific thinking). It might be argued that every domain has its necessary truths, and consequently phenomenology has since been applied to virtually every realm of human experience. But we do not find this range of interest in Husserl, and most of the questions that have accounted for the popular appeal and persistence of philosophy through the ages found no place in his voluminous writings. The problem that brought Husserl from mathematics into philosophy was the nature of arithmetic, and though this broadened as the years went by into a more general interest in necessary truth, Husserl's discussions of human experience always stay at a considerable distance from concrete daily life, even when he discusses such topics as the essential structure of perception. Despite his heavy emphasis on the self as the source of experience there is not even a hint of the moral self-engagement of Fichte, or the cosmic enthusiasm of Kant, Schelling, or Hegel, much less the striving wilfulness of Schopenhauer or Nietzsche. Husserl's self is a knowing self, with only occasional comments to the effect that it might also have such attributes as 'Affectivity and Volition'. It is as if Husserl is squarely in the middle of this grand tradition without in some important sense having any awareness of its dramatic nature.

And yet there are good reasons why Husserl had such a great influence on philosophers whose interests were much wider than his own. What influenced so many scholars and thinkers was not so much the substantive content of his philosophy as his integrity and conscientiousness. He provided more a model of how to do philosophy than a method as such. He insisted on a 'presuppositionless philosophy', and was always worried that there might be some unquestioned element in our thinking which was taken for granted. He called himself a 'perpetual beginner', and was continually rethinking his entire project, sometimes lapsing into despair that he never would, after all, find the certainty for which he was searching.

Thus, when he was doing mathematics he became concerned about the justification for the basic concepts of arithmetic, and was not willing to take them for granted. His first book, *The Philosophy of Arithmetic*, was an attempt to show that these concepts could be accounted for by a number of psychological observations about the nature of counting (a thesis similarly defended by John Stuart Mill in his *System of Logic* of 1872). It was a straightforward empiricist thesis, and ultimately denied the necessity of arithmetic and, by implication, necessary truth in general. Frege reviewed the book and convinced Husserl that he had confused logic and psychology, and had neglected the unique status of a priori as opposed to empirical knowledge. Husserl did a complete turn-around, and from then on vigorously rejected the reduction of logic and necessary truth to psychology (a thesis that he retrospectively called 'psychologism'). Beginning with a quote from Goethe, 'one is opposed to nothing more than one's own previous errors', Husserl's two-volume *Logical Investigations* is a thorough rejection of psychologism.

One of the considerations that led Husserl to reject psychologism was its affinity with scepticism. He became convinced that, if the truths of arithmetic were nothing more than empirical generalizations about the psychological processes of counting, it might well be that such processes would be different in different creatures or cultures. In any case they *could* be different, and even the possibility of different truths for different folks would undermine any sense in the idea that the statements of mathematics are necessarily true. If such statements were not true then the foundations of all of our knowledge would be nothing more than a tentative consensus of psychology or, perhaps, of anthropology (a thesis that Husserl similarly rejects as 'anthropologism'). As Descartes and Kant had argued before him, he insists that if any of our beliefs do deserve to be called 'knowledge', then some of them must be not only true but necessarily true, as the foundation for all of the others. So Husserl attacks psychologism, Dilthey's historicism, and all forms of naturalism—the reduction of necessary truth to any empirical science. Naturalism leads to relativism, for if necessary truths are empirical observations about the way we happen to think, then they may (and probably will) vary from creature to creature, and from culture to culture. Such relativism, Husserl insists, is an 'absurd' doctrine (inaccurately he blamed Hegel and the 'romantics' for relativism, with their 'doctrine of the relative justification of every philosophy for its own time'. He saw Dilthey's philosophy as 'the result of the transformation of Hegel's metaphysical philosophy of history into a sceptical historicism').

To avoid relativism it would be necessary to identify the essential foundations of experience within consciousness. To go outside of consciousness would be to invite scepticism once again, for any distinction between things 'in themselves' and the objects of experience introduces just that gap which makes scepticism possible. On the other hand, to look at consciousness in the ordinary way, seeking out 'associations of ideas' or various 'ways of thinking' would be to retreat to psychologism and, again, invite in the sceptic. What is necessary, Husserl concludes, is a new kind of description of experience which is valid regardless of whether or not the object is 'real' apart from our consciousness of it, and which does not vary no matter what the details of psychology might be. To make such a description possible Husserl formulates a series of methodological 'reductions', by which he does not mean to 'reduce' consciousness to anything else (as in psychologism), but rather to reduce our experience to the 'field of pure consciousness'. To do this requires a technique of 'transcendental reflection' in which one does not examine the objects of experience but rather the entire complex of our experience of objects, without regard to the actual existence of the objects themselves. Thus one would describe a perception, a hallucination, and a dream of the same object without allowing oneself to mention the fact that in the first case the object is real, in the second not, and in the third ambiguous; the difference between perception, hallucination, and dream would have to be discerned *within the experiences themselves*, and not by means of external reference. This intentional neglect of the existence of objects (and the causes of our experience) leads Husserl to describe phenomenology as 'the suspension of the natural standpoint'. Unlike the ordinary scientist, the phenomenologist is not concerned with objects except as they appear to consciousness, and unlike the psychologist he is not concerned with the cause of an object's conscious appearance but only the essential content of that experience. For Husserl consciousness thus appears as a separate realm of 'pure meanings', which is not available in the natural standpoint (the view of everyday life and ordinary empirical science) but only within the 'phenomenological standpoint'.

What is wrong, one might ask, with the natural standpoint? Nothing at all Husserl would reply, so long as one does not pretend to be doing philosophy, but in philosophy this ordinary way of thinking produces 'demonstrable absurdities'. For instance, philosophers often talk about consciousness in terms that are suited to material objects; they discuss ideas as being 'in' the mind, as if the mind were a physical container of some sort, and they talk about physical events causing mental events, as if the two sorts of events were comparable, and a causal connection between them were no more problematic than the effect of the motion of one billiard ball on another. But such talk has led to an entire history of absurdities; indeed, one might suggest that the history of Western philosophy since Descartes has been the history of just these absurdities. To deny that the mind is 'extended', as Descartes does, just exaggerates the problem, for what does it mean to say that the mind is not in space? To talk about the bodily cause of mental events seems to make sense until we realize that we know about bodily events only through our experience of them, and to say that those experiences are themselves caused by the same bodily events leads to troublesome paradoxes. But the most serious flaw in the natural standpoint (for philosophy) is its uncritical acceptance of the notion that objects are simply 'given' to us. We might doubt an occasional experience (an optical illusion, for example) but 'all doubting and rejecting of the data of the natural world leaves standing the general thesis of the natural standpoint'.[4] And this standpoint inescapably treats 'cognition as a fact of nature', and so as merely contingent—dependent upon our make-up as a particular kind of being. It assumes that all knowledge comes from experience, and tacitly denies, in Kant's words, that there must also be knowledge a priori which does not arise from experience. The natural standpoint takes its own validity for granted, but it cannot, without becoming 'involved in a vicious circle', testify on its own behalf.

To free us from and allow us to legitimate the natural standpoint, and to introduce us to the phenomenological standpoint, Husserl formulates what he calls the '*epoche*', the phenomenological reduction by which we 'suspend judgement' about the existence of the natural world and the causes of our experiences. Unlike Descartes, we do not actually *doubt* the existence of everything; we simply 'bracket' existence as inessential to experience as such. We describe our experience of things without worrying about the status of the things.

What we discover, having performed the *epoche*, is that consciousness is no poorer for this reduction; indeed it is every bit as rich—or even richer—than it was in the natural standpoint, for now we are in a position to appreciate it in full without the distorting judgements about the reality or the importance of things. We discover that, far from 'losing' the objects of experience, all consciousness is intrinsically and necessarily tied to objects, a feature of our every experience which Husserl calls 'intentionality', following his teacher Brentano. 'All consciousness is consciousness *of* something', he insists, and it does not matter, for the purposes of intentionality, whether this something is real or not. What we also discover, consequent to the *epoche*, is the self itself, the necessity—as Kant put it—of the 'I think' being able to accompany all of my representations, a transcendental ego which is quite different to, and independent of, the empirical self that in the natural standpoint each of us identifies as 'me'. In *Cartesian Meditations* Husserl goes so far as to suggest that the transcendental ego would remain in existence even if the entire universe was destroyed. But this bit of excess excused, it is clear that he is urging us to enter into and appreciate what is in one sense an entirely new realm of experience—the realm of experience as such.

What is the purpose of this novel experience? What phenomenology gives us, according to Husserl, is not just a new way of viewing things; it is the only *true* way. His rallying cry, 'to the things themselves' (*zu den Sachen selbst*), emphasizes phenomenology as a way of seeing the world without the distortions of philosophical theories which have infiltrated our perception and our conceptions of the world. It is, in other words, a description of experience and a philosophy that is without presuppositions, an experience of experience as such, an opportunity to see clearly and without doubts the essential structures of not only one's own consciousness but of every possible consciousness.

The reduction of experience to an intuition of pure consciousness allows us to recognize that, quite apart from the spaciotemporal 'natural' existence of objects, there are the objects of consciousness itself—intentional objects; and while we would not want to talk about their independent existence ('existence' belonging to descriptions from the natural standpoint) we do want to recognize their special status, and appreciate the fact that, whatever we know about objects in the 'outside world', we know them and about them only *through* the intentional objects of consciousness (thus Husserl adds that any sceptical claim that the objects themselves are different from objects as we know them is a 'logical absurdity'). The supposition of such 'third realm' entities is not unique to Husserl of course. Frege had argued an elaborate analysis of what he called 'the thought', and developed a complex ontology of meanings (*Sinne*) which he clearly distinguished from both psychological states and the objects to which they (usually) refer. Husserl's predecessor Meinong had suggested that we recognize a realm of objects that had *subsistence* rather than existence (see Chapter 7), though he did not particularly insist that these were to be found in consciousness. But Meinong, like Husserl, recognized that the *meaning* of experience could not be located outside of experience. Traditional empiricists had distinguished between sensations within consciousness and the objects outside which cause these and to which they correspond or refer, but they had ignored the need for meanings within experience and confused the mere sensuous matter of experience with the experience of objects as such. What Husserl means by 'meaning' is a complex study of its own, but at the basis of his theory is the view that the completeness of intentional objects is within our experience (as opposed to the view that experience has meaning only by reference to the material world outside of consciousness) and, second, to the *constitution* of objects through consciousness, the Kantian view that the structures of the world we experience are contributed by consciousness itself: 'What things are . . . they are as things of experience.'[5] But whereas Kant insisted that these basic categories had to be 'deduced' from the facts of experience, Husserl insists that they are 'intuited' directly, quite apart from the facts. Phenomenology thus takes the transcendental viewpoint one step further than the older idealists, for Husserl insists not only that the truth must be found in the self, but that it is the self itself that must find it there. Thus he assigns a double role to subjectivity— as both the locus of truth and as its discoverer—and a double source of objectivity—to be identified both in the essential structures of consciousness and in the essential features of the acts of intuition that the phenomenologist performs in order to intuit them.

In his early works Husserl emphasizes the importance of the necessary, or of the structures of transcendental consciousness, but with minimal dependency on a theory of the transcendental ego as such. In his later works he becomes more and more engaged in the importance of the ego, and at about the time of the *Cartesian Meditations* re-describes phenomenology as an 'egoology', the study of the essential structures of the ego. But the transcendental ego, like the essential categories of consciousness, is not a logical inference or deduction as in Kant, but a discovery, something intuited directly. In *Formal and Transcendental Logic* (1929), Husserl further insists that the transcendental ego exists 'absolutely', and everything else is relative to it. In his last book, *The Crisis of European Philosophy* (1936), he considerably weakens such opinions, and insists only that the transcendental ego is 'correlative' to the world, and he shifts from his extraordinarily individualistic view of the transcendental individual ego to the intersubjective community of individuals. In that same book he makes one of his very few acknowledgements of the importance of history, and the dependency of rationality and scientific knowledge on community practices and the unarticulated principles of daily life (the *Lebenswelt*). But he never pulled away from his central theses, that the truth was to be found in the self, and that this truth was universal and necessary. In Husserl's philosophy the transcendental pretence found one of its greatest modern defenders.

10

Two Discontents and their Civilization: Freud and Wittgenstein

> When I was young, the only thing I longed for was philosophical knowledge, and now that I am going over from medicine to psychology I am in process of attaining it.[1]
>
> Freud

> I used to think that there was a direct link between Language and Reality.[2]
>
> Wittgenstein

Nietzsche's indictment of the age as 'decadent' applied to nowhere better than to Vienna at the turn of the century, in the last days of the seemingly eternal Habsburg Empire, a time to which Karl Kraus sarcastically referred as 'the last days of humanity'. Under the reign of Mayor 'Handsome Karl' Lueger and the Emperor Franz Josef, anti-Semitism, universal hypocrisy, and conservative conformism, coupled with the revolt of ethnic and moral minorities, financial crises, and internal instability imposed an inescapable prognosis of doom. The metaphor of the age was that of the 'dark side' of brilliance, the golden surface ornament as a façade for anguish, alienation, neurosis, and despair. It was a period and a place that has come to define what we now identify as decadence, a way of life that was effete, elegant, lavish, fanciful, and on the brink of total disaster.

It was also a period of genius. Vienna in 1900 was the city of Mahler, Schoenberg, Berg, and Webern, of Kokoshka and Klimt, of Ernst Mach and Robert Musil. It was also the city of Sigmund Freud and Ludwig Wittgenstein. The founder of psychoanalysis and the inspirational figure of logical positivism may never have met but they shared a cultural heritage, a national neurosis, and, not surprisingly, a number of ideas as well. What they shared most of all was not so much an idea as an attitude of uncompromising intellectual and moral integrity. Whatever direction their investigations led them, there would be ferocious independence of thought, and that unmatched sense of culture and humanity that was the best product of the dying Habsburg culture.

The journalist and social critic Karl Kraus, although himself something of a crank and a misanthrope, was the pivotal figure in Viennese humanism. Single-handedly attacking the hypocrisy of the age, he called for a thoroughgoing 'critique of language'. He was anti-Freudian, and coined the now classic comment that 'psychoanalysis is the disease for which it purports to provide the cure'. He lambasted the 'nerve doctors', who diagnosed every deviation from 'normalcy', let alone manifestations of genius, as pathological; and he attacked a culture that placed such importance on ornamentation that no structure or significance remained visible. He rallied to the defence of prostitutes and homosexuals as victims of Viennese hypocrisy, and attacked the Press, its editors, the Church, the government, artists, art critics, phony styles, propaganda, the police, the military, the opera, Zionism, Jews, anti-Semitism, and the poetry of 'decadent' culture-hero Hugo von Hofmannstahl. His philosophical hero, if he had one, was Schopenhauer, and in temperament they were not dissimilar, but in place of Will and idea Kraus stressed the importance of truth and fantasy, which he complained were too often conflated and mutually quashed in the sexually repressed, wholly mercantile atmosphere of Viennese bourgeois society. His attack on psychoanalysis was in part a rejection of Freud's abuse of childhood and misuse of fantasy (as well, no doubt, as retaliation for a particularly vulgar analysis of Kraus's own alleged Oedipal complex by one of Freud's less talented disciples). Kraus, like Rousseau, thought of childhood as a happy period of fantasy, not as a series of traumas from which one could never emerge unscathed. Above all he defended the integrity of language and its power to express moral experience. It is not philosophically insignificant that he was the young Wittgenstein's hero.

Freud and Wittgenstein shared more than cultural origins. They were both men with scientific backgrounds who turned increasingly to the humanities. Both shared a particular interest in the nature and dimensions of the human mind, and rejected the Cartesian picture of consciousness with its insistence on the privileged access of the subject and the incorrigibility of self-knowledge. Both sought the structures of the mind, and looked for an understanding of consciousness in terms of language. Both developed an intense personal as well as theoretical interest in 'therapy', and struggled with the nature of the relation between society and the individual. There were also enormous differences. Wittgenstein was 33 years younger, the son of a wealthy steel magnate with a family fortune and all the best connections in the capital, while Freud's father was a modest Jewish wool merchant. Freud thought that much of the mind was 'hidden' from consciousness, while for Wittgenstein nothing is 'hidden' and the idea of an 'unconscious thought' is nonsensical. So too, Wittgenstein promotes therapy as a return to ordinary language, whilst Freud obviously intended much more for it. But they both explored the frontiers and limits of thought and language, and together they rendered many of the established presuppositions of European philosophy untenable.

Sigmund Freud (1856–1939) was not trained as a philosopher but as a physician, and psychoanalysis has ever since had the stamp of a medical mentality, obliterating the humanistic sentiments that motivate the entire enterprise. For example, at the heart of the Freudian model (or models) of the mind there is an implicit appeal to neurology. Freud's spatial and 'economic' metaphors explicitly rely on the possibility of future brain research, and his reliance on the concept of 'psychic energy' is borrowed straight from physics. In 1895 he wrote a short book, *Project for a Scientific Psychology*, in which he expresses his ambition (shared with Hume) to become the Isaac Newton of the mind. He there insists that, to be 'scientific', psychology should follow the materialist path of physics and chemistry and 'represent psychical processes as quantitatively determinate states of specifiable material particles'.[3] Consequently, for much of his career Freud's images of the mind are dominated by a 'hydraulic' model of some 'quantity' (called 'Q' in the project, 'psychic energy' thereafter), flowing through the neurons (just identified by Waldeyer in 1891), a quantity which, like water, could flow freely, be blocked up, or rechannelled. This mechanistic model or at least its ghost haunts Freud's writings until the end, and it is one of the favourite targets of his critics.

But Freud was not so single-minded, and the medical technology of his formal theories must be weighed against the evident humanism of his writing. Bruno Bettelheim has rejected the medical model at length, arguing that Freud's own terminology was not at all that of his translators, that he used terms such as 'spirit' and 'soul' more often than he did terms drawn directly from physiology.[4] Although Freud was a thoroughgoing determinist, his determinism was always in part teleological, and this clash between causal explanation and purposive understanding creates many of the crises and revisions of his psychology. If the hydraulic model permeates his 'metapsychology', the teleological concept of 'wish-fulfilment' dominates his clinical and descriptive essays. The key to many of his greatest insights is not his insistence on a possible causal explanation (that had been common to materialists since before the Enlightenment), but rather his extension of purposive inquiries into areas of human behaviour where they had long been considered inappropriate. To begin with the most notable instance, he inquired, in his masterpiece *The Interpretation of Dreams*, into the purpose and the intentions of dreams, answering that every dream is an instance of wish-fulfilment. In his study of *The Psychopathology of Everyday Life*—of revealing misstatements, unintended gestures, lost wedding rings, and other 'Freudian slips'—he again argues that all such behaviour has a purpose and an intention, even if these are not evident to the subject. And in neuroses in general he postulates a hidden cause which is an unspoken and typically unknown intention, whose frustration results in the familiar but mysterious symptoms of mental illness.

The key to all such explanations is the idea that we do not recognize, and may not even have access to, some of our own mental processes, which Freud captures with the quasi-spatial metaphor of 'the Unconscious'. Freud insists that he did not 'discover' the Unconscious; the philosophers before him did that. Indeed the history of the Unconscious—or at least the recognition that many of the motives of our behaviour may be unknown to us—encompasses the whole of modern German thought including Leibniz, Goethe, Kant, Schopenhauer, and Nietzsche, whose aphorism 'a thought comes when it will, not when I will' was much admired by Freud. But it is Freud who tried to turn this series of observations and speculations into a 'science' by describing in detail the Unconscious and its workings. The Unconscious is populated primarily by urges and impulses, many of them originating in personal traumas in childhood, but driven by what Freud famously calls the 'libido'. The unconscious libido urges us to do the unthinkable, the ghastly, the humiliating, the destructive; it is indifferent to the demands of good taste, self-preservation, or logic. It is kept in check, though often badly and always tenuously, by the ego. Our behaviour and mental health result from these two factors, the impulses of the Unconscious and the rational censorship of the ego.

It is not hard to appreciate the importance of Schopenhauer in Freud's model of the mind. The libido is an only slightly personalized version of Schopenhauer's Will, juxtaposed against a rational system of ideas. But unlike Schopenhauer he believes in the reality defined by the ego and its ideas, even if he insists that we struggle against the libido and, through self-understanding, free ourselves from its power. In fact Freud's theories of the mind virtually all work on the basis of some such fundamental opposition, between antagonistic instincts (for example the sex instinct and the ego-instincts), or between different 'agencies' of the psyche (the 'Ego–Id–Superego' model of his later years). Thus the theory is inherently dialectical, and the self turns out to be the product of violently conflicting forces. The terms of this dynamic dualism change frequently and dramatically throughout Freud's career, but the basic model of mind is easily recognized as the product of the past century and a half of philosophical and scientific thought.

The origins of psychoanalytic theory are not to be found in Freud's theoretical insights, however, but in a series of clinical observations, and in his traumatic self-analysis. Freud had studied with Charcot in Paris, the first clinician to identify and try to treat hysteria. With his friend Breuer, Freud began treating hysterical patients in Vienna, not through neurology (although they assumed it held the ultimate key to all mental illness) but through a 'talking cure' in which they and their patients would discover the *ideas* which were the proximate causes of the illness. The power of these hidden ideas impressed Freud, and from his treatment of hysteria he became convinced not only of the existence of the Unconscious, but also of the predominantly sexual content of unconscious ideas and impulses. These clinical studies led to the recognition of other abnormal behaviour and its aetiology in the Unconscious, then to normal but neglected behaviour such as dreams and slips of the tongue. In 1905 he published the most controversial of his works, the *Three Studies on Sexuality*, in which he argued not only the pervasiveness of sex in adulthood— which no one in Vienna could honestly deny—but also the centrality of sex in children, even in infants. To defend such a thesis he had to greatly expand the meaning of 'sex' so that it no longer had its exclusive focus on the genitalia and heterosexual intercourse. 'Sex' now referred to the release of tension (yielding pleasure) in any erogenous zone: the mouth or anus of the infant as well as the genitalia of a child or adult. But Freud was not being perverse in so stretching a word in a way that was sure to invite vilification; by his expansion of the notion of sex he also managed to forge a conceptual link between his hysterical patients and the childhood experiences they often reported in therapy. He hypothesized that adult neuroses might be the residuum, and sometimes also the re-enactment, of childhood sexual traumas. He further speculated—given the shocking numbers of respectable women who reported childhood abuses—that many of these traumas were fantasies rather than actual events, but that the force of such a trauma was no less powerful for that. Given this picture, the concept of the Unconscious took shape. It was not just a cauldron of ideas and impulses that were not acknowledged by the subject: it was a system of elements that *could not* be made conscious. These painful memories and desires had been repressed, and only the techniques of psychoanalysis could recognize and defuse them.

These clinical and 'metapsychological' considerations had coalesced into a grand theory by 1915. His concepts of 'the

Unconscious' and 'repression', his recognition of infantile sexuality and childhood trauma, and his observations of his patients against the backdrop of his materialist model of the 'psychic apparatus' yielded a powerful portrait of the human mind. It was a portrait that clashed at almost every point with the clarity of the Cartesian model; whole realms of one's own mind were inaccessible to oneself, and the principle of the mind was not freedom but determinism. Against Rousseau's happy discovery that the soul of humanity is intrinsically good, Freud gave us the bad news that the mind, even of children, contains the most perverse, hateful, and even murderous impulses imaginable. Much of the history of modern European philosophy was dedicated to the possibility of a harmonious, happy society (Kant's 'Kingdom of Ends' is an example), but Freud's pessimistic view was that civilization is possible only through the denial of the instincts. In contemporary Viennese society he saw all too well the cost of extreme and arbitrary sexual prohibitions mixed with moral hypocrisy, but the danger of unrepressed sexuality, he thought, would be even greater. In other words, the coexistence of harmony and happiness was an untenable dream.

After the war Freud's theories went through a number of important changes. He continued to move away from the psycho-physical shadow of his early neurology, and shifted from his early dualisms of sex and ego, Unconscious and consciousness, to his more complicated three-agency view of a mind consisting of the id, made up of mainly unconscious impulses, the ego, the 'rational' part of the mind, though still partly unconscious (as it is the ego that is responsible for censorship and repression), and the superego, 'the voice of the nursery' and the ethical imperatives drummed in long ago by one's parents. (On this view, Kant's categorical imperative is a product of regression and childish subjection to authority rather than the proud principle of practical reason.) More spectacular is Freud's postulation of a 'death instinct' which he opposed to the fusion of the ego and sexual instincts. This much criticized and celebrated suggestion occupied only a brief moment in Freud's career, and it followed, in one sense, from some of his most durable assumptions. Even in the *Project* of 1895 he had held that the key principle of all biological functioning—and of the psychic apparatus in particular—was the principle of 'homeostasis', the tendency of an organism to stabilize itself and, ideally, 'to divest itself of energy altogether'. The death wish (or 'Nirvana principle') might be viewed as the logical extension of this, which Freud seemed to think (at this point in his work) was even more powerful than 'the pleasure principle' which had also been one of his basic postulates since his earliest writings. But it should not be thought that he was essentially a (repressed) hedonist or that he was following Schopenhauer too closely here. A third basic principle of his theory was what he called 'the reality principle', and despite the impulses and distortions of consciousness due to the Unconscious even in the most 'normal' life, Freud always believed that a clear and untroubled vision of the real world was possible. In his *Future of an Illusion* he wrote, 'in the long run, nothing can withstand reason and experience'. He may have been a Schopenhauerian pessimist but he was ultimately a man of the Enlightenment. He pointed out the impotence of the intellect but he also shared with his critic Kraus an unshaken faith in the ultimate power of self-understanding and language to save us from ourselves.

'All philosophy is a "critique of language" ', wrote Wittgenstein (1889–1951) in his *Tractatus Logico-Philosophicus*, in a tribute to Kraus. He, too, was trained as a scientist—an engineer—but drifted towards romantic philosophy and the humanities through the medium of linguistics and mathematics. His dazzling career as a logic student and junior disciple of Frege and Russell, as the author of a book that G. E. Moore called a work of genius and which launched the powerful logical positivist movement, and his rejection of that same work, is well known, but it is not this account of Wittgenstein's career that will help us to understand his place in modern European philosophy. Wittgenstein may have been a brilliant logician and mathematician, but this is not how he saw his own work and not the context in which it can best be understood. As Janik and Toulman have pointed out in their *Wittgenstein's Vienna*, he was deeply engaged in philosophy before he met Frege and went to Cambridge to study with Bertrand Russell, and the philosophical problems that concerned him were not the technical ones of the new linguistic philosophy but the ethical questions that he inherited from his childhood in Vienna.[5] The new logic presented him with a vehicle to work out these questions; it was not the whole substance of his interests. Kraus, not Frege, was Wittgenstein's model, and it was Kierkegaard, not Russell, whom he most closely resembled.

Wittgenstein's concern was with the ability of language to express ethical matters. The background of this concern was not so much the continuing debate over Kant's categorical imperatives as it was the contemporary debasing of both language and morals in Viennese society. Freud saw the symptoms of repression, Wittgenstein the pathology of language abused. In one sense his efforts were neo-Kantian, to provide a thoroughgoing 'critique of language', but in a more profound sense his ambitions were Kierkegaardian, to draw the limits of ethics 'from the inside as it were', to separate ethics from the realm of rational discourse. It is a strange endeavour, and the structure of Wittgenstein's books—which resemble nothing so much as the experimental works of Nietzsche—displays this strangeness. His *Tractatus*, which he insisted was a book on ethics but which is virtually always read as being about logic and the philosophy of language, is almost wholly made up of questions of logical representation, with only a few cryptic remarks on ethics, death, and the meaning of life. The final sentence of that work, 'Whereof one cannot speak, thereof one should be silent', has often been dismissed as 'mysticism' and as secondary to the substance of the book, but Wittgenstein insisted that this was the whole purpose of the book, to make us realize that rational thought should be transcended. Here in particular Wittgenstein could not be more different from the Viennese positivists whom he inspired: they took the unsayability of metaphysics to prove that all questions of value and discussions of reality, except through science, were meaningless; for Wittgenstein it was the proof of their ultimate significance.

His project in the *Tractatus* was to reconceive and reconcile the descriptive language of science with the 'higher' nature of ethics. It begins with the extreme distinction—inherited from Kant—

between fact and value, knowledge and ethics. Like Kant, Wittgenstein wants to 'limit knowledge, to make room for faith', but where Kant sought to defend ethics and religion too as matters of reason, Wittgenstein—like Kierkegaard—wants to limit reason too, and defend a wordless, moral faith. There is little doubt that the philosopher who actually guides Wittgenstein's way in this project is that self-styled Kantian, Arthur Schopenhauer. Schopenhauer did not share Kant's faith in reason and the importance of principles; for him ethics consisted wholly of questions of character, as a matter of action and not intellect, and this is just what Wittgenstein wants to argue. What cannot be said can nevertheless be *shown*, and this emphasis on showing, on behaviour as well as abstract thought, characterizes his philosophy from beginning to end.

Wittgenstein owes another debt to Schopenhauer, not on the side of ethics but of knowledge, or rather, 'representation'. It was Schopenhauer who, in order to avoid the residual subjectivity of Kant's transcendental ego, suggested that one ought to make his notion of representation the central focus of philosophy (thus avoiding the ego-based idealism of Fichte). Wittgenstein follows Schopenhauer's lead in transforming Kantian questions about reason into ones about language, and one of the explicit quests of the *Tractatus* is to find the 'universal form of language', and to see how language 'represents' the world. His solution was that language 'pictures' the world, like a map or blueprint. Every proposition is a representative picture of a piece of the world—a fact. Taken together our propositions picture the world itself, which is defined in the first statement of the book as 'everything that is the case'. There are no thoughts apart from language, and no knowledge apart from what can be said. Wittgenstein is a holist in the *Tractatus*: every proposition in a language presupposes the entire language, just as every object presupposes the world. But against the idealists and Kant in particular, he insists that there is no necessity in the world, only in language, in the form of tautologies (trivial truths such as 'it is raining or it is not raining') and the equations of mathematics. 'Outside of logic', he concludes, 'everything is accidental.'[6] As sceptical as Hume, he argues that we cannot know even that the sun will rise tomorrow. With Schopenhauer he rejects the efficacy of our personal will: 'the world is independent of my will.'[7] Like Nietzsche he is thus not a determinist but neither does he believe in free will. Indeed the position that Wittgenstein provides in the *Tractatus*, even if it does not 'solve all of the problems of philosophy' (as he arrogantly announces in his preface), leaves us with very few.

The bulk of the *Tractatus* is an ingenious working out of the thesis that propositions are pictures of the world. What concerns us, however, is the short, final section of the book, which Wittgenstein took to be the heart of the project. If 'the world is everything that is the case', then it follows that 'everything is as it is, and everything happens as it does happen'. In the world, accordingly, there is no place for value: 'if value did exist', he remarks cryptically, 'it would have no value.' Values have no place in the world for they have to do with the way the world *ought* to be, not the way it is. Furthermore, he insists that values—unlike the facts of the world—do have necessity, and cannot be merely accidental. But if all that can be *said* are propositions that picture the world, then nothing can be said about values.

This is not a dismissal of ethics, as the logical positivists would argue. 'Unsayable things do exist', Wittgenstein tells us. Ethics are 'transcendental' and exist 'outside' of the world (6.4211). They belong to the transcendental subject, who is not in the world but is rather 'the limit of the world' (5.5632). But unlike Kant's transcendental ego, Wittgenstein's transcendental self is not primarily or exclusively the subject that has knowledge. It is rather the locus of value, and as such cannot be described or represented.

Self and value are not the only things that cannot be represented. Wittgenstein remarks, with conscious self-contradiction, that one cannot say that unsayable things exist. Nor can one use language to represent the way that language represents the world. The consequence of this denial is that the propositions that make up the *Tractatus* are, in a deep way, nonsensical. They are intended not to present us with a philosophical picture but rather to elevate us beyond philosophy and pictures to a 'higher' but unsayable position. Thus, 'whereof one cannot speak, thereof one must be silent'. Like many of the great works in the romantic tradition, the *Tractatus* is a brilliant intellectual defence of the most extreme anti-intellectualism.

A man of total integrity, Wittgenstein subsequently quit philosophy and academia—which he hated in any case—and went back to Austria. He gave away his considerable fortune and made every effort to live as simply as possible. He taught in a primary school, built a house, and considered joining a monastery. He probably thought very little about philosophy until 1929 when he returned to Cambridge. The direction of his work from that point was, remarkably, to attack virtually every aspect of the *Tractatus*. He rejected the distinction between fact and value, the 'picture theory' of language, the holism that held language and the world of the *Tractatus* together, and the notion of the transcendental self. What remains is his sense of intellectual and personal integrity, and the feeling that the purpose of his continuing 'critique of language' is and must be an ethical one. What was wrong with the *Tractatus*—not just in its details but its very conception—was that it failed to see language as well as ethics as primarily a social practice, and not the private concern of the transcendental self. Language, like ethics, is not a single descriptive enterprise: it consists of a plurality of activities, 'language games' which may have little to do with one another. Languages reflect not so much abstract forms as 'forms of life'. It is hard not to notice that Wittgenstein's thinking reflects the whole history of modern European thought, from solitudinous Rousseau and transcendental Kant to the public spirit of Hegel and Marx and ultimately, in style as well as strategy, the experimentalism of Nietzsche.

The main thrust of Wittgenstein's posthumously published *Philosophical Investigations* is the attack on the limited but holistic view of language in the *Tractatus* in favour of a rich and varied description of the many functions of language, which include commands, questions, puns, and jokes as well as the language of the natural sciences. The meaning of a sentence, he now argues, is its *use* in our activities. Once again he is attacking an overly intellectual and excessively narrow vision of human life in favour of one that is more expansive and less the privileged domain of language alone. But two other theses are worth mentioning here. First there is Wittgenstein's relentless attack on the entire Cartesian picture of the mind, which was still too much in evidence in the *Tractatus*. He rejects the very idea of 'private' meaning, something mental which corresponds to the facts of the world and is 'expressed' in language; language acquires its meaning in social interaction. Furthermore, he rejects the Cartesian idea of private mental entities in all of its forms, and with it the assurance that we have special 'inner' access to our selves.

Secondly, he turns increasingly to a notion of 'therapy', viewing philosophy as a kind of disease, as 'language going on holiday', and as a series of traps. In a way reminiscent of Kraus's view of psychoanalysis, Wittgenstein saw philosophy as a disease for which it presented itself as the cure. He had always looked for closure in philosophy, and more than any other philosopher in history he was tormented by uncertainties and self-doubts. It is easy to appreciate his remark that, like his father, he was a 'businessman', and wanted to get these problems *solved*. Life, he impatiently concluded, is in the living of it, in daily chores and useful work, not in the abstract speculations of the philosophers.

The Self Reinterpreted: Heidegger and Hermeneutics

> It was not that German idealism collapsed; rather, the age was no longer strong enough to stand up to the greatness, breadth, and originality of that spiritual world, i.e. truly to realize it. . . .

> The world is darkening. The essential episodes of this darkening are: the flights of the gods, the destruction of the earth, the standardization of man, the preeminence of the mediocre . . . [and] the misinterpretation of the spirit.[1]

> Heidegger

Martin Heidegger (1889–1976) was a student of Husserl, but he resisted his teacher's narrowness and rejected his reactionary Cartesianism. Heidegger seemed to see himself as a sage and prophet as well as a phenomenologist; what the twentieth century needed, he complained, was a new God. He presented his own views as 'the quest for Being', coupled with the curious complaint that Western metaphysics had 'forgotten' about Being ever since Plato. We once had a sense of the inviolate reality of ourselves in the world but this has been falling away from us since ancient times, and had all but disintegrated by the end of the already 'darkening' nineteenth century.

Heidegger saw himself within the Western philosophical tradition, but he also urged the jettisoning of much of what other philosophers had taken to be essential to that tradition in favour of something new and not altogether clear. Part of this unclarity is due to Heidegger's insistence that our very language has evolved in such a manner that our understanding of Being is blocked, and so he tries nothing less than to invent a new philosophical language. Any 'translation' of his thought into terms that we can understand, he argues, will most likely result in a misunderstanding. Similarly, any attempt to locate him in the tradition that he rejects will probably produce a false picture of his efforts. And yet he knew that tradition and was very much a part of it. He was an enthusiastic student of ancient Greek and medieval philosophy, saw himself as following in the footsteps of Kant and Schelling, and studied and wrote extensively about Hölderlin and Nietzsche. And, of course, he was deeply affected by his teacher Husserl. What he rejected from his very first works was Descartes and the Cartesian tradition in philosophy, with its schizoid division of mind and body, its lifeless view of the world as a mechanism detached from us and available for our exploitation, and its deductive quest for certainty. The fact that Husserl had so admired Descartes did not impress Heidegger; he saw in Husserl's phenomenology the means to undermine Descartes's dualism, the mechanistic vision of the world and the solipsistic, self-enclosed illusion of self that it fostered.

We should not be surprised by the fact that Heidegger attacks the Western philosophical tradition even while standing firmly within it. Rousseau was quite at home among the Enlightenment philosophers in his attempt to undermine traditional philosophy by seeking some Archimedean point of departure ('the state of nature'). Kant too begins with a 'critique' of traditional metaphysics, and a withdrawal from common sense and experience. Hegel begins by criticizing Kant and, even though he claims to absorb the whole of history in his philosophy, he nevertheless announces a brand new beginning. Kierkegaard and Marx attack Hegel in the name of subjectivity and science respectively, and Husserl claims to begin philosophy anew. Indeed, this rejection of the tradition is, perhaps, the heart of the tradition, as well as the heart of the transcendental pretence. Different philosophical views are not viewed as different opinions or perspectives but as alternative attempts at the Truth, which one will oneself succeed in grasping. Heidegger begins by rejecting the tradition for its wrong-headed approach to the problem of metaphysics, but it is not quite right to say that he considered that he provided an alternative approach which was not only superior but ultimately correct. Indeed the charm, if also the frustration, of Heidegger's philosophy is that he insists—increasingly so as his work progresses—that authoritative positions in philosophy are part of the problem, and so he refuses to give us one of his own.

The tower of Heidegger's philosophy is the metaphysical concept of 'Being', but the corner-stone is the more modest concept of '*Dasein*'—which we will cautiously characterize as 'human being' (though we will soon explain why this, like most readily accessible phrases, will not do for Heidegger). *Dasein* means simply 'being there'. It is an intentionally vague, non-descriptive, almost vacuous designation, virtually a pointing gesture rather than a proper subject for a philosophy. But this, according to Heidegger, is essential. He had learned from Husserl that philosophy should be 'presuppositionless', and it seemed to him that nothing would be a more flagrant presupposition than to assume that what one examines in phenomenology was a 'mind', or even a 'consciousness', which is clearly distinct from (even if mysteriously attached to) a body, which belongs to a certain kind of creature, which is similar to other such minds, and so on. What one finds at first is not an 'I think', nor even a 'conscious being' but simply a kind of brute fact, the fact of 'being there'. One has no right to assume that what one thus discovers is mind or consciousness, much less the mind or consciousness of a human being (hence our warning about 'human being' above). One has to start from a basic recognition which does not presuppose one's existence (much less one's *own* existence), and does not suggest or even allow for a distinction between mind and body, or between consciousness and anything else. There is simply 'Being-in-the-World', not a two-part experience of self and world but a 'unitary phenomenon' that we divide at our peril.

Being and Time, Heidegger's early master-work, announces itself as the study of Being but is largely devoted to the study of a particular kind of being, 'the being through whom we inquire about Being', namely *Dasein*. The leading theme is that *Dasein* is different from other being in that it is 'ontological'—that is, concerned with the nature of its own being, of what it is, how it came to be, and what its existence means. There is little doubt that the larger quest for Being is religious as much as metaphysical, concerned with the meaning of life as well as abstract knowledge. *Being and Time* is a substantial and striking interpretation of what it is to be human, and a philosophy of life (which Heidegger insists has nothing to do with 'ethics'). Inspired by Kierkegaard and Nietzsche, Heidegger is often said to be—and deserves to be recognized as—one of the leading 'existentialist' philosophers of this century, a title he rejected, however, because it was associated with Sartre and his Cartesian, atheistic humanism. And yet the key existentialist themes—of individual choice and 'authenticity', of temporal concern and *Angst* for the future, the emphasis on life and death issues and not just knowledge—these are all embodied in his thought, if sometimes obscurely. Much of what Sartre argued years later is more or less directly borrowed or adapted from Heidegger.

The problem of Being, as stated in Heidegger's *Introduction to Metaphysics*, begins with a strange question that Schelling had raised: 'why is there anything rather than nothing?' It is a question that prompts a metaphysical if not a religious answer, which is often supplied by belief in God. This is the import of Kant's teleology in the third Critique and the theodicy provided by Hegel as the history of Spirit. It is also an epistemological question, central to Husserl's phenomenology, which might be expressed as: 'what is it for a thing to exist?' or, 'what are *we* saying of a thing when we say that it exists?' But the temptation to provide a simple conceptual analysis, 'a mere dissection of words', will not do, for Heidegger has already insisted that our language reflects an inadequate and even dangerous way of (mis)conceiving Being. What philosophy must provide is not mere analysis but a rediscovery of how Being presents itself to us as phenomenon, of what Being means. 'Philosophy always aims at the first and last grounds of Being, with particular emphasis on man himself and on the meaning and goals of human being-there.'[2]

Our misunderstanding of Being—our 'fallenness from Being'—should not, therefore, be understood merely as a philosophical mistake, much less as a matter of intellectual neglect. Questions about metaphysics and ontology have dominated philosophy since its beginnings, but Heidegger nevertheless complains that modern, and even much of ancient and medieval thought, retreated from the grand question of Being to ask instead about beings, about particular objects and entities instead of about Being as such. Philosophers asked what it is for some particular thing to exist, but they failed to ask what it is that provides 'the ground' of their being. In Heidegger's immodest words: 'In *Being and Time* the question of the meaning of Being is raised and developed as a question for the first time in the history of philosophy.'[3] 'Being has become hidden from us', he claims; we cannot see Being for the beings, as a wood for the trees. Furthermore, ever since Plato there has been a serious confusion of Being with what Heidegger calls 'presence'. The idea is that existence has always been viewed in a single temporal mode—the present—in which beings *present* themselves to us. Husserl is just as guilty of this confusion as anyone else, and Heidegger suggests as an antidote a thoroughgoing investigation of the medium of *time*. Most philosophers, he complains, think of time as 'just another entity' (albeit a curious one), which can be and often is described by physical analogy—as like a river for instance. The key to *Being and Time* is the idea that time cannot be so understood, and that Being depends on all three dimensions of temporality, past and future as well as present. Being is absence as well as presence; a thing is what is not now present to us, as well as what presents itself.

Being and Time is almost unique in Western philosophy in its unrestricted emphasis on holism, its vision of our being-in-the-world as a seamless whole even more than in Hegel (who sees the whole as a result rather than a starting point). The negative thrust of the book is Heidegger's unrelenting attack on virtually all traditional dichotomies and dualistic vocabularies: mind and body, self and world, subject and object, self and other. He criticizes the dualism of the entire metaphysical tradition, not only since Descartes but since Plato who introduced, he argues, the idea of Being as presence in the first place. He criticizes even Nietzsche, who rejected the very idea of 'the external world' but only while accepting the fraudulent traditional distinction. Husserl, of course, continued to maintain the distinction between consciousness and its objects, and though he insisted periodically that these two 'correlates' could not be separated, he nevertheless argued throughout his career that the ego is distinct from the world it constitutes, and that one could and should 'reduce' or 'bracket' the world to get to the ego or consciousness and the phenomenological standpoint. But it should be noted that Heidegger sticks by his teacher even while rejecting most of his central theses. He utterly rejects the Husserlian *epoche*, the idea that one can 'bracket' the existence of objects and examine their purely conscious status, yet he retains the notion of 'phenomenology' (at least in *Being and Time*), and reinterprets the phenomenon as 'the showing-itself-in-itself' without implying any distinction between phenomenon and thing in itself. He rejects the idea of consciousness or the ego as the alleged residue of any such reduction, indeed he rejects the centrality of consciousness and ego altogether, yet holds on to the notion of 'transcendental constitution'. He rejects Husserl's catch-phrase 'to the things themselves', urging that this 'proves to be not only hasty but a highly questionable counsel',[4] but in his quest for Being he nevertheless upholds the general method of Husserl's phenomenology and its insistence on the first-person standpoint. But there is no denying the most dramatic differences between them. For Heidegger it is Being itself rather than the existence of beings that is in question, and our understanding of Being is not derivative of our knowledge of particular beings. And however we answer the question of Being ('why is there anything . . .') Heidegger makes it clear that it cannot be an ego that constitutes the world. But neither is this to say, in conventional pre-Kantian wisdom, that the world is simply there before us. This again is the myth of presence, and it reinforces the fatal dichotomy between ourselves as consciousness and the physicality of the world.

One of Heidegger's most ingenious theses is his turning topsy-turvy the very idea of how it is that we relate to and know 'things'. Since Plato (at least), philosophers have taken our primary relation to things as one of knowledge, and the nature of the things, accordingly, has been analysed in the terms in which we know them—in terms of visible properties and physical measurements for instance. Heidegger objects to this picture, and points out that our primary dealings with the world have to do not with things known but with 'equipment', tools and instruments that are 'ready to hand'. A hammer is first of all a tool before one studies it or even looks at it, perhaps even before it has a name or is fitted into a category of objects. The distinction between consciousness and the object that seems so self-evident to a philosopher who is sitting back and observing the hammer, is not at all in evidence when one is actually using it. The object 'hammer' has certain properties, for example, the property of being black, but colour is not at all relevant to the hammer-in-use, and indeed a hard-working carpenter may well be incapable of describing to us some of the more 'obvious' properties of the hammer he has been using for hours. What we know is *how to use* a bit of the world, not necessarily *that* this bit of the world is a distinct object with certain properties.

Heidegger attacks the over-emphasis on epistemology and knowledge in philosophy in a particularly forceful way, and with it undermines the main source of the dualistic image we have developed of ourselves and the world. It is before we step back and take notice of what we are doing and what we are using that we recognize our primary involvement in the world, not after we have taken that step and removed ourselves from the things we are using. Indeed, we begin to take notice of the world as a collection of 'things' or 'objects' when we are prompted to do so by the loss or breakdown of tools. One loses the pen with which one has been writing for the past few days, and finds oneself struggling to describe it. Prior to the search, one did not notice the pen; one only used it. One examines the hammer for the first time when the head starts slipping loose, and the hammering loses its force. Knowledge is secondary to involvement in the world, or what Heidegger calls 'concern'. Knowledge often arises only when we give up this primary concern and detach ourselves from the world. And though knowledge breaks up the world into individual objects and things, the world as equipment is essentially a totality: 'there is no such thing as equipment. To the Being of any equipment there always belongs a totality of equipment, in which it can be this equipment that it is.'[5] The categories we invent to understand ourselves and the world are thus prone to grave misunderstandings.

From this picture of the world as 'equipment' we can get a

much clearer view of Heidegger's concepts of Being and *Dasein*. Whereas so much of philosophy—including the German idealists—takes the world to be primarily something known, something of which we are conscious, Heidegger points out that there is an enormous part of our lives that is not primarily concerned with knowledge, and in which, in a perfectly ordinary sense, we are not 'conscious'. This is not to say that we are 'unconscious' of course: a carpenter hard at work trying to make a perfect cabinet corner does not pass out, but he is so concerned with the task in hand that there is little self-consciousness, little awareness of what else is going on that is not directly involved in the cabinet-making process. Nor is he aware of any profound distinction between himself and the cabinet; indeed, such awareness will probably arise only when he becomes frustrated with his clumsiness, and consequently self-conscious. As for the traditional Cartesian distinction between mind and body, it would be difficult to distinguish which aspects of the craft are mental, which physical; indeed, the distinction seems to make no sense at all. Similarly, the fragmentation of the world into separate objects is a falsification of one's experience: the world is organized according to one's task, and the ontological separation of 'things' does not enter into it.

Dasein is thus, first of all, engaged in the world of which it is an intrinsic part. This is not to say that it is just another being in the world; on the level of equipment, there are no beings, only Being-in-the-world. On reflection, however, *Dasein* becomes ontological, though its primary search becomes easily misled by the detachment from concern which is its precondition. What Heidegger urges, therefore, is a 'fundamental ontology' in which we do not allow ourselves to be misled by this detachment, and always remember that *Dasein* is itself different from all other beings, in that it cannot ultimately take a detached view of itself, cannot treat itself as a mere thing—as much of the history of science and philosophy has urged us to do. But '*Dasein* is an entity which does not just occur among other entities', Heidegger tells us; 'it is peculiar to this entity in that with and through its Being, this Being is disclosed to it.'[6] Insisting on this uniqueness Heidegger repeats again and again that '*Dasein* is ontically distinctive in that it *is* ontological'; in other words, *Dasein* is different from other beings in that it thinks about and is concerned with the nature of its own existence in the world. Furthermore, because *Dasein* is always asking such questions of itself, there is never a final answer to the question 'what am I?' for one has to work out rather than simply find out what one is, through living. This is an important point for the existentialists and Sartre in particular, who borrows Heidegger's characterization of *Dasein*, 'its existence precedes its essence', as one of the catch-phrases for his philosophy.

The emphasis on practicality, holism, and the self-questioning of *Dasein* in a world of equipment leads us to see why the self, for Heidegger, must be a much more complex and intriguing matter than it could ever have been for Descartes, Locke, Hume, or even for Kant, Hegel, and the other idealists and romantics. If the self is first of all a practical function of living in the world, then it cannot be primarily a matter of knowledge, whether the simple self-reflection of Descartes, the introspection of Locke and Hume, the deduction of Kant, or the grand recognition of Spirit in Hegel. Like the self of the idealists *Dasein* is an activity rather than a thing, but it is not in any sense a pure activity, an activity 'behind the scenes' that can be distinguished from the world in which it acts. *Dasein* also shares with the transcendental self of the German idealists its supra-human status. That is, just as Being-in-the-world cannot be broken up into different aspects, it is a falsification of *Dasein* to assume that it is in any clear sense personal, that it belongs to or is inherent in an individual human being. The boundaries of *Dasein* are not self-evident, nor do they become evident with protracted study and phenomenological observation. *Dasein* does not begin with and cannot be assumed to have an individual self, a troubling state of affairs which Heidegger characteristically expresses as a paradox: that the 'who' of *Dasein* is not at all 'the "I myself" '.[7]

The question of selfhood has a curious status in Heidegger's philosophy, as does the transcendental pretence. On the one hand, following Husserl, phenomenology, and the method of first-person description, the self is at the core of Heidegger's philosophy, and though he may insist that *Dasein* is not yet a self, and that self and world are not to be separated, the basic stance of the whole modern movement since Descartes, Rousseau, and Kant is already built into Heidegger's project. One's experience (whatever the scope of that 'one', and however one understands 'experience') is considered to be rich and expansive, and the sole basis for understanding the world (or Being-in-the-world). On the other hand, Heidegger has doubts about the notions of self and subjectivity even in *Being and Time*, and in his later works persistently tries to remove subjective bias from his philosophy, moving further and further away from the concepts of modern European thought, and closer to the wholly self-less speculations of the pre-Socratic philosophers. But in *Being and Time* and the early essays on metaphysics—which are the works that mainly concern us here—the notion of the self is always central, if obscured, and *Dasein*'s most persistent question is not 'what is Being?' but 'who am I?'

One of Heidegger's most famous (if unintended) contributions to the existentialist tradition was his employment of Kierkegaard's notion of 'authenticity' (or literally, 'own-ness'). For Kierkegaard 'being authentic' clearly referred to making one's own life-choices autonomously, passionately, and without the rationalization or excuses that would make one's decisions any less one's own. Living 'inauthentically', by contrast, meant 'going along with the crowd', not making one's own decisions, and not even facing up to the questions. Philosophers like Hegel were Kierkegaard's favourite examples of inauthenticity, who lived in terms of very different categories than those they wrote about, who allegedly rationalized everything and felt nothing, who denied the individual in favour of abstract concepts like 'Spirit'.

Heidegger retains some of these features of authenticity, but he is by no means so sanguine as Kierkegaard about the identity of the individual. Making choices that are 'one's own' is far more problematic than it appears to be. To understand his notion of authenticity and its contrary, we have to understand more about Heidegger's central notion of *Dasein*. We can already surmise that *Dasein*'s authenticity will have something to do with being ontological and asking the right questions about Being, and in particular its own Being, and we can be sure that falling into the

Cartesian view of the world will be a paradigmatic form of inauthenticity. Above all, we can be certain that treating oneself as a mere thing will be the height of inauthenticity for *Dasein*. And yet it is in pre-reflective activity that we are, in one sense, most ourselves, and it is in self-reflection that we lose ourselves. 'Ontically, we are *Dasein*, each one of us,' Heidegger says, 'but ontologically, we are farthest from ourselves.'[8] Self-knowledge, in other words, will not be a simple matter of self-recognition.

Dasein is not undifferentiated, and Heidegger fills most of *Being and Time* with its analysis, and the distinctions between the various structures that constitute (what we would call) experience. We have already employed the distinction between the 'ontic' and 'ontological' aspects of *Dasein*, the former consisting of facts about *Dasein* (notably the fact that it is at all), the latter referring to those thoughts that *Dasein* has about itself and the world. We might also mention Heidegger's distinction between those experiential structures that are essential to *Dasein*'s unique sort of being—which Heidegger calls 'existential'—and those which are inessential and common to 'things' (which he calls '*existentielle*'). His analysis of *Dasein* is an investigation into its essential (a priori) existential structures (or 'existentialia'), which are themselves pre-ontological but are to be described ontologically (that is, they are necessarily there before the philosopher finds them). The primary existential structure of *Dasein* is its Being-in-the-world, its holistic unity which includes not independent objects (as in Husserl's notion of intentionality) but rather the whole world, 'the worldhood of the world'. It is a world that cannot be 'bracketed', a world that is not so much there 'for us' as one from which we cannot distinguish ourselves (Heidegger sometimes writes dramatically of our 'being thrown' into the world). The idea of a world known by us which is distinct from the one in which we act (as in Kant's 'two world' view) is unintelligible, and another primary structure of *Dasein*, consequently, is *care*, a generalized notion of 'concern' which refers to the necessity of our engagement in the world. In this it parallels, in an active way, Husserl's insistence on intentionality, but it is more akin to Kierkegaard's insistence that 'the real subject is not the cognitive subject [but] the ethically existing subject'.[9] Being-in-the-world and care are the basic structures from which all other existentialia of *Dasein* are derived. In other words, if we were isolated selves who only tried to know but did not care about the world, we would not be—in the most obvious sense—the beings that we are.

Dasein's primary concern, however, is its own identity. This is the 'ontological character' of *Dasein*, which is an existential (that is, necessary) structure of it, and one of the keys to the notion of authenticity: 'in its very being this being relates to its being.'[10] It is by virtue of this self-concern that *Dasein* relates to other *Dasein*s and objects in the world, not just in the world as equipment (which is relatively unselfconscious) but in the conscious (ontological) lifelong effort to find our own identity, defining ourselves for ourselves and for others. But the fact that each of us is self-concerned does not mean that we already have a self, much less our 'own' self. Quite the contrary, each of us is at first not ourself at all, but rather a kind of pre-conscious social construction that Heidegger calls '*das Man*' (from the German for the pronoun 'one', as in the phrase 'one is . . .'). Just as our primordial experience of the world is the holistic one of being involved in a task with tools, our primary awareness of self in the world is as a self that is wholly defined by other people, in the roles that we play and the expectations that others have of us. '*Das Man*' refers to just this more-or-less anonymous sense of self, anonymous in the sense that we are nothing more than a place-holder, the one who happens to be the oldest son, the biggest or smartest kid in the class. But such characteristics are strictly comparative and contrastive, not 'one's own' characteristics at all. Who we are, consequently, is dependent upon this anonymous *das Man*, the 'they' (as in 'they say that potatoes grow best in clay') that tells us what to do and who to be. We are not ourselves: we do not have selves, much less our own selves. The philosophical assurance that each of us is an 'I' gives us at most a 'non-committal formal indicator'. It does not tell us who we are (or whether we are anyone) at all.

The break with *das Man*, and the origin of the authentic (one's own) self come not just with ontological reflection but with a kind of action, a 'taking hold' of oneself, a profound kind of choosing, a *resolution*. Inauthenticity as well as authenticity begins with a recognition of the challenge so to take hold of oneself, but the former flees it while the latter accepts it. This ability to take hold of oneself and make choices is what Heidegger calls *Dasein*'s *Existenz*, and it is, again, a concept borrowed from Kierkegaard, who stressed the importance of individual choice in order to really 'exist'—as opposed to the 'so-called existence' of those people who drift through life. For Heidegger too this is an essential structure of *Dasein*. But the fact that each of us has this capacity does not mean that we will successfully exercise it. '*Dasein* decides its existence, whether it does so by taking hold or by neglecting.'[11] It is possible for us to neglect or ignore our choices in life. Indeed, our *Existenz* only presents us with possibilities; there are other possibilities as well.

One of these, which is just as essential to *Dasein* as *Existenz*, is our tendency to 'fall' back into everyday routines, and block out our awareness of alternatives and the 'big picture' of our lives. Heidegger calls this essential tendency 'Fallenness'—which we met earlier in its specifically philosophical version as the neglect or denial of the question of Being. What we fall into he calls 'average everydayness', and it is that unthinking engagement in tasks that Heidegger has already told us is our primary dealing with the world. But although we define ourselves through our choices (including the negative choice of 'falling' back into our daily activities) we cannot choose whatever we like. We are limited by another existential structure of *Dasein* which Heidegger calls our 'facticity', the fact that we find ourselves engaged in a world in which tasks are already there for us. Authenticity, we may anticipate, has much to do with recognizing and exercising one's *Existenz* and its possibilities. Inauthenticity, by contrast, has to do with Fallenness, falling back into average everydayness and the anonymous self of *das Man*. Facticity is forever present to both of them, as the world in which one must decide one's existence.

Heidegger links the three existential structures of *Existenz*, facticity, and fallenness to the three dimensions of time, which now becomes itself an existential structure of *Dasein*. *Existenz* refers to the future, facticity to the past, fallenness to the present (as in 'getting caught up in the moment'). Indeed he goes on to redefine 'care' as 'ahead-of-itself-already-being-in as being-near-to',[12] where the first phrase refers to *Existenz*, the second to facticity, and the third to 'falling captive to the world'. But if time and self-awareness are essential structures of *Dasein*, then it would seem to follow that one essential aspect of our identity must be the one absolutely unavoidable future event, one's own death (which Heidegger perversely calls our 'most necessary possibility'). Not only does death make us keenly aware of our own temporal limitations, it also becomes the key ingredient in our coming to terms with and identifying ourselves. *Das Man* defined each of us anonymously in terms of roles and expectations that might just as well apply to someone else, and so the question arises what is there that each of us can do wholly for ourselves, in which we cannot be replaced by anyone else? The answer is that we die for ourselves, and by ourselves. No one can die for us. (Sidney Carton, who in one sense died for Charles Darnay in Dickens's *Tale of Two Cities*, is not a counter-example to Heidegger's thesis.) Each of us is a 'being-unto-death', not just in the sense that each of us will die, but in the more profound sense that it is by having one's own death that one becomes—or can become—an authentic self. Death is not only necessary: it is our 'ownmost possibility', that which makes us ourselves.

The centrality of death in Heidegger's philosophy provides a fertile field for inauthenticity as well as authenticity, and offers us an excellent example of the former. There is an obvious sense in which we all know that we will die, but most of us, for most of the time, take this to be an abstract and inapplicable bit of knowledge. A physician who sees death every day in the hospital nevertheless finds himself shocked when, at the age of forty, he suffers from his first life-threatening illness. It is hard to imagine anyone being more aware of human mortality than such a doctor, but facing up to one's own death is a very different matter. Inauthenticity manages to absorb the terrifying knowledge of one's own death, and treat it as an abstraction; facing death as one's own thus becomes a hallmark of authenticity.

Such existential attitudes toward the importance of individual choice, resolution, and anxiety (*Angst*) about death only indicate half of Heidegger's philosophy of authenticity, the half he inherited from Kierkegaard and Nietzsche. The other half he inherited from Hegel, and it consists of the recognition that an individual life means very little in isolation, that what we are is defined by our place in a community and in history. We make our choices only within a social and historical context, and they have no significance outside such a context. Thus Heidegger, like Hegel, emphasizes the historicity of *Dasein* and the ultimate insignificance of the individual even while he praises individual resolution. Our resolution is not (as in Kierkegaard and Nietzsche) one of going against the crowd but rather of giving it our personal affirmation. Taken as a whole the message of Heidegger's philosophy is unabashedly conservative.

The final effect of Heidegger's analysis of *Dasein* is a powerful portrait of human existence submerged in history but faced with choices concerning self-identity, while always tempted to 'forget' both history and choice, and remain lost in present tasks and narrowly defined social roles. Facing the future inevitably causes *Angst*, while losing oneself in the moment allows an illusory complacency even in (or especially in) the midst of the most frenzied daily routine. There can be little doubt that he is offering us an ethics and telling us how we should live our lives, and yet he repeatedly tells us that he is not giving us 'ethics' (by which he means something along the lines of Kant's categorical imperative). But it is evident that he is urging us to be authentic, to see ourselves as part of history, and to avoid falling into the traps of the moment, and, worst of all, falling prey to the fragmented vision of our being-in-the-world that is represented by traditional metaphysics. It is true that he insists that authenticity and inauthenticity are both our possibilities, and the basic structures of *Existenz*, facticity, and fallenness are common to all of us, but Heidegger clearly has an ethics, nevertheless. Ultimately he urges us to care about the world and our place in it. Care may be an existential structure of *Dasein*, but it is also a virtue that had been forgotten by generations of philosophers too concerned with problems of knowledge.

But what about Being, which seems to have dropped out of the discussion of *Dasein*? In *Being and Time*, *Dasein* is explicitly introduced as the proper approach to Being, as 'the entity that with and through its Being, its Being discloses itself'. But the danger is that one will not get past *Dasein*, that in spite of all Heidegger's caution it may yet be too subjective, too human, too intent on *imposing* its concepts on Being rather than just 'letting Being be'. In his later works he becomes increasingly disenchanted both with his most influential book and with the history of metaphysics as a whole, whose destruction he now sees as his philosophical task. The main problem is the idea of 'presence', the ancient and still powerful vision of a world that confronts us, and even *Being and Time* is still affected by this. In a number of essays on metaphysics and truth he begins to spell out his alternative, beginning (as his predecessors Kant, Hegel, and Nietzsche had begun) by attacking the commonsensical notion of truth as 'correspondence' to a fully formed reality 'outside of' us. The notion of an 'external world' makes no sense, and we can talk about truth at all only insofar as we are 'in' it, not searching for it outside of experience. Thus Heidegger shifts the language of truth from correspondence to 'disclosure' and 'revelation', and as his work progresses moves increasingly away from any taint of subjectivity. He gives up phenomenology, and talks less and less about *Dasein* as the key to Being. Indeed, he worries about whether human language can adequately describe Being at all, not only because language has 'blunted the word ''Being'' ' but because our logic and grammar make the expression of Being impossible. He urges us to liberate ourselves from grammar, in the form of poetry and a special form of 'thought' that is not rational (or irrational either). Ultimately he despairs of our ever appreciating Being, for as he complains in his massive study of Nietzsche, we always hit 'the impasse of our own humanity'. But in giving up subjectivity, and the last vestiges of humanism and the Cartesian picture of philosophy, he is by no means signalling a return to the old absolutism. What we are given instead is an increasingly obscure picture of indeterminacy, a view from nowhere that is not objective nor subjective, but is often analysed as a form of mysticism (a label which Heidegger himself, of course, would reject). It would seem that he agrees with Schopenhauer and Wittgenstein, that in the end one should be silent—or at least very obscure.

Heidegger's influence has been, like his philosophy, ambiguous and difficult to chart. Two philosophers in France have taken him in exactly opposite directions: Jean-Paul Sartre along the lines of existentialism, with renewed emphasis on the self, consciousness, and responsibility; and Jacques Derrida against the presumptions of the existentialists, with a radical rejection of the self and its autonomy. In Germany and elsewhere there are groups of philosophers who claim to be his followers, but there is one development in particular that has had a dramatic impact far beyond the boundaries of academic philosophy. It is called 'hermeneutics', and received its twentieth-century impetus in the central pages of *Being and Time*.

Hermeneutics had its origins in a method of biblical interpretation formulated by Friedrich Schleiermacher (1760–1834) while he was at the University of Berlin (with Hegel). The main point of it was to capture the 'spirit' of the author, the inner dynamics of the work. In the singular case of the Bible, of course, attention to the author and His spirit had very special significance, but when Dilthey picked up the notion of hermeneutics later in the century he insisted that all texts—and indeed all human activities—could and should be subjected to the same rigorous technique of interpretation not on the basis of extraneous information, causes, and influences but rather on the basis of the intrinsic meanings of the work itself. It is on this basis that Dilthey sharply distinguishes the natural from the human sciences ('*Geisteswissenschaften*'): the natural sciences employ causal explanation, but the human sciences require interpretation of meanings, the meanings which are already in every human enterprise as its point and purpose. What Heidegger added to this tradition was an ontological turn: not only texts and human activities could be interpreted according to their intrinsic meanings, but the world itself was filled with such meanings. He rejected the division between human and natural (as he rejected virtually all such dichotomies), and considered Dilthey still far too Cartesian, too concerned with 'objectivity'. For Heidegger, '*Dasein* occurs as a givenness of meanings before actively reflecting on these. *Dasein* is the projection of a world of structures that constitute possibilities in life.'[13] These 'foremeanings' are not 'constituted' by us (as in Kant, Hegel, or Husserl) but given to us, not by an 'external world' but by the indivisible complex that is *Dasein*. *Dasein*, ultimately, is the 'disclosure of meaning'.

Heidegger did not pursue this particular line of thought, for as he put less emphasis on *Dasein* he consequently had less room for such a distinctively human activity as interpretation, but one of his students, Hans-Georg Gadamer (b.1900), became the leading figure in hermeneutics, devoting his life to working out the method and implications of Heidegger's few terse paragraphs, and much of contemporary continental philosophy (in France as well as in Germany) is indebted to Gadamer's work.

The central concern of Gadamer's hermeneutics is nothing less than the problem that has carried us through the history of modern philosophy, the problem of truth. Questions of interpretation raise this problem in small, specific ways—what is the 'true' interpretation of one of Kafka's parables?—but the problem facing Gadamer is the grand philosophical problem: what does it mean to say that anything is true? Since Kant (and before), two extreme views have emerged in reply to this. On one side Kant, Husserl, and Frege, for instance, insist that if the word 'truth' means anything at all, then there must be some single, timeless 'objective' truth independent of particular perspectives or methods. On the other, Nietzsche, for example, insists that there can be no such thing as 'the Truth', that there are only perspectives, only a variety of incommensurable truths that change through history and from culture to culture. The first position, which we might call 'objectivism' (or 'transcendentalism'), accepts the role of the subject in constituting meaning in the world, but refuses to accept the Fichtean corollary that there might be different meanings and no single 'true' meaning. The latter takes the self-constitution of meaning, combined with the postulate of our own freedom and/or individuality, and concludes that there can be no Truth as such, only various truths 'relative to' this or that individual or society. But both of these options are open to objection: the first is dogmatic, the second irresponsible. Gadamer's hermeneutics is an attempt to steer us between the Scylla and Charybdis of objectivism and relativism, and give us a notion of truth that has neither of these faults.

What Gadamer takes from Heidegger, above all, is the insistence that any philosophical attempt to distinguish 'subject and object' can only cause trouble, and consequently that any notion of having 'removed' oneself from temporality—as when one attempts to formulate such a 'timeless' method as transcendental phenomenology—must be an illusion. For Gadamer, as for Heidegger, our situation is essentially historical, and there is no escaping the context in which we as philosophers attempt to assay our existence. But this realization need not 'degrade truth' or lead to the conclusion that there is only a multitude of irreducible and incompatible interpretations. Having given up the subject and the notion of the subject's constitution of meanings the hermeneuticist comes to appreciate the availability of meanings already in the world, and by interpreting these meanings we find, in Gadamer's words, 'a radically new possibility in the face of classical historicism'. Gadamer rejects the formulation of 'methods' as a way to the truth, for it is the multiplicity of methods, not truths, that leads to relativism. The problem with traditional relativism is that it paid almost exclusive attention to purely theoretical and methodological concerns, the questions of science and the abstract problems of philosophy for example. But the unifying theme that will allow us to understand one another, and move beyond the Babel of competing voices is not in the realm of theory but rather of *practice*. We share a historical situation, a world, and by comparing and contrasting our various interpretations, *in this historical context*, we can achieve a 'fusion of horizons' despite our differences. The ultimate aim of hermeneutics, according to Gadamer, is a familiar Hegelian ambition: 'reawakening consciousness of solidarity of a humanity that slowly begins to know itself as humanity, for this means knowing that it has to share the problem of life on this planet.'

It is with this sounding of the Hegelian theme that we should mention one other leading hermeneuticist—although he has long refused to accept that too-Gadamerian label. Jürgen Habermas (b. 1929) is not a disciple of Heidegger but a faithful student of Hegel and Marx. He too has attacked the philosophical over-emphasis on purely theoretical issues, and emphasized instead human *praxis*, the practically oriented forms of human life. Where he differs from Gadamer—and the two have often confronted one another in public and in print over the past several decades—is in his insistence on the *critical* function of interpretation, not just expounding the meanings that are given in life but also criticizing them, finding some Archimedean point from which to reject certain meanings and institutions, and defend others. Habermas is sceptical of Gadamer's claims for the universality of hermeneutics and the 'fusion of horizons', since he is concerned much more than Gadamer with the various social and practical factors that distort and disguise the meanings that hermeneutics is to disclose. In a perfect world hermeneutics might be as consensual and universal as Gadamer claims, but in this world, which is far from politically perfect, communication and interpretation are systematically distorted. Both men agree (with Heidegger) that much of this distortion is due to the exaggerated importance of science and technology, which they attack as 'scientism', but Habermas spends much more time diagnosing and criticizing this distorting influence, and formulating modes of interpretation and communication that might lead to a more genuine and faithful understanding of ourselves in the world.

Much has been made of the disagreements between Gadamer and Habermas, but for our purposes it is more important to appreciate their shared vision. Both insist, following Heidegger and Hegel respectively, on the inescapability of historical consciousness and social context. Both emphasize the practical dimensions of human life, and reject the overly abstract and scientific. Both reject the traditional emphasis on method and the authority of experts, who 'degrade practical reason to mere technological control' (Habermas). Both reject the traditional dualisms of the Cartesian tradition, and insist that, while objectivism is unacceptable, relativism is not the only alternative. Both assure us of the possibility of a harmonious, universal consensus, although Gadamer tends toward romanticism while Habermas is very much a child of the Enlightenment. Indeed, there is a strong strain in Habermas that resembles an attempt at transcendental argument, just as there is—despite his denials— an unavoidable tendency toward historicism, with or without universal consensus, in Gadamer. But both emerge as rationalists with confidence in human reason and the future, because of that 'quiet but obstinate, never silent claim to reason' that permeates even the worst periods of human history.

12

The Self in France: Sartre, Camus, de Beauvoir, Merleau-Ponty

> One of the chief objections levelled against existentialism
> is that the precept 'to will freedom' is only a hollow for-
> mula and offers no concrete content for action. But that is
> because one has begun by emptying the word freedom of
> its concrete meaning; we have already seen that freedom
> realizes itself only by engaging itself in the world: to such
> an extent that man's project toward freedom is embodied
> in him in definite acts of behaviour.[1]
>
> de Beauvoir

It would not be too unreasonable to suggest that the culmination of
modern Continental philosophy and the transcendental pretence
is the position widely known as existentialism. The name was
coined by Jean-Paul Sartre (1905–80), who is still recognized as *the*
existentialist, although the term embraces a large group of his one-
time friends (many of whom rejected the label) including Albert
Camus, Maurice Merleau-Ponty, and Sartre's lifelong companion Simone de Beauvoir. Existentialism owes a heavy debt to both
the Enlightenment and romanticism (Iris Murdoch once called
Sartre a 'romantic rationalist'). Sartre's philosophy in particular
owes much to both Rousseau and Kant, while Hegel, Marx,
Husserl, Heidegger, and Nietzsche figure prominently in several
of his central ideas and formulations. The structure of his philosophy is undeniably Cartesian, and its emphasis on individual subjectivity in many ways represents both the full fruition and the
degeneration of Rousseau's original celebration of the self and its
domain.

Sartre is, perhaps, the ultimate individualist. While he read and
borrowed much from Hegel, Marx, and Heidegger, he utterly
rejected any suggestion that the individual was determined or

dominated by history. 'Man makes himself', he proclaimed in one of his famous slogans: it is the individual who gives meaning to history, not the other way around. And while the scope of the self is much reduced from Hegel's grand notion of Spirit or Husserl's transcendental ego, Sartre insists that the individual self has a unique and extraordinary power which he calls 'absolute freedom'. Human consciousness is free to choose, and with this freedom comes an irreducible and unavoidable sense of responsibility. Although there are no necessary choices, no 'categorical imperatives', freedom itself is both universal and necessary, common to all men and women in every conceivable circumstance. The transcendental pretence, in other words, is alive and very well in Sartre's philosophy.

Sartre began as a dedicated phenomenologist. He had studied Husserl, and his first attempts at philosophizing—he was writing short stories, novels, and political tracts at the same time—were contained in a series of amplifications and modifications of Husserl's phenomenological method. Most important among these is an essay published in 1936, 'The Transcendence of the Ego', in which he reconsiders the very idea of a phenomenological reduction that leaves us with an irreducible self or ego at the basis of consciousness. Following Heidegger, he rejects Husserl's *epoche* or 'reduction', and insists that phenomenology cannot be just an examination of consciousness but must be, at the same time, an examination of the actual world. Again following clues from Heidegger but going beyond (and circumventing) him, he insists that there is no self at the core of consciousness, that self and consciousness are—contra Husserl—completely different. Ignoring Heidegger's rejection of the vocabulary of 'consciousness' in favour of his original language of '*Dasein*' (a word Sartre frequently uses, nevertheless), Sartre continues to insist that consciousness exists in confrontation with the world. The self, however, is not to be found in consciousness but rather in the world, 'like the self of another'. The 'transcendence of the ego' means that the ego is never given in consciousness (as Descartes, Locke, and Husserl all believed), and furthermore that consciousness is always reaching ahead of itself in search of the self, which (as in Heidegger) is created only through living, that is by virtue of our actions and our relations with other people. One of the curious consequences of this theory, according to Sartre, is that the long-standing suspicion that all our actions are basically selfish makes no sense; we cannot be always selfish if there is no inner self to be served. Consciousness in general is selfless and unselfconscious; it is 'pre-reflective' and unaware of itself. Sartre's example of running for a streetcar is illustrative: my consciousness is not of myself but only of 'streetcar-to-be-overtaken'. There is no 'I' in pre-reflective consciousness, and Sartre utterly rejects the need for a transcendental self to give meaning to our experiences. Merleau-Ponty similarly argues: 'In so far as I am a consciousness, that is, in so far as something has meaning for me, I am neither here nor there, neither Peter nor Paul; I am in no way distinguishable from an "Other" consciousness.'[2] Consciousness is one thing, self and personal identity another.

No matter how freely the French existentialists may have borrowed from their German teachers and predecessors, their basic philosophical intuitions are unmistakably French, and this means Cartesian. Sartre, Camus, and Merleau-Ponty all adopt the metaphysical dualism of consciousness and the world (it is partly for this reason that they never considered the break between Husserl and Heidegger as serious, much less as a schism in the very idea of phenomenology as such). Sartre divided his 'phenomenological ontology' into two forms of Being, which he calls (after Hegel) 'for itself' and 'in itself', the former the being of consciousness, the latter the being of things in the world. Camus writes in *Myth of Sisyphus* of the confrontation between 'rational man and the indifferent universe', and Merleau-Ponty, although he denies the intelligibility of a disembodied consciousness, develops his philosophy along the lines of embodied consciousness seeking meaning in the world. They all accept Descartes's basic model of a free and rational consciousness set against a mechanical, physical world. One thing that they do not accept from Descartes, however, is the 'third substance' of his model, that is an omnipotent, omniscient, eternal God who created and watches over minds and world. Although there have been, and still are, important religious existentialists

(Kierkegaard most notably), these French existentialists are committed and sometimes belligerent atheists, and it is the rejection of God that leads Camus and Sartre to conclude that the universe is ultimately meaningless and, Camus adds, 'absurd'.

The Cartesian starting-point, coupled with their allegiance to phenomenology, keeps Sartre and Merleau-Ponty focused on the importance of consciousness (for Merleau-Ponty, embodied consciousness), but their recognition of Heidegger's importance leads them to reject at least one central theme in Descartes and Husserl, the possibility of separating consciousness and the world, in Descartes through the method of universal doubt, in Husserl through the methodological reduction, the *epoche*. Sartre, Merleau-Ponty, and Camus as well are all unabashed realists, taking the 'givenness' of the world at face value, and having no time at all for epistemological scepticism. Merleau-Ponty holds on to the phenomenological reduction as a device for suspending common-sense prejudices, but he also insists that 'the most important lesson which the reduction teaches us is the impossibility of a complete reduction'.[3] Sartre too insists that there is no separating appearances from the thing itself: 'that is why we can equally reject the dualism of appearance and essence. The appearance does not hide the essence, it reveals it; it is the essence.'[4] In his early novel *Nausea*, Sartre presents us with a character (Roquentin) who is nauseated by the brute reality of objects, in particular by the gnarled and sprawling root of a chestnut tree: 'Never had I understood the meaning of "existence" . . . And then all of a sudden, it was clear as day; existence had revealed itself. It had lost the harmless look of an abstract category; it was the very paste of things, this root was kneaded into existence.'[5] Camus uses the same image in the *Myth of Sisyphus*: 'Here are trees and I know their gnarled surface, water and I feel its taste . . . how shall I negate this world whose power and strength I feel?'[6] The rejection of the *epoche* is not a mere technical disagreement, however. The point of this dispute is, as in Heidegger, nothing less than a reorientation of philosophy away from pure questions of knowledge back to questions about our active and emotional involvement in the world. Merleau-Ponty writes: 'the world is not what I think but what I live through.'[7]

On purely philosophical considerations, Merleau-Ponty (1908–61) is the most sophisticated of the French existentialists, and he alone seems to have grasped the depth of Heidegger's quarrels with Husserl. After his break with Sartre he frequently accused his former partner of remaining caught in the 'subject–object' dichotomy, and though he retains the word 'consciousness' in his writings he is quite clear—as Sartre is not—that the connection between consciousness and the body is not at all Cartesian (Sartre confuses the issue by insisting that the relation between them is not contingent, but there is nothing in his analysis of consciousness to indicate why this should be so). Merleau-Ponty accordingly replaces the Husserlian notion of 'intentionality' with the more bodily notion of 'motility', and declares that consciousness is 'not originally "I think" but "I am able to" '.[8] Like Sartre in 'The Transcendence of the Ego', Merleau-Ponty adopts the concept of a pre-reflective consciousness, or 'preconscious intentionality'. Following Heidegger he declares that not only is there no self at one pole of this consciousness, there is no object at the other, just the world of 'equipment' and tasks to be done which we later try to translate into objective knowledge. And yet the Cartesian, subjective position remains at the heart of his philosophy: 'all my knowledge, even my scientific knowledge, is gained from my own particular point of view. . . . I am not a "living creature" nor even a "man" nor a "consciousness". . . . I am the absolute source.'[9]

For Sartre, Merleau-Ponty, Camus, and Simone de Beauvoir the key questions of philosophy are not epistemological or phenomenological but always tied to the self, to the nature of the individual, to the question of what it means to be a good human being. Unlike Husserl and Heidegger, and even more than Hegel and Marx, the French existentialists were steeped in practical politics, and their philosophies, even at their most technical, bear the imprint of their political concerns. They were all in Paris during the Nazi occupation, and were all deeply affected by the resistance movement. The questions that pursued them there were not questions of knowledge but, as for their tormented predecessor Rousseau, questions about the ultimate goodness of human nature, the ability of an individual to withstand ominous social pressures and influences, and the proper locus of responsibility for the ills of the world. Their aim was not absolute truth but rather, in Merleau-Ponty's words, a 'dialogue with the world'.

The key idea of French existentialism, which set it apart from most of the German philosophy that had inspired it, was that human existence has no essence. It was an idea inherited from Heidegger—the existentialists even borrowed his phrase 'existence precedes essence'—but they stated their thesis more boldly and clearly than he ever could have. Philosophers had always asked about the essence of human nature, and a variety of popular answers had come down through the ages: 'man is a social animal', 'people are basically selfish', 'human beings are by nature religious', 'men and women naturally tend to love one another'. Sartre's thesis—one shared with modifications by his friends—is that all such hypotheses are not only false: they are self-deceptive. People are not essentially anything whatever, except that they are essentially free. They are free to choose what they will be, and collectively they are free to choose what humanity will be. If people choose to be selfish then human life will be, as Hobbes wrote, 'a war of all against all'. If they choose to be saints then humanity will be saintly, as in Kant's holy 'Kingdom of Ends' in which every person obeys the Moral Law, and assumes that everyone else will too. But there is no final truth about human beings; they are what they choose to be. Of course one can always twist this around and claim that we do after all have an 'essence' according to the existentialists, namely freedom. But this sort of paradox—for which Sartre himself has a special fondness—does not undermine the position. If our essence is freedom, then it follows that whatever we do is bound by that essence. We are and will be what we make of ourselves; the rest is self-deception and cowardice.

It is easy to see how such an idea could have become so compelling in the paranoid, humiliating situation of war-torn Paris. In normal circumstances we might have a lax and flexible notion of when someone is free and responsible and when he is not. If a neighbour cuts his leg on the lawn-mower one is not likely to upbraid him for not finishing the lawn, but a soldier on the battlefield could not use a similar injury as an excuse. A student might be excused from class because of a pain in his tooth, but a prisoner in the hands of a Gestapo inquisitor will not be excused when he gives in to the pain, no matter how extreme it may be. It was in such extreme circumstances that the French existentialists constructed their polemical picture of human nature. Not for them the niceties of morality at high table. The questions of human freedom and responsibility are to be answered in the most urgent situations, in which 'reasonable expectations' do not apply. No matter how serious the injury or excruciating the pain, these are circumstances in which one is never let off the hook and forgiven: the ultimate explanation of one's behaviour is always that one *chose* what to do.

If one wanted to summarize Sartre's existentialism in a short phrase it would be that there are 'no excuses'. Whatever one does, one chooses to do. Whatever the reasons, one is responsible. There is no saying 'I couldn't take it any more', only 'I decided not to take it any more'. There is no appeal to the obstacles and interferences of the world, only the fact that one has given in to them. There is no excuse because of 'the way one is'— 'I couldn't help it, I'm a coward'; one chooses to be a coward by choosing to behave as one does. In this sense Sartre's philosophy is merciless: one never breaks free of responsibility. He even says, in a sense to be explained later, that one is responsible for being born, an event which, in any familiar terms, one certainly did not choose. It is this harsh view of 'absolute freedom' that in part undermined his friendships with Camus and Merleau-Ponty, both of whom argue that there are circumstances that mitigate these conditions. It also caused tension with de Beauvoir, for the absolute freedom of choice that Sartre suggests fails to take into account the difference in power and social place between men and women.

Before we examine these crucial issues of freedom and responsibility more closely, it is necessary to look at the very special concept of consciousness developed by Sartre, and with modifications by Merleau-Ponty. The basic ontology Sartre accepts is, as we noted, a Cartesian one with consciousness on one side and the physical world on the other. Sartre calls these two types of being, 'being-for-itself' and 'being-in-itself'. He has little to say about being-in-itself except that 'it is, it is what it is, and it is as it is'. As an unabashed realist his concern is not whether consciousness can know the world, but rather how consciousness deals with the world, and more importantly how it deals with itself. Consciousness, accordingly, is called 'for itself', and its concern is its own nature and well-being. The problem is—to introduce a difficult notion without warning—that consciousness is itself nothing. It is not, as in Descartes, a substance. It is not even, as in Kant, a form of transcendental activity. It is, in Sartre's early metaphor, 'like a wind, blowing from nowhere toward everything'. The world is rich and full of things. Consciousness is utterly empty. It has no 'contents'. It is not an object of any kind (accordingly it is not subject to physical laws, such as the law of causation). It exists only in its awareness of itself and the world. This is the basis of its freedom, but also the source of its dilemma: it is nothing but wants to be something. It always 'is what it is not, and is not what it is'.

What Sartre intends by this series of paradoxes is fairly clear, even if the ontological implications are complex and confusing. To speak of 'nothing' here is a way of freeing consciousness from the causal chain, a ploy earlier used by Kant, Hegel, and Schopenhauer. Consciousness is not an object for consciousness, and as such it is not subject to the categories which consciousness applies to all objects, including the all-important category of causality. Furthermore in his second (practical) Critique Kant argues that, for an agent, to think oneself free is to *be* free. We might note that Sartre (like Kant) is perfectly willing to accept determinism in the realm of science. What he refuses to do is to allow the concept of causal determinism—which would deprive us of any meaningful notion of responsibility—to intrude into the domain of human action. But this curious notion of 'nothingness' that characterizes consciousness does not just refer to its non-objective status, but also to its primary activity, which Sartre calls 'negation'. Consciousness (unlike every kind of being-in-itself) has the ability to negate the world by making plans and envisioning possibilities. One might say that a giant meteor too has the ability to 'negate the world', or at least a large part of it, but Sartre points out that any such natural alteration of the world, no matter how devastating, is so only in *our* eyes. In the indifferent eyes of the world it makes no difference whether the meteor is still streaking out into space or firmly mashed into that earthly plot that *we* know as 'London'. Destruction and devastation are such only because of consciousness. Change matters (counts as change) only because we are conscious of it. Consciousness thus differs from all other forms of being not just in its nothingness but in its ability to negate, to see the world as it was or as it might be, as well as the way it is. Here is its power which, in action, is what Sartre means by 'freedom'.

Consciousness can also negate itself: one can be disgusted by what one is, and can resolve to be different. Since consciousness is nothing *in* itself anyway, there is no limit to what it can envision. Indeed Sartre sometimes insists that what we all really want is nothing less than to be God. On a smaller scale we all have plans and what we somewhat disparagingly call 'dreams' which far exceed any apparent possibility at the moment. The 'one is what one is not' paradox refers to this ability of consciousness to 'transcend' itself, to look ahead (and behind), and to want always to be more than it is.

Obviously the world resists our intentions. Our freedom cannot be just the free play of imagination, but must be tied to action, to particular situations, limited by the harsh realities of the world. How, then, are we free? Sartre's position, stated in somewhat banal terms, is that one is always free to *try*, to do *something*, even if it is only to change our attitude. Like many other French writers (including Camus in *The Stranger*) he uses the metaphor of the prisoner to illustrate the notion of freedom. A prisoner in chains would seem to be the paradigmatic example of unfreedom, but Sartre makes the point that one is never so conscious of one's freedom as when it is brutally limited. The prisoner still has the freedom to shout or spit at his captors, or to despair, or to make plans for his escape or his future, or to formulate revolutionary philosophy, or to spend his time watching the flies on the wall. In his dramatic writings Sartre sometimes employs the device of a momentary glance which expresses an attitude of defiance, even in the last moment of dying. The thesis of absolute freedom is not the (nonsensical) claim that one can do anything that one chooses to do, but rather the negative claim that one is *never* in a position such that one cannot choose, and is not responsible for what one is or does.

Borrowing heavily from Heidegger, Sartre fills out his existential ontology by distinguishing two aspects of the human condition which he calls 'facticity' (taking the term directly from Heidegger's *Being and Time*) and 'transcendence' (a confusing term that is *not* the same as our central Kantian adjective 'transcendental'). Facticity is, as in Heidegger, the sum total of facts about us and the situations in which we have been 'thrown'. One's facticity is, in particular, one's past, those deeds and events that are over and done with, but whose consequences largely determine the present circumstances, and constitute a significant part of who or what we are. A person who has murdered is, and in one sense always will be, a murderer. A man who was crippled in a childhood accident must live with his handicap for the rest of his life. A woman who did brilliantly at school will always carry that advantage with her, whether or not she succeeds in making anything of it. A person is, in part, his or her facticity, and at death—when one has nothing but facticity—one is nothing but what one has done. Thus Sartre says, in retrospect, 'Proust's genius is nothing other than Proust's works'. In his play *No Exit*, he casts his characters, all of whom have just died, into Hell to judge for themselves what they have become.

Transcendence is similar to what Heidegger called '*Existenz*', and it consists of our various possibilities. But Sartre emphasizes what Heidegger takes for granted, that such possibilities apply only to consciousness, not to things. An acorn has the potential of becoming an oak tree, but it does not have the possibilities that make up transcendence. An acorn does not anticipate becoming an oak; it does not look forward to it, or fear that it will fail, and does not plan its steps and stages. A student on the other hand has the possibility of becoming a lawyer, not just because it is 'possible', but because he or she is capable of looking ahead, deciding what to be, and taking steps to fulfil that ambition. Transcendence, Sartre insists, is not just an act of imagination, although imagination is essential to it, but is tied to action, and it is the formation of intentions to act that ultimately constitutes our freedom.

Facticity and transcendence are the essential components of being human. Facticity defines our situation and who we are—up to that point. Transcendence opens up the world of possibilities—what we can make of that situation and ourselves—given who or what we are so far. One rarely has a clean slate, an opportunity to establish oneself without baggage from the past. One can try to establish a new identity in a new town, but though the situation is novel one nevertheless carries the past with one—in habits and expectations, in memories, and in one's face. Facticity and transcendence are sometimes in brute opposition, as when one tries to change an old habit or a way of life, but most of the time they fit together, transcendence 'gearing itself' to facticity, and facticity being reinterpreted according to one's transcendence. Our plans usually fit our circumstances: indeed it is the circumstances that circumscribe if not dictate (but do not determine) our plans.

In *Being and Time* Heidegger outlined three existential structures: *Existenz*, facticity, and fallenness. *Existenz* and facticity become transcendence and facticity in Sartre, but Sartre also has a notion similar to fallenness. He calls it 'bad faith', and it is perhaps the most striking and important concept of his philosophy. Bad faith is not just a tendency to 'fall' back into the routines of everyday life, but is nothing less than a betrayal of one's self, a lie in which one deceives oneself about oneself. The most prevalent example of bad faith is the denial of one's freedom in the form of an excuse, typically beginning with 'I couldn't help it . . .'. With his insistence on absolute freedom Sartre refuses to acknowledge the legitimacy of any such excuse. No matter how oppressive and overwhelming the circumstances that constitute one's facticity, there is always transcendence and one's ability to envision—and act on—alternatives. Bad faith, in other words, is a denial of one's transcendence by way of an appeal to one's facticity. It includes the sort of example that Sartre is particularly concerned to expose, the instance of the Nazi soldier or policeman who insists: 'I was just doing my duty; I could not do otherwise.' One can always do otherwise: one can quit, or run away. The cost might be enormous, but it is never a case of 'cannot', always of 'will not'. One chooses to continue to be a Nazi: it is not determined by one's nature.

Bad faith can also be the denial of one's facticity. Sartre gives the example of a woman who, while the object of seduction, refuses to acknowledge herself as a desirable woman, pretends that her companion is interested only in her sparkling intellect, and 'disowns' her hand which is being fondled as she talks. It is not that she decides not to have sexual relations, but rather that she does *not* decide and denies that the relevant choice is hers, that puts her in bad faith (notice that this form of bad faith conspires with the other as well). Similarly, a person who continues to entertain extravagant artistic ambitions despite repeated demonstrations of lack of talent is in bad faith because of a refusal to adjust plans and expectations to reality. But notice here too that the line between bad faith and persistence is not easily drawn, and the case has more to do with the degree of self-deception than the divergence of ambition and ability as such.

Sartre's most developed example of bad faith and its dilemmas is the case of the homosexual in *Being and Nothingness* who is forced to decide, in very practical terms, whether or not he *is* a homosexual (a literary illustration of the same case is Sartre's character Daniel in his novel *The Age of Reason*). On the one hand the man in question has had a considerable number of homosexual encounters in the past. He continues to find men attractive and thinks about them erotically. His facticity, in other words, would seem to indicate that he is a homosexual. On the other hand, he has his doubts, his sense of humiliation, his disgust, and has resolved more than once to change his life and 'go straight'. From the point of view of transcendence, in other words, he is not a homosexual but only a person who has had homosexual experiences in the past. Next time he will resist temptation, and he will try to avoid circumstances in which he will be tempted. The dilemma, which focuses on (but does not reduce to) the very philosophical word 'is', concerns whether the person should think of himself as a homosexual or not. To make matters more complicated Sartre introduces an antagonist whom he sarcastically calls 'the champion of sincerity' (who also appeared in his early novel *Nausea*) who offers the unsympathetic advice, 'why not just admit that you are a homosexual?' But to do so would be the height of bad faith, for a person never *is* anything, in the way that a tree or a stone *is* something, at least not as long as he is alive. To admit that one *is* a homosexual is to deny one's transcendence, and undermine one's willingness to change, but to insist that one is not a homosexual is to deny one's facticity, including not only one's past but one's present desires and inclinations as well.

The place of desires and other conscious urges in Sartre's ontology is illustrative and interesting. Most philosophers (Kant and Schopenhauer, for instance) treat these as compulsions, whether as natural causes or the manifestations of irrational will. Freud, notoriously, suggests that much of our behaviour is determined by desires whose source is the Unconscious. For Sartre, however, desires, emotions, and all mental events and processes are objects *for* consciousness, not *in* consciousness, since consciousness is nothing, and can have no contents. But this means that we can and must take an attitude toward our own motives and feelings much like that which we take toward external threats and obstacles. We *choose* to give in to them or not. One has a pain, but whether or not one gives in to it is not dictated by the pain itself, no matter what its intensity. It is part of our facticity, something to be considered, interpreted, weighed, and acted on. According to one story, the germ from which the whole edifice of *Being and Nothingness* grew was Sartre's experience of fatigue while on a hike. He realized that, no matter how painful his exhaustion, at every step it was his choice whether to continue or to 'give in' to the fatigue that was troubling him. Similarly, a motive, no matter how urgent or compelling, is not *in* consciousness but *for* consciousness. It does not determine our behaviour, but only contributes to the situation in which *we* determine our behaviour. No one is compelled to act as he or she does, and no one can appeal to their motives as an excuse. One might explain one's behaviour in terms of motives, of course, but what one does thereby is to explain *which* motive one chose to follow, and perhaps why one did so.

Sartre's insistence on the ultimate voluntariness of our behaviour places him in direct confrontation with Freud. Freud's model of mind is a thoroughly deterministic one, where the motives for many of our actions are not known to us. Sartre, on the contrary, insists that consciousness has no content—much less an inaccessible basement—and that none of our behaviour is determined in the fashion that Freud suggests. Accordingly he launches a full-scale attack on Freud's model, and introduces his own form of 'existential psychoanalysis'. He specifically rejects the Freudian concept of the Unconscious, and in a series of arguments shows that the very notion of 'unconscious intentions' is contradictory. His central claim is the phenomenological one that consciousness is thoroughly 'translucent'; it has no unconscious part, 'no corners' to hide in. His argument against Freud is essentially this: if one part of consciousness hides information from itself, then it must both know and not know the information in question. But how can one hide knowledge from oneself? And if one suggests some inner agency as Freud does, a 'censor' which keeps the information from consciousness, then the same paradox arises in the case of the censor, for it must both know and not know the same piece of information. In place of Freud's inaccessibility of the deterministic unconscious Sartre substitutes bad faith, the *refusal* to attend to what we know. What we are and what we do is never beyond our conscious responsibility.

Sartre ignores or bypasses Heidegger's attack on Cartesianism, retaining not only such disputed terms as 'consciousness' but also the dualistic ontology that, according to Heidegger, has been responsible for so much philosophical misunderstanding. His assault on Freud is a Cartesian one, based on the separation of the deterministic world-in-itself and consciousness-as-freedom. Freud, according to Sartre, conflated the two. But if his neglect of Heidegger allows Sartre to retain his strong, central conception of individual responsibility, it deprives him of that sense of meaningfulness enjoyed by Heidegger and the subsequent movement of hermeneutics. Descartes saved the notions of value and meaning despite his dualism because he believed in God. Heidegger recognized that *Dasein* already found itself in a world filled with meanings which it did not itself constitute. But for Sartre, who is Cartesian and an atheist, neither God nor the givenness of the world is sufficient to make it meaningful: 'The existentialist finds it extremely embarrassing that God does not exist, for there disappears with him all possibility of finding values in an intelligible heaven.'[10] Values are, he admits, given at every moment, 'like little signposts that say, ''keep off the grass'' ', but these are not yet *our* values, and the question is how any values can be made our own, indeed whether there *are* any values, in a meaningful sense, at all.

This aspect of Sartre's philosophy is anticipated and dramatized by Albert Camus (1913–60), particularly in his *Myth of Sisyphus*. Camus recognizes that the separation of the world and human consciousness (without God as intermediary) leads to hopeless frustration. Our rational expectations of justice and satisfaction confront the 'indifference [albeit ''benign''] of the universe'. He refers to this inevitable frustration as 'the Absurd', an irreducible gap between our demand for values and meaning, and the neutral meaninglessness of the world. Whatever meanings there may be, we have put them there, but knowing that they are only our projections is sufficient for Camus to conclude that they cannot be real or significant, and the upshot of his early philosophy is that all values in life are futile and illusory: it is only life itself that is of ultimate value. From this he draws the disturbing conclusion that all questions of the 'quality of life' are pointless: there is only quantity. 'There is no substitute for twenty years of experience.' On the other hand, his characters often find themselves facing death (for example Meursault in *The Stranger*) and discovering that it does not make any difference: 'one has to get through this business of dying some time.' Adopting the Being-unto-death theme from Heidegger, Camus argues that life is meaningless because ultimately we all have to die. But what he says about values in life gives us no reason to suppose that life would be any more meaningful if we did not have to die. Indeed, his mythological character Sisyphus has the dubious advantage of being immortal, but this is little compensation for his endless and meaningless task of rolling his rock up a mountain again and again, each time to have it fall back to the starting-point. 'There is no greater punishment', Camus's gods reasoned, 'than pointless toil.'

Camus's 'Absurd', we can see, is not a single concept but a

family of considerations: our objective insignificance in a universe trillions of light-years in size and billions of years old, our inevitable end in death, the ultimate futility of our every act and gesture, and the metaphysical gap that separates our demands and expectations from the world that could (but will not) fulfil them. But beneath this bewildering array of images there is a singular sense of hopelessness combined with a perverse satisfaction, a feeling that was summarized in the last century by Dostoevsky as the joy of despair, which Camus declares in his brief preface to *Myth of Sisyphus* to be 'the sensibility of the age', and there is a deeper realization that this sensibility may be not just a fashion but an essential structure of the human condition. If values are not given, if they are only our projections on to the world, then they are not real. Consequently, Camus finds himself only limply and inconsistently defending the value of human life itself, as he tries to establish a strong and sensitive humanist position in the midst of political turmoil without being able to formulate anything even vaguely resembling an ethics.

Sartre, like Heidegger, claims that his 'phenomenological ontology' is not, and does not yield, an ethics, but there can be no doubt that he does provide us with an ethics as well as with a lesson in how to live our lives. Like Nietzsche, he sees that 'there are no moral facts', and the multitude of values and demands that are before us at every moment are nothing more than considerations, possibilities for action, but certainly not 'categorical imperatives' that tell us what to do. Yet Sartre has in his philosophy a solid foundation for an ethics, even if it is not the sort that recommends specific courses of action, and that is the notion of 'bad faith'. One might add that appeal to practical reason or any other authority is just another example of bad faith. Despite Sartre's strategic denials, 'bad faith' clearly *is* bad, and to be avoided as much as possible. If he suggests that there may ultimately be no escaping from bad faith (as there would be no avoiding Original Sin), that does not mean that it is commendable or that it does not matter whether one is more or less in bad faith. Sartre's ethics consists, in a phrase, of the insistence that we recognize our own responsibility, and though few concrete consequences may follow from that general prescription, there can be no doubt that it separates the good from the bad. In his attack on anti-Semitism, for example, it is the bad faith of the anti-Semite that Sartre employs as his ultimate weapon against him. In his attacks on the Communist party, again, his primary objection is the neglect of responsibility and the bad faith of economic determinism. Like Kierkegaard, he holds that it is not *what* one values but *how* one values that is crucial, but he always seems to manage to defend the 'right' values by attending to the question of 'how' they are held.

The 'how', of course, refers to freedom, the necessity of freely choosing and committing oneself to a course of action but also to defending freedom, one's own and others'. One can refuse to make a decision, pretending that one has no power or responsibility in the case, but then one is 'choosing not to choose', in Sartre's famous formulation, and so one is guilty not only of a sin of omission, but more seriously in Sartre's estimation, of bad faith. One can excuse one's actions by appealing to some 'higher court', to orders from one's commander or the principles of rationality, but this too is bad faith. The question is not so much the action one decides upon, nor even its success, as the self-awareness of the decision: ' "to be free" does not mean "to obtain what one has wished" but rather "by oneself to determine oneself to wish" '. 'In other words,' Sartre concludes, 'success is not important to freedom.'[11]

It should be evident that Sartre's ethics, despite his very different starting-point, is closely akin to Kant's and Rousseau's in its uncompromising insistence on the importance of the individual and individual freedom, and the recognition that it is good intentions rather than results which determine moral worth. Sartre does not share Kant's emphasis on reason, nor Rousseau's optimistic portrait of man as intrinsically good, but he does share Kant's emphasis on very general principles, even if (as he argues) the principles are endorsed by one's actions rather than the other way around. And with Rousseau, he does believe that what one is (that is, the clarity and commitment with which one acts) is much more important than what one actually does or succeeds in doing. Referring to the situation of a slave, Sartre comments: 'it is necessary fundamentally to choose himself on the ground of slavery and thereby to give a meaning to this obscure constraint. The life of a slave who revolts and dies in the course of this revolt is a free life.'[12] What is more, despite their very different approaches Sartre actually agrees with the categorical imperatives of Kant's philosophy. 'Act in such a way that others should act that way also', and 'treat others as ends and never merely as means' characterize Sartre's ethics as well as Kant's, for in the first instance he argues that our every action is an example for the rest of humanity (indeed, our own contribution to the definition of human nature), and in the second he says that to treat someone as an 'end' is precisely to treat them as free. Indeed, with freedom as the heart of his philosophy we can expect that—in ethics or politics—whatever increases freedom will be a good thing, and whatever decreases it will most likely be an example of bad faith.

It is worth noting that we have said virtually nothing about other people in this account of Sartre's philosophy, a serious omission to be sure. Some of the philosophers previously discussed also appeared as lone individuals in isolation from society—notably Rousseau, Kierkegaard, and Nietzsche—and others spent too little time considering the interpersonal dimension of human life—for instance, Kant, Husserl, and Heidegger. Sartre does not just extol the lone individual, but recognizes that we are irreducibly social beings. Nor does he ignore or minimize the role of other people: indeed he insists that the category of 'being-for-others' is 'ontologically primary' and 'on a par with the other two', namely, being-for-itself and being-in-itself. But his analysis of being-for-others (even the name has a certain paranoid ring to it) starts with the proposition that our primary relations with other people are based on *conflict*, and as if this is not harsh enough, one of his characters in the play *No Exit* utters the brutal definition: 'Hell is other people.'

Sartre's account of being-for-others and its various complications in love and hatred is based on Hegel's master–slave parable in which two self-consciousnesses fight for each other's recognition (see Chapter 4). In Sartre's philosophy each person wants the other to recognize his freedom, but as one person's views and expectations of another restrict and interfere with one's opinions of oneself, this recognition is inevitably frustrated. One wants to see oneself as a charming, trustworthy, wholly likeable fellow, but the fact that this other person finds one crude, untrustworthy, and generally detestable makes that opinion hard to retain. And so we try to 'prove' ourselves through a series of devices, each aimed at either making the other a supporter of our own opinions, or failing this, of 'reducing' the other to an object (being-in-itself), and retaining one's own freedom. The resulting fight is not (as in Hegel) to the death, but rather a convoluted interpersonal battle, employing looks and caresses rather than more mortal weapons. With what Sartre calls 'the look' one renders another painfully self-conscious, reducing him or her to a category, a thing. In *St Genet*, Sartre tells how the young Jean Genet became a thief when one day an adult came upon him when he was removing an object from a drawer, and with a look and a word 'pinned him like a butterfly', rendering him forever a 'thief'. Human relations, according to Sartre, are a battleground on which each of us tries desperately to preserve our sense of ourselves 'for ourselves', against the intrusive manipulations of others. This is not merely Heidegger's *das Man*, nor even Nietzsche's hateful 'herd'. It is a portrait of the individual as wholly embattled, for whom freedom is first of all an inner resource but ultimately freedom from others as well. The portrait is familiar: it is that of Rousseau. And though there is some distance between Rousseau's lonely walk in the woods and Sartre's embattled Parisian existence, we can see that they are two of a kind, at least in their acceptance of the transcendental pretence.

This view of our social existence would not seem to be a promising starting-point for a social and political philosophy, but Sartre had always been deeply involved in politics, and in the years following *Being and Nothingness* he increasingly devoted his attention to the development of an existentialist social philosophy. The result was his *Critique of Dialectical Reason*, published in 1956. Sartre uses Marxism as 'an ethics of deliverance and salvation', and declares that 'Marxism is the inescapable philosophy of our time', but his specific concern in the Critique is to move beyond the excessive individualism of *Being and Nothingness*, and discover a type of group activity in which the conflict between individuals is overcome. Not surprisingly he finds this in the activities of revolutionaries who are fighting together for their freedom. He still insists that group membership is never merely a matter of 'belonging' but of renewed individual commitment ('the pledge'), and he continues to reject traditional ('vulgar') Marxism because of its emphasis on economic determinism. He continued his old existentialist attack on bad faith but now with an explicitly social flavour: bourgeois 'business as usual' is always an option facing us, but it is only an option, never a necessity. Sartre's own career illustrates his existentialist attitude. He spent years fighting beside communists but always refused to join the party. He chose his own battles, and he broke entirely with the communist left after the Russian invasion of Hungary in 1956. He wrote for the world but refused the world's recognition when he turned down the Nobel Prize in 1964. He was always, in his own eyes, an individual, but like Rousseau he also saw himself as a representative of humanity.

The last word, however, belongs not to Sartre but to his closest friend, Simone de Beauvoir (1908–86). She is the only woman to be mentioned in our story, and one should ask why. Is it that European philosophy is a man's game, uninteresting to women? Or is it that men, while writing in the name of humanity ('man'), were unwilling to let women play the game at all? Are these philosophies—which claim to analyse human nature—in fact expressions of distinctively male attitudes, representing slightly less than half of our species? If we dare to generalize on this treacherous ground, we might not expect a female philosophy so dramatically to emphasize the abstract universal and the isolated individual to the exclusion of interpersonal relations with others, or to ignore the body as a source of significance, and refer quite so exclusively to the faculties of the mind. Perhaps we would even do without the transcendental pretence, in which case the history of the past two and a half centuries might have been very different.

In *The Second Sex* de Beauvoir announces her viewpoint as an 'existentialist ethics'. In an earlier work, *The Ethics of Ambiguity*, she had mainly expounded the ethics that Sartre had so far declined to give us, emphasizing the centrality of 'humanity' and analysing the ways in which people evade their humanity through irresponsibility, apathy, and childish obedience. The 'ambiguity' in her title (the term actually comes from Merleau-Ponty) refers to the twin temptations of facticity and transcendence, to be overcome through free choices and commitments. Morality—a concept that Sartre avoids—is constituted in these choices and commitments. Where de Beauvoir starts to move beyond Sartre is in her keen awareness of the importance of caring for others and respecting their freedom. For Sartre the freedom of others presents a threat, and relationships are bound in conflict. De Beauvoir is well aware of the conceptually dependent status of women. 'A man never begins by presenting himself as a member of a certain sex', she writes. The relationship between the sexes is not symmetrical. While a woman is a woman by virtue of her 'ovaries, and uterus', a man 'superbly ignores the fact that his anatomy also includes glands'. 'A man thinks of his body as a direct and normal connection with the world, whereas he regards the body of woman as a hindrance, a prison.' A woman's peculiarities 'imprison her in her subjectivity'. De Beauvoir's analysis explores the significance of embodiment and the essential nature of our bonds with others with a sensitivity and at a depth avoided even by Sartre. At the core of her discussion, however, is both an attack on male presumptions and an existentialist stimulus aimed at women. The 'truly feminine' is a concept that has been fashioned through history by some of the same philosophers whom we have watched delineating the nature of humanity. Her work is a pioneering attempt to define an alternative conception, in which sexual differences are both a recognized reality and existential possibilities. In *The Second Sex* de Beauvoir's analysis flies in the face of the transcendental pretence, for once we acknowledge this one major split in the idea of humanity, it will be difficult to deny any number of others.

Supplement

The End of the Self: Structuralism, Post-Modernism, Foucault, and Derrida

> The goal of my work . . . has been to create a history of the different modes by which, in our culture, human beings are made subjects.[1]
>
> Foucault

Sartre's existentialism was too Cartesian, too ontologically conservative, too personally and politically radical to have much of an impact in Germany, especially after the devastation of the Second World War, and in the face of the bold developments in critical theory and hermeneutics, and the renewed interest in the philosophies of science and language. But in France the reaction against Sartre's philosophy was as dramatic as the existentialist craze itself had been. As always, the reaction was not aimed at a single philosopher but at the entire modern movement in philosophy. Not surprisingly then, some of its lesser advocates—who prefer titles to ideas—dubbed this reaction 'post-modernism', and it did indeed become the systematic rejection of the most basic premises of modern European philosophy: the celebration of the self and subjectivity, the new appreciation of history, and most of all the already flagging philosophical confidence in our ability to know the world as it really is. It was, in a phrase, the wholesale rejection of the transcendental pretence.

It is always impossible to be definitive in evaluating the significance of philosophical figures and movements, especially when trying to gauge a more or less contemporary phenomenon, and particularly in France. The philosopher who is all the rage one year may be unknown the next, and this generation's rewriting of the history of philosophy may well turn out to be a dead end, or

just another footnote to the same old line. But in its broad outlines the current history of philosophy in France seems to look
something like this: post-modern philosophy, which means
essentially the reaction against Sartre, Descartes, and the
German thinkers between them, begins with a reply to Sartre, not
from another philosopher but from an anthropologist, Claude
Lévi-Strauss (b. 1908). His discipline is uniquely suited to
explode the pretensions of any armchair theory of human
nature—including the existentialist theory that holds that there is
no such thing as human nature. Lévi-Strauss accuses Sartre of
projecting his own peculiarly urbane Parisian consciousness on
to humanity as such, of falsely assuming that bourgeois freedom
is universal, and of denying, without any thorough investigation
or appreciation of history, the universal structures of the human
mind. Lévi-Strauss utterly rejects the idea of the Cartesian subjective self, and in its place imposes an ambitious and ominous
theory of universal structures, not based in the self (as in Kant, *et
al.*) but in language, and ultimately in the structure of the human
brain. Lévi-Strauss and his theory, called 'structuralism', thus
occupies an important but peripheral role in our story. On the
one hand, he rejects the transcendental pretence in the form that
has dominated European philosophy since Descartes and
Rousseau, but on the other hand he reintroduces it in a new and
more 'scientific' form. One might say that he has just abandoned
the self and subjectivity in order to tighten the grip of the claim to
universality and objectivity. Nevertheless, he also demonstrates
an appreciation of cultural differences that is immensely refresh-
ing after three centuries of chauvinist talk about 'man'.

Post-modernism proper begins with a second revolution, the
rebellion against Lévi-Strauss and structuralism which is accordingly called 'post-structuralism'. The two main figures in this
rebellion, from a current vantage point, are Michel Foucault and
Jacques Derrida. Foucault was a radical historian who rejected
first the name 'structuralism', and then the philosophy, and
whose own philosophy came to stress the discontinuities in history, and the central place that power plays in knowledge.
Derrida was a student of Husserl and Heidegger who, under the
influence of the latter, saw the folly of the former, and with that

the erroneous ways of the entire metaphysical tradition stretching back not only to Rousseau and Descartes but perhaps to ancient times. Rousseau, as always, occupies an important but ambiguous role in post-modernism: he is reinterpreted by both Lévi-Strauss and Derrida as a figure who not only initiated modern philosophy but also sowed the seeds of its destruction.

Post-modernism in philosophy is an attack not only on the pretensions but also on the premisses and presuppositions of modernism: its expansive sense of self, its confidence in our knowledge, its a priori assurance that all people everywhere are ultimately like us. Lévi-Strauss—still a 'modernist'—begins the attack by rejecting not only the self but also the idea of the subject and subjectivity. The self had been distinguished from the subject (or from consciousness) by any number of modernists, from Hume to Sartre; that in itself was no longer a radical move. But however much the self had been denied or displaced, expanded to cosmic proportions or dissolved in the cosmic Will, the emphasis on the first-person standpoint, the inescapability of subjectivity remained. Even Heidegger's *Dasein*, which tried hard to avoid the entire vocabulary of subjectivity, still depended on the phenomenological standpoint and thus first-person description (whether or not it was a person), and so in the important sense it was still unavoidably subjective. Lévi-Strauss rejects not just the self but entire first-person framework that had been accepted without question in modern philosophy. He rejects the significance of Descartes's famous premiss, 'I think, therefore I am', and the pretensions of Rousseau's great discovery in the forest. He agrees that there is no escaping our own cultural and conceptual context, and maintains that the important truths about ourselves are not to be found in consciousness. They are to be found in the world, in our expressions and our creations, in what we produce, including our literature and our stories, our language and our cultures. It is by comparing these—across cultures—that we will get a glimpse of the universal structures of the human mind.

We are not first of all consciousnesses but rather social creatures, products of genetics, language, and culture-bound education. The subject–object distinction that is taken as a premiss or a problem in philosophy is itself an anthropological curiosity, and Lévi-Strauss intends to have done with it, not by redefining it once again but by ignoring it altogether. Structuralism is a science, not another version of Cartesian or Kantian phenomenology. It does not insist, as did Dilthey and the hermeneuticists, on a sharp distinction between the methods of the social and natural sciences, indeed it rejects not only the significance of the subject in its research but the importance of 'meaning' as well. Structuralism is the scientific search for objective laws of all human activity, beginning with the classification of its basic elements (actions and words) and the ways in which they are systematically combined. For example, Lévi-Strauss investigates the systematic interaction between the three concepts 'raw', 'cooked', and 'rotten' and their actual structure in specific societies. Elsewhere he discusses at length the Oedipus myth and its invariant structures across a spectrum of very different societies. There is no room for talk about transcendental constitution here, only for the concepts and rules that determine the structure of the activity. But although Lévi-Strauss rejects transcendental notions as such, he retains and renews the modern confidence in the availability of universal knowledge, knowledge about human nature as such. The structures discovered by structuralism are not the manifestations of a priori rules of consciousness, but they are nevertheless reliable evidence about the universal structure of the human brain.

One of the concepts central to structuralism is the notion of a 'difference', a shorthand way of expressing the relativity of terms *vis-à-vis* each other. The vowel sounds in 'Mary', 'marry', and 'merry', for example, are distinguishable only by contrast, and speakers with slightly different accents might pronounce different terms the same way. The sound 'a', in other words, does not by itself have a determinate place in the phonetics of our language: its place is determined by contrast with other vowels, by its 'difference' rather than by its absolute identity. This concept, introduced by the linguist de Saussure, becomes central to structuralism, for structuralism (at least Lévi-Strauss's variety) distinguishes between the *possible* permutations of a system of elements, and the *actual* deployment of any element in a system of differences. It is worth emphasizing again that, for Lévi-Strauss, the *meaning* of these elements (whether sounds or cultural concepts) is not of significance; it is only their place in the system that counts (it is as if the brain can only dictate relations, while meaning is something added and inevitably subjective). The aim of the structuralist is not to tell us what something means but only to identify the elements of a system, their oppositions (raw/cooked; natural/cultural; male/female), and the rules concerning them. The results of such an analysis will give us both concrete empirical knowledge of the differences between societies, and solid theoretical knowledge about human nature, neither of which was or could have been forthcoming from the self-centered transcendental tradition.

Michel Foucault (b. 1926) rejects the name 'structuralist', though this familiar assertion of philosophical individualism should not be given any particular significance. He prefers to call the method of his historical research 'archaeology', but admits that 'the results are not entirely foreign to what is called structuralist analysis'. Archaeology differs from structuralism in two ways: first, it does not concern itself with the possible permutations of a system but only with its actual, historical instances; and secondly, there is no attempt to eliminate meanings from discussion. Indeed, since language ('discourse') is the subject of much of Foucault's research, dispensing with meaning is virtually unthinkable. Like Lévi-Strauss, Foucault is a holist in his insistence that an element can be identified only by its place in a system, and has no identity outside this. But he also insists that, just as one cannot define an element outside a system, so one cannot formulate a table of possible permutations of elements, and one will not find objective laws concerning such permutations that are cross-cultural and timeless. One can only describe actual situations and the changing transformations of meaning.

In direct opposition to Lévi-Strauss and the structuralist ambition of formulating a general theory of human nature, Foucault's central thesis is the inevitable disintegration of the human sciences, and the 'end of man'. From his earliest work he has been extremely sceptical about the possibility of an all-embracing concept of humanity, and as his work has proceeded this doubt has become something of a war-cry. But even in his first, historical works the presentation of this thesis is, to put it mildly, dramatic. His first book is about madness, and its aim is to capture a domain of the human condition in which the traditional attempts to describe universal meanings—and the structuralist attempt to identify universal structures of language—break down. The distinction between reason and madness itself is shown to be discontinuous and closely related to the power relations in society. He points out that in the seventeenth century the insane were often classified (and interned) with the poor, the sick, and the homeless, and this should be understood not as bad medical science but rather as early experiments in social control, which Foucault links to the laws, ethics, and economics of France at the time. These are themes that will pervade all of his works: the centrality of language in understanding social practices, the 'illusion of autonomous discourse', the discontinuity of history, the systematic oppression of people through classification and confinement, and the central place of political power in what the authorities prefer to present as scientific knowledge. Other philosophers and social scientists preserve the illusion of rationality and continuity by studying the established institutions of society; Foucault prefers to study 'discursive practices', the seemingly aimless, shifting behaviour that betrays the ultimate meaninglessness of human activity.

'Archaeology', as opposed to both transcendental and structuralist methods, makes no promise about the continuity or mutual meaningfulness of the layers of meaning it excavates. Foucault believes in meanings, but rejects the idea of 'serious' meaning. He believes in history but does not at all believe in progress, and while he resists talking about the post-modern situation in terms of 'decline' (as that would indicate the possibility of progress gone wrong) there is no question but that Foucault thinks that we currently face 'the greatest danger', not so much from nuclear extinction (which is real enough), but from that same general threat of technological take-over ('bio-power') that haunted Heidegger in his last years. In his later works Foucault rejects nihilism and any method of mere 'deconstruction', but his opposition to all established practices, and what he calls his 'hyperactive pessimism' do not offer even the 'cheerfulness' of Nietzsche's *amor fati*. Indeed, one might well see Foucault as the final inversion of Rousseau, a man alone in the jungle of (post-) modern society, filled with revulsion not only with that society but with the human self. Rousseau was expansive with the pregnant sense of humanity within himself; Foucault is indignant at the very thought of humanity's invasion of self, and has no faith in human nature to suggest that it just might come out right.

Jacques Derrida (b. 1930), on the other hand, displays little sense of danger, or of the seriousness that Foucault tried to undermine. Indeed Derrida's most vocal critics (unfairly) accuse him of wholly ignoring social and political issues and the problems of the world in favour of the philosophical 'play' which is so evident in all of his books, which abound with (and are sometimes based upon) puns, plays on words, the seemingly endless teasing-out of metaphors, and other varieties of verbal swordsmanship. But the point is that Derrida, who is himself a serious scholar and knows the tradition he criticizes, finds that tradition utterly bankrupt and pretentious, defined by claims that it cannot possibly defend, and pumped up with a confidence that it cannot possibly sustain. In particular, these claims and this confidence come down to what Derrida summarizes (following Heidegger) as 'the myth of presence', whether this takes the form of the immanent presence of God, or of the world as a determinate entity, or of the self as an 'inner' certainty. This 'theo-ontological tradition' refuses to consider the possibility that there are no such certainties, and even the language we use to talk about philosophy is riddled with distinctions and words that make this myth unavoidable. Consequently, Derrida's style is not to offer a counter-hypothesis but rather, as in guerrilla warfare, to attack quickly and run back, to puncture and parody, and to defuse through refusing to take a thesis seriously. Derrida has called this way of doing philosophy 'deconstruction', though he insists that this is not a method (as Gadamer insists that hermeneutics is not a method, and for much the same reason: methods are already biases, and restrict—even as they aim for—the truth).

One uses language but does not subscribe to its premisses. Derrida's truly perverse way of putting this is to declare that all language is now *written* language ('in the broad sense'), but what he has in mind is not the absurd literal sense of this but the anti-transcendental claim that it is with writing that language takes on the appearance of what Foucault called 'autonomous discourse', without an author, without intention or interpretation, and outside of space, time, and context. Thus Derrida's arguments are often pointedly *ad hominem*, bringing the author to the surface, exposing the conditions of his writing, and at the same time deflating his pretensions. For Derrida, as for Lévi-Strauss and Foucault, there is no constitution of meaning by a transcendental subject, a point that he makes with characteristic hyperbole by insisting that 'texts have no author'. Consequently texts do not and cannot express universal meanings, and the point of deconstruction is to do away with 'the transcendental signified'. He too accepts the fact that one cannot escape from one's historical and cultural context, but he turns this even against Foucault, who could not possibly understand the madness he describes in his work (Foucault, in return, dubbed Derrida '*le petit pedagogue*').

Of course Derrida cannot avoid using the traditional terms of metaphysics, but he insists on doing so, as he puts it, 'under erasure'—in other words: 'I am using these terms because I cannot avoid doing so, but do not take me literally or too seriously.' He shares with Nietzsche an intense distrust of metaphysics, including the metaphysics of self, and again like Nietzsche he writes in such a way as to continuously undermine even his own presuppositions, and expose his own metaphors as nothing more than metaphors (ironically, many students take these same devices as literal truths and as part of a philosophical method— exactly the opposite of what is intended). The histories of metaphysics and of our language, according to Derrida, are histories of self-enclosed and consequently inescapable systems of metaphors ('presence', 'essence', 'existence', 'experience', 'consciousness', 'subject', 'object'), and the point of philosophy is not to defend or account for these systems, but to '*deconstruct*' them. This is not to 'destroy' them (for they are inescapable), but neither is it to construct some other system to take their place. Consequently philosophy has no substance, and Derrida tries to make up for it in style.

The place of Foucault and Derrida in the story of modern European philosophy is unsettled, for the story is far from over. Other recently important figures, Jacques Lacan and Althusser for instance, have already dropped out of the picture, and it would not be too surprising if all those discussed in this chapter were to drop out too, wholly eclipsed by some dashing new philosophy of the year 1999, or viewed in retrospect by some neo-Heideggerian as 'just more of the same', a final, negative expression of the old transcendental pretence. But for now, if there is a lesson to be learned, it is that the intellect is prone to self-aggrandizement, and that intellectual arrogance will always take a fall. We can learn that intellectual integrity and intellectual despair are never very far removed from one another, and that the quest for the absolute may end not in scepticism but in the merely academic denial of both ourselves and the world. But there is a middle ground, one not readily found in modern or post-modern European philosophy, but summed up well by the American philosopher George Santayana in his fairly unsympathetic book on the German idealists. Dismissing the transcendental pretension to absolute self and absolute knowledge as a façade for scepticism and nationalistic arrogance, he urges us instead to have 'courtesy in the universe . . . discarding the word "absolute" as the most false and the most odious of words'.[2] The lesson of the transcendental pretence is that in order to be human we do not need to be more than human, and in order to be ourselves we should not want anything more—or less—than that perfectly modest sense of self that precedes the pretensions of philosophy. Between the self as absolute Spirit and the self as nothing at all there is, it turns out, very little difference—as Kierkegaard in particular told us some time ago.

References

Where publication and translation details are not given, they are to be found in the Select Bibliography (pp. 207–10).

Introduction

1. *Religion and Philosophy in Germany*, p. 137.

Setting the Stage

1. In W. T. Jones, *Kant and the Nineteenth Century* (New York, 1952), pp. 2–3.
2. *A Treatise of Human Nature*, p. 451.

Chapter 1

1. Quoted from E. Cassirer, *Rousseau, Kant and Goethe* (New York, 1963), p. 22.
2. *Confessions*.
3. *Emile*, iv. 306; cf. *Second Discourse*, pp. 202–3.
4. *Confessions*, p. 17.
5. Ibid., p. 166.
6. *The Social Contract*, p. 15.
7. Ibid., p. 18.
8. *Second Discourse*, pp. 141–2.
9. Ibid., p. 195.
10. *Emile*.
11. *Confessions*.

Chapter 2

1. *The Critique of Practical Reason*, p. 166.
2. *The German Ideology*, p. 206.
3. *Prolegomena to any Future Metaphysics*, p. 67.
4. *The Critique of Pure Reason*, p. xv.
5. *Prolegomena to any Future Metaphysics*, p. 116.
6. *The Critique of Pure Reason*, p. 75.
7. Ibid.
8. *Groundwork of the Metaphysics of Morals*, p. 9.

Chapter 3

1. In a letter to Schelling, April 1795, quoted in W. Kaufmann, *Hegel* (New York, 1966), p. 303.
2. *Science of Knowledge*, p. 16.

Chapter 4

1. *The Encyclopaedia of the Philosophical Sciences*, iii. 377.
2. *The Philosophy of Right*, p. 13.
3. *The Phenomenology of Spirit*, p. 130.

Chapter 5

1. *The World as Will and Idea*, p. 130.

Chapter 6

1. *Concluding Unscientific Postscript*, p. 33.
2. *Early Writings* (Bottomore), p. 64.
3. *Journals*, 1837.
4. Feuerbach, quoted from H. Hoffding, *History of Modern Philosophy*, trans. B. E. Meyer (New York, 1950), ii. 281.
5. *Theses on Feuerbach*, no. 11, in *Early Writings* (Colletti), p. 423.
6. *Early Writings* (Bottomore), p. 124.
7. *The Communist Manifesto*, p. 82.

Chapter 7

1. *Selected Writings*, p. 162.

Chapter 8

1. Beyond Good and Evil, 6.
2. *Thus Spake Zarathustra*, Prologue, 4.
3. Ibid., iii. 20.
4. *The Birth of Tragedy*, 5.
5. *Beyond Good and Evil*, 11.
6. *Twilight of the Idols*, 3, 2.
7. *Human, All Too Human*, 517.
8. *The Will to Power*, 387.
9. *The Antichrist*, 47.
10. *Twilight of the Idols*, 5, 1.
11. *The Will to Power*, 667.
12. *The Gay Science*, 270.
13. *The Will to Power*, 370.

Chapter 9

1. *Ideas*, p. 166.
2. Ibid., p. 76.
3. *Cartesian Meditations*, p. 33.

4. *Ideas*, p. 96.
5. Ibid., p. 133.

Chapter 10

1. *The Origins of Psychoanalysis*, p. 162.
2. *Letters from Wittgenstein*, p. 97.
3. *Project for a Scientific Psychology*, p. 295.
4. B. Bettelheim, *Freud and Man's Soul* (New York, 1983).
5. A. Janik and S. Toulmin, *Wittgenstein's Vienna* (New York, 1973).
6. *Tractatus Logico-Philosophicus*, 6. 3.
7. Ibid., 6. 373.

Chapter 11

1. *Introduction to Metaphysics*, p. 37.
2. Ibid., p. 8.
3. Ibid., p. 70.
4. Ibid., p. 67.
5. *Being and Time*, p. 68.
6. Ibid.
7. Ibid., p. 115.
8. Ibid., p. 15.
9. *Concluding Unscientific Postscript*, p. 281.
10. *Being and Time*, p. 41.
11. Ibid., p. 12.
12. Ibid., p. 192.
13. Ibid., p. 312.

Chapter 12

1. *The Ethics of Ambiguity*, p. 78.
2. *The Phenomenology of Perception*, p. ix.
3. Ibid., p. xiv.
4. *Being and Nothingness*, p. lv.
5. *Nausea*, pp. 170–1.
6. *Myth of Sisyphus*, p. 15.
7. *Sense and Non-Sense*, p. 144.
8. *The Phenomenology of Perception*, p. 160.
9. Ibid., pp. viii, ix.
10. *Existentialism as a Humanism*, p. 33.
11. *Being and Nothingness*, p. 591.
12. Ibid., p. 673.

Supplement

1. 'The Subject and Power' in H. Dreyfus and P. Rabinow, *Michel Foucault: Beyond Structuralism and Hermeneutics* (Chicago, 1983).
2. G. Santayana, *Egotism in German Philosophy* (New York, 1915), p. 165.

Select Bibliography

Introduction

Descartes, R. *Meditations*, in *The Philosophical Works of Descartes*, trans. and ed. E. S. Haldane and G. R. T. Ross (London, 1967).

Heine, H. *Religion and Philosophy in Germany*, trans. J. Snodgrass (London, 1981).

Setting the Stage

Hume, D. *A Treatise of Human Nature* (Oxford, 1951).

Chapter 1

Rousseau, J.-J. *Emile*, trans. A. Bloom (New York, 1979; London, 1950). *Confessions*, trans. J. Cohen (London, 1954). *The First and Second Discourses*, trans. R. Masters (New York, 1964). *The Social Contract*, trans. C. Frankel (New York, 1947).

Chapter 2

Kant, I. *Groundwork of the Metaphysics of Morals*, trans. H. J. Paton (New York, 1964). *Prolegomena to any Future Metaphysics*, trans. L. W. Beck (New York, 1950). *Religion within the Bounds of Reason Alone*, trans. T. H. Green (New York, 1960). *The Critique of Judgement*, trans. J. C. Meredith (Oxford, 1956). *The Critique of Practical Reason*, trans. L. W. Beck (New York, 1956). *The Critique of Pure Reason*, trans. N. Kemp-Smith (New York, 1966).

Chapter 3

Fichte, J. *Science of Knowledge*, trans. P. Heath and J. Lachs (New York, 1970). *The Vocation of Man*, trans. W. Smith (Chicago, 1946).

Schelling, F. *On Human Freedom*, trans. J. Gutmann (Chicago, 1936).

Schiller, F. *Letters on the Aesthetic Education of Man*, trans. R. Snell (New York, 1965).

Chapter 4

Hegel, G. W. F. *Reason in History*, trans. R. Hartman (Indiana-polis, 1953). *The Encyclopaedia of the Philosophical Sciences*, trans. W. Wallace (Oxford, 1971). *The Phenomenology of Spirit*, trans. A. V. Miller (Oxford, 1977). *The Philosophy of Right*, trans. T. M. Knox (Oxford, 1967).

Chapter 5

Schopenhauer, A. *Parerga and Paralipomena*, trans. E. F. J. Payne (Oxford, 1974). *The World as Will and Idea*, trans. E. S. Haldane and J. Kemp (London, 1948–50); reprinted in R. Stern and E. Robinson, *Changing Concepts in Art* (New York, 1983).

Chapter 6

Kierkegaard, S. *Concluding Unscientific Postscript*, trans. D. Swenson and W. Lowrie (Princeton, 1944). *Either/Or*, trans. D. Swenson, W. Lowrie, and H. Johnston (New York, 1954). *Journals*, trans. A. Dru (London, 1938).

Marx, K. *Early Writings*, trans. and ed. T. Bottomore (London, 1963). *Early Texts*, trans. D. McLellan (Oxford, 1971). *Selected Writings*, ed. D. McLellan (Oxford, 1977).

Marx, K. and Engels, F. *Early Writings*, ed. L. Colletti (London, 1975). *The Communist Manifesto*, ed. A. Taylor (London, 1967). *The German Ideology*, trans. W. Lough, C. Dutt, and C. P. Magill (New York, 1970).

Chapter 7

Brentano, F. *Psychology from an Empirical Standpoint*, trans. A. Rancurello et al. (London, 1948).

Dilthey, W. *Pattern and Meaning in History* (New York, 1962). *Selected Writings*, trans. and ed. H. P. Rickman (London, 1976).

Meinong, A. 'Theory of Objects' in R. Chisholm (ed.), *Realism and the Background of Phenomenology* (New York, 1960).

Chapter 8

Nietzsche, F. *Beyond Good and Evil*, trans. W. Kaufmann (New York, 1966). *Human, All Too Human*, trans. M. Faber (Lincoln, Nebraska, 1984). *The Birth of Tragedy*, trans. W. Kaufmann (New York, 1967). *The Gay Science*, trans. W. Kaufmann (New York, 1974). *The Will to Power*, trans. W. Kaufmann and R. J. Hollingdale (New York, 1968).

Thus Spake Zarathustra, *Twilight of the Idols*, and *The Antichrist*, trans. W. Kaufmann (New York, 1964).

Chapter 9

Husserl, E. *Cartesian Meditations*, trans. D. Cairns (Hague, 1960). *Ideas*, trans. W. R. Boyce-Gibson (New York, 1931). *Philosophy as a Rigorous Science*, trans. Q. Lauer (New York, 1965).

Chapter 10

Freud, S. *Standard Edition of the Complete Psychological Works of Sigmund Freud* (in 24 vols.), trans. and ed. J. Strachey (London, 1966): *Project for a Scientific Psychology* (vol. iii); *Interpretation of Dreams* (vol. iv); *Three Contributions to the Theory of Sexuality* (vol. vii); *Introductory Lectures on Psychoanalysis* (vol. xv). *The Origins of Psychoanalysis*, ed. M. Bonaparte, A. Freud, and E. Kris (London, 1954).

Wittgenstein, L. *Letters from Wittgenstein*, ed. P. Engelmann, trans. L. Furtmuller (Oxford, 1967). *Tractatus Logico-Philosophicus*, trans. C. K. Ogden (London, 1922).

Chapter 11

Gadamer, H.-G. *Truth and Method*, trans. G. Barden and J. Cumming (New York, 1975).

Habermas, J. *Knowledge and Human Interests*, trans. J. Shapiro (Boston, 1971). *Theory of Communicative Action*, trans. T. McCarthy (Cambridge, Ma., 1984).

Heidegger, M. *Being and Time*, trans. J. MacQuarrie and E. Robinson (New York, 1962). *Introduction to Metaphysics*, trans. R. Mannheim (New Haven, 1958).

Chapter 12

Camus, A. *Myth of Sisyphus*, trans. J. O'Brien (New York, 1955). *The Stranger*, trans. J. O'Brien (New York, 1946).

de Beauvoir, S. *The Ethics of Ambiguity*, trans. B. Frechtman (New York, 1948). *The Second Sex*, trans. H. M. Parshley (New York, 1953).

Merleau-Ponty, M. *Sense and Non-Sense*, trans. H. Dreyfus (Evanston, Il., 1964). *The Phenomenology of Perception*, trans. C. Smith (London, 1962).

Sartre, J.-P. *Being and Nothingness*, trans. H. Barnes (New York, 1956). *Existentialism as a Humanism*, trans. P. Mairet (New York,

1947). *Nausea*, trans. L. Alexander (New York, 1949). *No Exit*, trans. S. Gilbert (New York, 1947). *The Transcendence of the Ego*, trans. F. Williams (New York, 1957).

Supplement

Derrida, J. *Of Grammatology*, trans. G. Spivak (Baltimore, 1976). *Speech and Phenomena*, trans. D. Allison (Evanston, Il., 1973).

Foucault, M. *Madness and Civilization: A History of Madness in the Age of Reason*, trans. R. Howard (New York, 1965). *The Order of Things* (London, 1970).

Lévi-Strauss, C. *The Savage Mind* (Chicago, 1966).

Index

romanticism (*die Romantik*), 12–15, 16, 43, 44–55, 95, 171, 173

Rousseau, Jean-Jacques, 1–2, 6, 14, 16–21, 26, 28, 40–1, 47, 48, 52, 59, 61, 63, 67, 68, 69, 70, 87, 90, 94, 95, 103, 112, 113, 118, 124, 140, 145, 150, 153, 173, 177, 189, 190, 194, 196, 200

Russell, Bertrand, 146–7

Sade, Marquis de, 8

Santayana, George, 202

Sartre, Jean-Paul, 129, 160, 164, 168, 173–92, 194, 195

Saussure, Ferdinand de, 197

Say, Jean-Baptiste, 96, 97

Scheler, Max, 103

Schelling, Friedrich, 52–5, 56, 60, 65, 76, 86, 162

Schiller, Friedrich, 21, 39, 45–6, 47, 48, 60, 69, 94

Schlegel, Friedrich and August, 47

Schleiermacher, Friedrich, 168

Schopenhauer, Arthur, 47, 75–85, 90, 108, 112, 116, 123, 132, 140, 143, 146, 148, 149, 167, 185

Science of Knowledge (Fichte), 51

Second Sex, The (de Beauvoir), 192–3

self (ego), 1–2, 4–6, 14–16, 17–19, 57–8, 61–4, 71, 126, 130, 143, 149, 153, 157, 160–1, 163–4, 174–5, 177, 202

self-interest, 21, 97, 178

sexual desire, 81, 82–3, 144

Sittlichkeit, 70–1

scepticism, 26, 28, 29, 31, 36, 99, 129, 176

slave morality, 120–4

Smith, Adam, 96

Social Contract, The (Rousseau), 9, 48

Socrates, 5, 44, 113, 121

Spinoza, Baruch, 52, 54

Spirit (*Geist*) (Hegel), 57–8, 61–4, 75, 79, 87, 91, 202

structuralism, 195–8

Stumpf, Karl, 103–4

Sturm und Drang, 27, 45, 46, 49, 60

Symposium (Plato), 81

teleology, 27, 42–3, 50, 53, 63–5, 108, 125

Thus Spake Zarathustra (Nietzsche), 112, 124, 125

time: in Bergson, 109–10; in Heidegger, 156, 164–5

Tolstoy, Leo, 3

Tractatus Logico-Philosophicus (Wittgenstein), 146–51

transcendence, 182–3

transcendental, 31–5, 137: aesthetic, 32; analytic, 32–4; argument, 31–3; deduction of the categories, 32–3; dialectic, 34–6; ego (self), 33–4, 52, 149, 160, 177; idealism, 31–4, 55, 56

transcendental pretence, 1–2, 3–7, 12, 15, 31–2, 54, 64, 71, 75, 106, 110, 138, 174, 193, 194, 195, 202

Treatise of Human Nature, A (Hume), 14

Übermensch, 112, 124–5

Unconscious, the, 141, 142–3, 144, 159, 186

Unhappy Consciousness, 66

universalism, 11, 31, 46, 117–18, 190

Upanishads, 84

Voltaire (François-Marie Arouet), 8, 10, 13, 16, 17, 21, 41

Will, 40–1, 77–81, 82, 83, 84, 108, 116, 118, 123, 143, 149

will to power, 112, 115

Wittgenstein, Ludwig, 91, 139–41, 146–51, 167

World as Will and Idea, The (Schopenhauer), 75–85

World Soul, 5, 54, 60

Zarathustra, see *Thus Spake Zarathustra*

OXFORD

MORE OXFORD PAPERBACKS

Details of a selection of other books follow. A complete list of Oxford Paperbacks, including The World's Classics, Twentieth-Century Classics, OPUS, Past Masters, Oxford Authors, Oxford Shakespeare, and Oxford Paperback Reference, is available in the UK from the General Publicity Department, Oxford University Press (JN), Walton Street, Oxford OX2 6DP.

In the USA, complete lists are available from the Paperbacks Marketing Manager, Oxford University Press, 200 Madison Avenue, New York, NY 10016.

Oxford Paperbacks are available from all good bookshops. In case of difficulty, customers in the UK can order direct from Oxford University Press Bookshop, 116 High Street, Oxford, Freepost, OX1 4BR, enclosing full payment. Please add 10 per cent of published price for postage and packing.

A HISTORICAL INTRODUCTION TO THE PHILOSOPHY OF SCIENCE

Second Edition

John Losee

Since the time of Plato and Aristotle, scientists and philosophers have raised questions about the proper evaluation of scientific interpretations. A *Historical Introduction to the Philosophy of Science* is an exposition of positions that have been held on issues such as the distinction between scientific inquiry and other types of interpretation; the relationship between theories and observation reports; the evaluation of competing theories; and the nature of progress in science. The book makes the philosophy of science accessible to readers who do not have extensive knowledge of formal logic or the history of the sciences.

PHILOSOPHERS AND PAMPHLETEERS

Political Theorists of the Enlightenment

Maurice Cranston

The philosophers of the French Enlightenment wrote for a large public with the aim of promoting political reforms. In this lively and readable book, Maurice Cranston demonstrates the richness and variety of their ideas.

Professor Cranston studies Montesquieu's parliamentarianism and Voltaire's royalism as rival ideologies reflecting competing interests in the *ancien régime*; he analyses Rousseau's debts to the republican experience of the city-state of Geneva, traces the movement from utilitarianism to liberalism in the thought of Diderot and Holbach, and examines Condorcet's endeavour in the first years of the French Revolution to reconcile democracy with the rule of the wise.

MODERN BRITISH PHILOSOPHY

Bryan Magee

Bryan Magee's general survey of contemporary British philosophy originates in a series of radio conversations with leading British philosophers. In them, he elicited their views on chosen subjects, ranging from influential philosophers, such as Russell, Wittgenstein, Moore, and Austin, to the relationship of philosophy to Morals, Religion, the Arts, and Social Theory.

'Under Magee's sensitive guidance a remarkably coherent interpretation of this period emerges.' Marshall Cohen in *The Listener*

'Bryan Magee has done everything possible to get these philosophers to put themselves in a nutshell.' Kathleen Nott in *New Society*